THE FRENCH
NEW CRITICISM

THE FRENCH
NEW CRITICISM

An Introduction
and a Sampler

Laurent LeSage

THE PENNSYLVANIA STATE
UNIVERSITY PRESS
University Park & London
1967

Library of Congress Catalog Card Number 66–26270

Copyright © 1967 by the Pennsylvania State University
All rights reserved

Printed in the United States of America

Designed by Marilyn Shobaken

AUTHOR'S NOTE

Last year in France, the publication of a small pamphlet started a literary quarrel that soon involved every columnist and critic in the land. Not for years had the public been treated to such a spectacle. A professor from the Sorbonne, that stronghold of tradition, had spoken out to denounce a new trend in literary criticism. In his pamphlet, he anathematized this trend in the name of reason, clarity, and responsibility, cited instances of philosophical pretentiousness or linguistic extravagance, alluded to texts even defamatory to the institutions of the nation. If his colleagues were content to applaud discreetly, many columnists and reviewers jumped for joy: the New Critics had received a proper thrashing. Stinging from the blows, the champion of the opposition retorted. His supporters lent aid by hurling taunts and accusations of murderous intent. With the verse that they display in their literary essays, the New Critics pictured their opponents as being after real blood, stimulated by an archaic tribal instinct to rid the community of all dangerous elements.

What finally burst forth in a loud polemical exchange and put literary criticism in the news had been brewing for some years. A new school of criticism, lofty in its ambitions and its claims, has developed in France to oppose the traditional approaches to literature. French intellectuals—friends or foes—recognize the importance of the movement and acknowledge that among its adherents are some of the most brilliant and original literary minds of the day. It is still little known in America, and the greater part of the French New Criticism still awaits translation. Yet it deserves to be known—and possibly even to be judged. That is the reason for this book. Of course, with a young and active movement like the French New Criticism, any definitive picture is impossible at the present moment. Facts are incomplete, may sometimes be erroneous; appraisals and interpretations are subject to revision. Yet a sketch such as this book represents, can be of service, and future surveys of the scene will complete the picture and correct the faults of vision that will be found in this first one.

LAURENT LeSAGE

University Park, Pennsylvania,
and Paris, 1966

ACKNOWLEDGMENTS

The author's thanks are hereby made to the following publishers for permission to use the materials indicated:

To L'Arche for an extract from *Jean Racine, Dramaturge*, by Lucien Goldmann.

To Editions de La Baconnière, S.A., for an extract from *Paul Valéry et la Tentation de l'Esprit*, by Marcel Raymond.

To George Braziller, Inc., for an extract from *Saint-Genet*, by Jean-Paul Sartre (tr. by Bernard Frechtman).

To Cahiers du Sud, for an extract from *L'Ame Romantique et le Rêve*, by Albert Béguin.

To Librairie José Corti, for extracts from *L'Eau et les Rêves*, by Gaston Bachelard; *Forme et Signification*, by Jean Rousset; *Des métaphores obsédantes au Mythe personnel*, by Charles Mauron; *L'Imagination d'Alfred de Vigny*, by François Germain; *De Baudelaire au Surréalisme*, by Marcel Raymond.

To Editions Gallimard, for extracts from *Situations* (I) and *Saint-Genet*, by Jean-Paul Sartre; *Le Dieu caché* and *Pour une sociologie du roman*, by Lucien Goldmann; *Le Livre à venir* and *La Part du Feu*, by Maurice Blanchot; *Sur un héros païen*, by Robert Champigny; *L'Ecrivain et son Langage*, by Manuel de Diéguez; *Raymond Roussel*, by Michel Foucault; Introduction to the *Œuvres complètes de Jean-Jacques Rousseau*, by Marcel Raymond; *L'Œil vivant*, by Jean Starobinski; *Genèse de l'Œuvre poétique*, by Jean-Paul Weber; *Essais Critiques*, by Roland Barthes.

To Editions Bernard Grasset, for an extract from *Mensonge romantique et Vérité romanesque*, by René Girard.

To Hill & Wang, Inc., for an extract from *On Racine*, by Roland Barthes (tr. by Richard Howard).

To Humanities Press, Inc., for an extract from *The Hidden God*, by Lucien Goldmann (tr. by Philip Thody).

To The Johns Hopkins Press for extracts from *Deceit, Desire, and the Novel*, by René Girard (tr. by Y. Freccero); *Studies in Human Time* and *Interior Distance*, by Georges Poulet (tr.

by Elliott Coleman); "Les Deux Critiques", by Roland Barthes (*Modern Language Notes*).

To Editions de Minuit, for an extract from "Qu'en est-il de la Critique", by Maurice Blanchot (*Arguments*).

To Orion Press (c/o Grossman Publishers) for an extract from *Poetics of Space*, by Gaston Bachelard (tr. by Maria Jolas).

To Peter Owen, Ltd., for an extract from *From Baudelaire to Surrealism*, by Marcel Raymond.

To S. G. Phillips, Inc., for an extract from *Literary and Philosophical Essays*, by Jean-Paul Sartre (tr. by Annette Michelson) (Criterion).

To Librairie Plon for extracts from *Etudes sur le temps humain* (*La distance Intérieure*) by Georges Poulet; *Jean-Jacques Rousseau, la transparence et l'obstacle*, by Jean Starobinski.

To Presses Universitaires de France for an extract from *La Poétique de l'Espace*, by Gaston Bachelard.

To Editions du Seuil for extracts from *Sur Racine*, by Roland Barthes; *Rabelais par lui-même*, by Manuel de Diéguez; *Poésie et Profondeur*, by Jean-Pierre Richard.

To Skira for an extract from *Balzac Visionnaire*, by Albert Béguin.

To *The London Times* for an extract from "Criticism as Language", by Roland Barthes.

To the University of Edinburgh Press for an extract from *Etudes sur le temps humain*, by Georges Poulet.

To the Indiana University Press for an extract from *Stages on Sartre's Way*, by Robert Champigny.

To the author, for an extract from *Le Genre poétique*, by Robert Champigny.

The author wishes to express his appreciation to the Central Fund for Research of The Pennsylvania State University and to the Fulbright Commission for their assistance during certain phases of the research for this work.

Translation of the selections from works unavailable in English is by the author.

CONTENTS

INTRODUCTION TO
THE NEW CRITICISM

INTRODUCTION TO
THE NEW CRITICISM

Modern French literary criticism, as the manuals of literature
tell us, begins with Sainte-Beuve (1804–1879). He represents
a definitive break with the past, with criticism that was
chiefly the judging of a given piece of literature on the basis
of pre-established standards. With Sainte-Beuve, criticism
becomes more description than evaluation; and, although to
appraise a work will remain part of the critic's task, it will not
be according to a model of genre or a pattern of previous
attainment. Evaluation, what there is of it, is based on the
personal opinion of the critic, whose principal duty is, however, to explain the work. To this end, he describes not only
the work but the writer as well, for the better we know him
the better we will understand what he writes. "La production
littéraire n'est point pour moi distincte ou du moins séparable
du reste de l'homme." [1] So Sainte-Beuve painted portraits of
authors in as much detail as he could, including traits of their
character and facts of their life, often of the most anecdotal
sort. "On ne saurait s'y prendre de trop de façons et par trop
de bouts pour connaître un homme." And to set off the
portrait, he sketched in the time and the place.

Since Sainte-Beuve, there have been few attempts to return to the absolute criticism practiced before him. The part
that judgment plays in criticism has been progressively reduced. Modern criticism has moved forward along two lines:
the scientific and the impressionistic, both of which depart
from the author of the *Lundis*.

Hippolyte Taine (1828–1893) made of literary criticism a
branch of positivistic enquiry. "On peut considérer l'homme
comme un animal d'espèce supérieure, qui produit des phi-
losophies et des poèmes à peu près comme les vers à soie font

[1] Sainte-Beuve, *Nouveaux Lundis*, III, "Chateaubriand."

3

leurs cocons et comme les abeilles font leurs ruches." [2] By studying a work as the product of time, place, and race, he situated it as a phenomenon in history and in sociology; by studying its author as a personality dominated by a "faculté maîtresse," he situated him as a case history in psychology. Emile Faguet (1847–1916) cared little about situating a work, but followed Taine in the assumption of a dominant faculty as the key to a personality. To define it was his main concern in the essays he devoted to French writers. Ferdinand Brunetière (1849–1906), imbued with the scientific mystique of the age, applied to literature the principles of Darwinian evolution. For him, genres arose, flourished, and then disappeared in the manner of natural species. Within a given genre, a work is bound by genealogical ties, and it is the critic's task to identify them. The scientific tradition in criticism, which these writers illustrate, can claim derivation from Sainte-Beuve, for it was he who adopted for literature the descriptive and classifying devices of the nineteenth-century naturalist. But Sainte-Beuve never committed literature to rigid systems or scientific laws. On the basis of the suppleness of his criticism and its unbridled personal tone, the impressionistic tradition in modern criticism can, just as the scientific, claim derivation from Sainte-Beuve.

Impressionistic criticism became strong at the end of the century, as part of the general reaction to "scientism." Jules Lemaître (1853–1914) denounced the objective pretensions of the positivistic critics and declared that criticism could never be more than the impression that a certain work at a certain time makes upon a critic. He therefore presented his articles as only "impressions sincères notées avec soin." [3] Anatole France (1844–1924) defined a good critic as one who "raconte les aventures de son âme au milieu des chefs-

---

[2] *La Fontaine et ses fables*, préface.
[3] *Les Contemporains*, première série, avant-propos.

d'œuvre." [4] These two critics, who opposed Brunetière and the practitioners of scientific criticism, argued on the basis of the inevitable subjectivity of the critic. It was for Remy de Gourmont (1858–1915) to shift emphasis from the critic to the artist in the matter of subjectivity and bring impressionistic criticism closer to the Beuvian ideal of contact with another soul. If the critic's idea of beauty was individual, so was the artist's. What Gourmont sought to discover, therefore, were an author's unique qualities. Gourmont's relativism in criticism is attested to by the preface to his first *Livre des Masques*: "Nous devrons admettre autant d'esthétiques qu'il y a d'esprits originaux et les juger d'après ce qu'elles sont et non d'après ce qu'elles ne sont pas."

The antidogmatic tradition in criticism continued during the between-wars period, particularly in the writings of contributors to *La Nouvelle Revue Française*. Although animated by a common desire to safeguard artistic values, they conceived of criticism more as discovery than as judgment. Albert Thibaudet (1874–1936) was the greatest among them; his criticism can be summed up in the words description and delectation. This generous critic recognized the legitimate claims of all types of criticism. He saw them as essentially three: that of the professors, that of the artists, and the kind he called spoken or spontaneous criticism. We need not be concerned here with the last two, for the criticism of creative writers as well as that of simple reviewers and columnists figures for very little in the development we are tracing. We can likewise dismiss from our discussion the criticism tainted by strong political or religious bias. On the other hand, the criticism of professors is important enough to warrant more explicit description.

Professorial criticism has its roots in nineteenth-century positivism. Taine, Faguet, and Brunetière, chief exponents of

[4] *La Vie littéraire*, I, iii.

criticism as a science, spoke from their chairs at the university. In spite of differences in point of view and in focus, they subscribed to a basic principle of science—dispassionate objectivity. By the time of Gustave Lanson (1857–1934), nothing else remained of the scientific concept of criticism. Lanson favored no system, had no theory to test or to prove. Although he suggested that his type of work might serve an end other than itself, he was content to limit his own activity to factual investigation. Modern literary scholarship has modeled itself on Lanson's work. The method is well known: verification of the text, its classification in literature, and its establishment in time and space. The tools are documentation and analysis. Erudite or "university" criticism ranges widely over the fields of biography, history, and sociology in pursuit of its material; but, committed to facts and scientific objectivity, it remains, as it were, outside the work. The university critic does not presume to commune with an author, relive the experience of his work, or use his work as a pretext for his own creative expression. The Lansonian method has been often ridiculed for its sterility and its futility, justifiably so when it has been used without discretion. Recently it has been attacked on philosophical grounds as an expression of outmoded "scientism." It remains, however, strong in the university; and, so long as literary history is deemed a valid subject for inquiry, the method to which Lanson gave his name cannot be altogether discarded.

After World War II, criticism, while still following the lines we have traced from Sainte-Beuve, took on a new and distinctive coloring.[5] That is to say, although the technique remained basically descriptive, the purpose of criticism became far more concentrated upon the ethical value of literature. This meant that, without returning to evaluation in a

---

[5] C.-E. Magny presents the platform of the postwar critics in an article in *Une Semaine dans le Monde:* "Critique sage et critique 'partiale, passionnée, politique,'" April 17, 1948, pp. 1–2.

pre-Beuvian sense of absolutism, criticism would often include judgments—praise and condemnation—based upon
the ethical content of the work or the reflection of life that
the critic saw in it. Jean-Paul Sartre, in his essays on Mauriac
and Giraudoux, written before the war, planted the seeds for
the criticism that flourished after the war. In a style marked
by a blending of vehement journalese and pedantry, Sartre
described and judged the moral universe implicit in an author's works.

The postwar generation of critics drew from writings of the
time models of deportment to follow or reject in a world
where old humanistic values no longer pertained and where a
confidence in the rational nature of man was no longer
possible. The characters of Sartre and Camus were most
often cited, but so were many other heroes of anguish and
the tragic vision. Albérès pushed way back to Nietzsche and
to Kierkegaard in his *Portrait de notre héros* (1945). The
subsequent monographs of Albérès are additional portraits of
rebels, fugitives, and other "Promethean" figures which he
found in twentieth-century French fiction. Gaëtan Picon
used the same word "Promethean" to describe Malraux's
heroes, whom he saw as desperate prisoners in a world dark
and abandoned. Pierre-Henri Simon, although personally re-
gretting the contemporary alienation from humanism, made
the history of that alienation the subject of his books, sugges-
tively entitled *L'Homme en procès*, *Procès du héros*, and
Témoins de l'homme. French criticism during the late 1940's
and early 1950's was chiefly concerned with presenting literature as a mirror of life and writers as spiritual directors for the
new generation. In the name of this generation, young Pierre
de Boisdeffre examined the literary great among his elders,
rejected most of them, and called for a general spiritual re-
generation. Maurice Nadeau, in *Littérature présente* (1952),
declared that works that leave the reader unchanged are
worthless.

Towards the esthetic aspect of literature, the postwar French critics were indifferent or hostile. Nadeau said flatly, "Je n'ai pas l'admiration esthétique." [6] Boisdeffre declared, "La critique, telle que je l'entends, peut tracer des routes, déchiffrer des secrets, éclairer des consciences." And he added, "Et nous paraissent désormais bien vains les livres qui ne nous apprennent rien sur la condition humaine." [7] Only Gaëton Picon seems to have remembered that the subject of discussion was an art. His *Ecrivain et son ombre* was a serious probing into the nature of esthetics to determine whether it is something besides the philosophy, the science, the history, or the criticism of art. But Picon's book was of course a work of theory, and in the actual criticism of the time, literature was not discussed as an art but as philosophy or ethics.

Some observers did not hesitate to point this out with disapproval. As early as 1944, Henri Hell noted what he called "une certaine tendance pseudo philosophico-poétique qui plonge de plus en plus la critique littéraire dans un charabia prétentieux et creux." [8] One may argue that it is only normal that a criticism directed towards a literature itself philosophical should be philosophical in nature. This would not excuse the jargon employed, which is probably what Hell had in mind.

The lexicon of a recent star pupil in the philosophy class is only part of the general rhetoric that distinguishes this generation of critics, who took as their motto Baudelaire's declaration that criticism should be "partiale, passionnée, politique." Young Albérès was given to apocalyptic conjurations; Boisdeffre, to fiery denunciations; Picon, to bursts of bravura. Nadeau and Simon were quieter, but the former was none the less polemical and could be very biting, while the

[6] *Littérature présente*, préface, p. 17.
[7] *Métamorphose de la Littérature* (1950). See Preface by André Maurois, p. 12, and p. 16.
[8] "Critique de la critique," *Fontaine*, XXXII (1944), 223.

latter, who was considerably older than the others, was simply preachy. The general impression is of a criticism actively "engaged." Some of its exponents had definite religious or political *parti-pris*—the Catholic Boisdeffre, the Christian humanist Simon, the leftist Nadeau—and all were concerned with seeking a proper philosophy of life for the postwar world.

Within a very few years, the young Turks of postwar criticism turned, however, into literary historians and pundits. Albérès, now professor at the University of Fribourg, surveys the contemporary scene from his column in *Les Nouvelles Littéraires*; Boisdeffre, program director of radio and television, periodically reissues his *Histoire vivante de la littérature contemporaine*, a treasury of factual information; Picon, director of arts and letters in the government, still writes monographs and reflections on his reading; Simon, retired from his university teaching, is literary critic for *Le Monde*; Nadeau, who has occupied several editorial positions, put out a survey of the French novel a few years ago. They remain prominent figures on the literary scene. But they figure no longer in the militant advance guard; rather do they tend to play the part of elders who regard with some dismay the generation which has succeeded them.

The critics of the new generation, which it is the purpose of this volume to present, have in common with their immediate predecessors a dead seriousness of intention, an intellectual background deeply influenced by Existentialism, and a disposition towards jargon and high-flown rhetoric. In their concept of criticism, however, these French New Critics differ considerably. Not "engaged" and not at all in pursuit of answers from literature as to how to live and why, they give all their attention to the work itself—that is, the work and the author so far as he is involved in the work. Significant as this new emphasis is, in the light of history it can be seen as but the latest development of modern descriptive criticism, and the New Critics' quarrel with cousins and ancestors does not remove them from the family tree.

In proselytizing for their particular interest, the New Critics are concerned neither with historical perspective nor always with objective justice. One or the other has attacked all French criticism since Sainte-Beuve except that of their immediate predecessors, whom they ignore. Impressionism has been dismissed as trivial, scientific criticism as being postulated on false premises. Sainte-Beuve has been a principal target, particularly because of his concern for externalia. *Contre Sainte-Beuve,* the title of Proust's posthumous essay, could serve as motto for the New Critics, who exploit to the fullest the distinction Proust made between the creative personality and the everyday personality of an artist. The Lansonian criticism in the university, their chief foe today, has been attacked on the same grounds of externalia. Criticism, they insist, belongs on the inside—within the work itself and the creative personality that produced it. Biography, history, sociology belong on the outside. Professor Claude Pichois, of the University of Basel, doubts that the New Critics can ever accept literary history. After the 1963 meeting of the International Association of French Studies, he wrote, "La coexistance pacifique que je souhaitais s'est réalisée autrement que je la souhaitais: les tenants de la nouvelle critique nient l'histoire littéraire; quant à celle-ci, elle renforce ses positions dans toutes les facultés françaises, en ironisant sur les acrobaties arachnéennes de la critique. Dialogue de sourds. Ou plutôt: monologues de byzantins éperdus." [9] The Barthes-Picard exchanges of 1964–65 would seem to substantiate Pichois' pessimism.[10] On the other hand, all clear-cut distinctions between New Criticism and university criticism are

---

[9] *Cahiers de l'Association Internationale des Etudes Françaises,* March 16, 1964, p. 119.
[10] This will be spoken of again in connection with Roland Barthes.

false, and theses along the lines of New Criticism are being accepted in increasing numbers by French universities.[11]

On the basis of their vehement denunciation of the biographical method, the French New Critics call to mind certain groups abroad such as the Anglo-American "new critics," Russian formalists, or German descriptive critics. There seems little evidence of direct borrowing but there are unmistakably basic points in common. Chief among them is of course the effort to avoid the "biographical fallacy" and the concentration upon the work itself as an art form. From this basic position, all the groups have explored in several directions and meet in one or another. Yet certain directions seem characteristic. The Russian view of a work as a closed system of relations and oppositions seems to have led into linguistics. Anglo-American "ontological" criticism, although concerned with syntax and semantics, has remained more purely literary in its work of explication and exegesis. The French New Critics show more affinity with the German school, which springs from Existentialist philosophy. Heidegger advocated for literary criticism a phenomenological technique—description rather than explanation. Before the work the critic is first to feel, then to analyze his feelings, then experience feeling enriched by knowing. Certainly Maurice Blanchot and Georges Poulet must be aware of Heidegger's views. Poulet must certainly know Heidegger's disciple Emil Staiger, who is a colleague, teaching German literature at the University of Zürich, and a fellow student of time in literature. But although some among the New French Critics may know German critics like Staiger or Kayser, English or American critics like Eliot or John Crowe Ransom, Croce, or Slavic writers like Roman Jakobson, none makes mention of a foreign debt or influence. The only debt we can be sure of is indirect; it stems from Existential philosophy which,

[11] See "Quoi de neuf à la Sorbonne," *Les Nouvelles Littéraires*, April 14, 1966, p. 9.

through Jean-Paul Sartre, has permeated the intellectual life in France during the last two decades.

There need not be any direct influence from abroad, since in France itself the way was already prepared for the New Critics. During the between-wars period, Charles Du Bos found widespread approval for his criticism by empathy or collaboration, whereby the critic identifies with the author in his creative process. Paul Valéry made fun of the biographical method, saying, "Il sera bien temps de traiter de la vie, des amours et des opinions du poète, de ses amis et ennemis, de sa naissance et de sa mort, quand nous aurons assez avancé dans la connaissance poétique de son poème." [12] Jean Prévost concurred, "Nous ne croyons plus expliquer un écrivain par sa vie: ce serait expliquer la perle par l'huître." [13] All three advocated an "integral" type of criticism to replace the scientific or impressionistic. The theorists of Surrealism, too, could well be counted as precursors. But the recognized sources of inspiration for the French New Critics are two professors who, dissatisfied with the conventional perspective and method of literary enquiry, set out for something new. It may be that the example of German criticism helped orient them. Both are Swiss, both taught at the University of Basel. One taught for a time in Germany and can be considered a student of German letters.

Marcel Raymond (born in Geneva in 1897) taught at the University of Basel until 1936 and then at the University of Geneva, where he still occupies the chair of French literature. His book *De Baudelaire au Surréalisme* is celebrated for having traced the history of modern poetry not by influences and conscious borrowings but by inner affiliations and relationships. Although Raymond claims to have rejected the

[12] "Questions de poésie," *Variété III* (Gallimard, 1936), p. 44.
[13] Cited by Claude Bonnefoy, "En 10 ans la 'Nouvelle Critique' a renouvelé notre vision de la littérature," *Arts*, February 19–25, 1964, p. 5.

objective method, his work itself does not seem particularly at odds with the university tradition, and one may wonder if the reverence expressed by Georges Poulet and others is not based more on the quality of the book than on its originality. Albert Béguin, four years younger than Raymond, replaced his elder at Basel and remained there until 1945, when he forsook the university for a career in the publishing world of Paris. Béguin's work is a monumental thesis, *L'Ame romantique et le rêve.* In revolt against the classic ideals of reason, clarity, and harmony, Béguin turned to German Romanticism for the prestige it gave the mystic and oneiric experience. The revelation of this book was the part played by the subconscious in artistic creation. Béguin, like the German poets and the Surrealists, declared that the material of poetry is the dream. This pioneer in the study of creative processes had the opportunity, before his death, of giving his blessing to the new school. Too long, he wrote in an article for *Esprit,* has literary criticism been in the service of history, psychology, or sociology. He categorically opposed the scientific method, wondering even if literary history is possible. According to him, Georges Poulet and Gaston Bachelard, plus some young writers like Jean-Pierre Richard and Roland Barthes who also limit themselves in their studies to the literary phenomenon, are the only critics worthy of our attention today. Thus Béguin announced as early as 1955 the movement in criticism that is imposing itself today, and named some of its major exponents.

Georges Poulet acknowledges Raymond and Béguin as his masters in criticism. He was born in Belgium in 1902. Between 1927 and 1952 he taught French literature at the University of Edinburgh, then for five years at Johns Hopkins, finally at the University of Zurich, where he still teaches. In his studies of French writers, Poulet has been concerned exclusively with the theme of time and space. However, as he uses the terms, they are quite elastic, now shrinking to become almost synonymous, now stretching to stand for all sorts of things about an author and his work that we do not normally associate with temporal or spatial concepts. He does not lift his eyes, nonetheless, from the text itself, finding all his evidence and his inspiration in the author's work. One is astonished at Poulet's ability to find so much grist for his mill and, upon reflection, may decide that a more objective searcher would reject a great deal of it. But then Poulet is not a scientist or even a philosopher. The subject of time and space is only a theme for brilliant, highly subjective explications of text. As such, his essays are held up as models of what criticism should be today, and his theme of time and space has become a major touchstone in the analysis of literature.

New Criticism owes much, also, to a distinguished Sorbonne professor, Gaston Bachelard, who died a few years ago at the age of seventy-eight. Bachelard cast interesting light upon the workings of the poetic imagination through his studies of the representation made by the human mind of the four elements—fire, water, air, earth—which he spoke of as complexes. Although a philosopher of science, Bachelard had gradually lost faith in the basic assumptions of science and had defected to phenomenology which, wary of abstract formulations, limits itself to a description of nature reflected in the mind and of the reflecting processes themselves. Phenomenology, imported into France along with Existentialism, has won great favor with the young intellectuals and is behind both the New Novel and the New Criticism. Especially instructive to the young critics was the distinction Bachelard made (in spite of his psychoanalytical vocabulary and his debt to Jung) between his phenomenological approach and psychoanalysis. Psychoanalysts, he declared, are concerned primarily with the man behind the work of art, whereas he, Bachelard, is interested only in the poetic act. The image that one finds in art, he added, is not a copy of nature but a subjective creation, a product of the uncon-scious—at times, of the collective unconscious.

Jean-Pierre Richard (born in Marseilles in 1922), at pres-ent professor at the French Institute of Madrid, calls him-self a disciple of Poulet and Bachelard in his analyses of the creative imagination. Approaching his subject as a phenom-enologist, Richard studies a work to obtain a notion of the writer's affective consciousness and instinctive reactions. The characteristic patterns he detects are called "structures" or "themes," and they constitute a writer's basic "coherence." These terms are common in French New Criticism—they carry the special meaning indicated here. If the terms and philosophical wrapping are new, the basic method is not. At bottom, Richard's work does not differ from traditional sty-listic studies in imagery and theme. But the traditional inves-tigation into such matters is usually a very prosy affair. Ri-chard, on the contrary, seems at times more poetic than the poet he is treating. At times it is apparent that the imagery and symbolism we are reading about is not the poet's so much as the critic's. Like Poulet, Richard depends upon a very personal intuition and a very personal vocabulary. Such criticism may therefore be literally less valid than a forthright piece of scholarship; on the other hand, it is highly stimulat-ing and can bring back to life for us certain authors mum-mified in our manuals of literature.

A New Critic who has been stimulating to the point of being the one among the group most often attacked is Ro-land Barthes (born in Bayonne in 1915). His essays on sociological and lexicographical aspects of literature have called forth the accusation of a Marxist bias; and his "psy-choanalysis" of Michelet, the charge of eroticism. It is his interpretation of Racine, however, which transformed scat-tered attack into concentrated polemic. According to Barthes, our traditional idea of Racine's "psychology" is wrong; his characters, asserts Barthes, are but primitive or archetypal figures. One can understand the irritation of scholars before the inflated rhetoric of Barthes, typical of the young critics. He calls the room represented on the Racinian stage the site of tragedy and adds, "Le lieu tragique est un lieu stupéfié, saisi entre deux peurs, entre deux fantasmes; celui de l'étendue et celui de la profondeur." Such linguistic verve expresses ideas that are also pure rhapsody. If the principal room is the place of tragedy, the adjoining vestibule symbolizes for Barthes flight and liberty. Beyond the vestibule is the sea, which stands for escape. Striking as such interpretations are, they must indeed be recognized as brilliant fantasies rather than contributions to knowledge.

The controversy which Barthes' *Racine* occasioned has led to an identification of the New Critics as the antiuniversity group. Barthes himself encouraged such identification by his article "Les Deux Critiques," first published in *Modern Language Notes* in 1963. In it he scores the literature departments for their alleged hostility towards "interpretive" criticism and their esteem for the outmoded positivistic criticism inherited from Lanson. He admits, however, that the New Critics are professors themselves for the most part and that several of their most important contributions have been accepted by the university as theses.[14] Since the dispute that they have occasioned involves professors on both sides, the university is not a very satisfactory basis of identification.

To refer to the New Critics as the Swiss school is not exact either, despite the importance of Switzerland in the development of New Criticism. The proximity of that country to Germany, where a similar philosophical and critical thinking has long been flourishing, and the knowledge of German literature and civilization which certain Swiss critics demonstrate, suggest that Switzerland has served as a relay station for the movement of critical ideas from Germany into

[14] See "Quoi de neuf à la Sorbonne," *Les Nouvelles Littéraires*, April 14, 1966, p. 9.

France. Be that as it may, Swiss universities have been vital centers in the development of New Criticism: Basel, where Raymond and Béguin taught, Zurich, where Poulet still teaches, Geneva, where Raymond, Starobinski, and Rousset now make up a strong concentration. Although it cannot properly serve as a designation, nationality must be included in any description of the New Criticism.

Both Jean Starobinski and Jean Rousset were born in Geneva, Starobinski in 1920 and Rousset in 1910. As critics, they pursue the sort of thematic or structural investigation that characterizes the New Criticism. Starobinski has been especially interested in the literary incidence of looking or seeing—"le complexe du regard." In Rousseau he finds the obsession of guilt translated into an imagery of spying and surveillance. In Corneille, it is the thirst for glory, the need to dazzle, that expresses itself in sight images. In Racine, it is love. Two objections to Starobinski's system immediately arise. First, it tells more about the author than about the work, a pitfall that phenomenologists no better than psychiatrists seem to avoid. Second, it discovers the obvious in finding vision an important basis for figurative language. There is nothing extraordinary in an expression like "I see" in the sense of "I understand." Jean Rousset is mainly concerned with patterns of plot, which he would like to prove inseparable from the meaning of the work. It is not difficult to see the x-ray pictures he takes; it is less easy to ascribe to them anything but subjective validity and to tie them in with the author's meaning. Moreover, as with Starobinski, if we can reduce complicated and flowery discourse to simple statement, we often find before us the commonplace and self-evident.

Starobinski's leaning towards psychoanalysis suggests the names of other New Critics likewise tending in that direction. Manuel de Diéguez (born in 1922) demonstrates what he calls Existential psychoanalysis in his book on

Chateaubriand. He sees the author of *Atala* struggling between two attracting forces: history and poetry. Antagonisms, tensions, ambivalences, paradoxes have become basic to the "mystique" of contemporary criticism everywhere. Diéguez, like Richard, demonstrates the proneness of French New Critics to find the structural foundation of a work in some movement in opposing directions. The great number of examples of Hegelian dialectic in the subconscious of an author makes us suspect that it is the critic who puts it there and that it "structures" his essay better than the work under discussion.

The "thematic" criticism of Jean-Paul Weber is quite close to psychoanalysis, but differs by its singleness of theme and by its personal nature. In classical analysis the theme is multiple—there may be many complexes within a single individual—and impersonal. What Weber looks for is, on the contrary, one very personal traumatic experience in childhood that proliferates throughout an artist's entire production. For example, Vigny and the clock. Noting the frequent occurrence of a clock motif in this poet, Weber suspects an obsession. For confirmation, he turns to biography and uncovers its source in an early traumatic event. Then he returns to the work, which, with the magnifying glass of Sherlock Holmes, he scrutinizes for all possible symbolic expression involving clocks. In his first book, Weber finds in eight authors similar key themes, and adds to this number in his second.

Alfred de Vigny, long neglected by critics, has recently returned to favor. François Germain studies Vigny's creative imagination in a huge Sorbonne thesis, which is one of the first examples of New Criticism to be presented for a degree. Germain's work claims to establish the "topography" of Vigny's imagination—his heaven and his hell—by representing in spatial terms the poet's complexes, his conflicts, and his ideas.

Among the practitioners of literary "psychoanalysis" one might include Robert Champigny (born in 1922), on the basis of his first study, which is an Existentialist analysis of Alain-Fournier. But this critic has since moved out of the area of Sartrian influence into a field reminiscent of criticism before Sainte-Beuve. Like Northrop Frye, Champigny seems to be working back towards a criticism based on a strict definition of genre. His latest essays propose, in effect, lines of demarcation which will separate the novel, the poem, and the play.

It is doubtless an abuse of a medical and scientific word to speak of studies in the creative imagination as psychoanalysis. To qualify it by the word "Existentialist" is even more abusive. Some critics prefer "phenomenological," "thematic," or "structural" to emphasize their focus on the author rather than on the man. We have seen that this focus is badly maintained. But if the critics commit the "biographical fallacy" in a new sort of way, they are not, for that reason, any more psychoanalysts. Neither, actually, is Charles Mauron (1898–1966), although his abundant references to psychoanalysis and a concentration upon the subconscious may lead one to think of him as such. Professor Mauron calls his technique psychocriticism, and it involves bringing together texts that point to an obsession or fixation. Among the younger men, Weber seems closest to Mauron. But Mauron does not push exclusiveness of theme as Weber does. Such individual differences and similarities among the new critical approaches complicate the problem of definition by a specific descriptive word. Particularly so when the words in use are improper—like psychoanalytical—or do violence to conventional usage—like phenomenological, thematic, or structural. Yet definition of the New Critics by description is somewhat more satisfactory than by nationality or by opposition to a "university" method.

Defining on the basis of description of method cannot

establish separate categories among the New Critics: the tangle of individual similarities and differences is too great. But it can locate certain focal points of activity. Weber and Mauron look for obsessive patterns; Germain, Richard, and Poulet map out the creative imagination; Barthes and Bachelard go beyond the personal towards the archetype; Diéguez and Richard emphasize ambivalence and antagonisms. The criticism of René Girard (born in 1923), like that of Rousset, aims at the organizational structure of a single work. Where Rousset finds various patterns, however, Girard has only one, which, with necessary modification, he would apply to every work of fiction. From his study of the hero's motivation, Girard concludes that the hero's will never acts spontaneously or independently—Don Quixote's values are copied from those of Amadis of Gaul; Madame Bovary's, from her notion of what high society considers good. In Girard's words, the line between the hero and the object of his desire is never straight; but, deflected towards a second character, it forms a triangle which becomes the inner architecture of the novel. Needless to say, this architecture becomes very complicated if it is to be that of all novels, and Girard's theory often seems to get lost in a maze of classification and distinction. One wonders if all the pains do more than affirm the obvious imitative factor in personality.

Lucien Goldmann (born in 1913) has been quick to see in Girard's triangle scheme that the "referred good" can be equated with a social ideal and therefore can be useful in furthering his own type of investigation, which is the sociology of literature. Goldmann is a Marxist critic, a disciple of Georg Lukàcs. He endorses the New Critics' approach to literature, but he would show how the intimate structures of a work reflect social values. He calls his work genetic-structural analysis.

Independent of the New Criticism, yet closer to it than

to any of the older types still practiced today, is the work of
Maurice Blanchot (born in 1907). Like Goldmann, Blanchot pursues extraliterary aims in his criticism. He does not
concern himself with society, however, but with philosophy.
Imbued with Hegelianism, his essays are solemn meditations
on the nature of literature and its fate. The dichotomy of
language and life has provided Blanchot with an inexhaustible theme. Michel Foucault (born in 1926) reminds one of
Blanchot. He, too, is fascinated by language as a phenomenon, and he expresses himself on the subject in a manner
that seems very close to Blanchot's.

On the basis of the nature of their work it has not been
possible to discern quite separate groups among the New
Critics. Indeed it is not possible to define by description the
group as a whole, except in general terms and in terms of
what they are not or profess they are not. We know them as
students of the creative processes of an author, interested
particularly in the spontaneous and unconscious function of
those processes as they manifest themselves in an author's
work. We know that they rely heavily upon their own intuition, which, since they have, along with a superior culture,
brilliantly original minds and great powers of imagination,
produces a type of criticism which is in itself creative. We
know that they are not content with simple scholarship,
biographical work, or any criticism which does not involve
the intimate elaboration of a literary work within the creative
faculties. We know that, as a group, they are not ideological
or political critics, and do not seek extraliterary values in the
works they study.

To compensate for what is vague or too general in a
definition by description, we might further sharpen our historical focus. The relationship with the postwar critics, German philosophers, and certain scholars like Béguin and Raymond has been pointed out. Jean-Paul Sartre, on the other

hand, has not received the emphasis he deserves. If the earlier, postwar critics were inspired by Sartre's metaphysical and ethical ideas, the New Critics, accepting his metaphysics as a matter of course, have ignored his ethics to concentrate on his psychology and its implications for literature. It is worth recalling that one of Sartre's earliest books was an essay on the imagination, the mechanics of which the New Critics have made their particular concern. Sartre's works on Baudelaire and on Jean Genet developed the techniques of Existential psychoanalysis, which have provided the New Critics with a method. Sartre, although never acknowledged by them as a guide or master, propagated the philosophy upon which their criticism is built, and he himself erected the first model structure.

The French New Critics, like the French New Novelists, are deeply in Sartre's debt. Second generation Existentialists, both occupy now the center of the literary stage in France. The novelists appeared first in the limelight, but the critics have now joined them. We cannot, in spite of the definite reservations we may feel about each and every one of them, but greet them with applause. However excessive their theories and their rhetoric may be, the New Critics stimulate rereading and rethinking in all areas of literature. Their contribution in exploring the underside of art is a very real one. Perhaps, too, they may gradually move to the upperside. We have seen that since World War II critical interest, first fixed upon content, has moved in the direction of form. But since it has so far been chiefly concerned with unconscious design, we can scarcely speak of an esthetic interest. The esthetic aspect of literature has been almost completely neglected and universally disdained by contemporary French critics. Perhaps before long, to give a proper balance to their research, they will look again at the conscious intention of the artists, which may be after all the greatest factor in the creation of a work.

GENERAL REFERENCES

"Où en est la critique, aujourd'hui?" *Arguments*, January, 1959, pp. 34–51.

Barthes, Roland. *Essais Critiques* (Seuil, 1964): "Les deux critiques," pp. 246–251; "Qu'est-ce que la critique," pp. 252–257.

——. *Critique et Vérité* (Seuil, 1966).

Berl, Emmanuel. " 'Anciens' contre 'Modernes': un match nul," *Preuves*, June, 1966, pp. 73–79.

Bonnefoy, Claude. "En 10 ans la 'Nouvelle Critique' a renouvelé notre vision de la littérature," *Arts*, February 19–25, 1964, p. 5.

Bonnefoy, Yves. "La critique anglo-saxonne et la critique française," *Preuves*, January, 1959, pp. 68–73.

Brée, Germaine and Zimmerman, Eugenia. "Contemporary French Criticism," *Comparative Literatures Studies*, III (1964), 175–196.

Carloni, J. C. and Filloux, Jean C. *La Critique Littéraire* (Presses Universitaires de France, 1955).

Diéguez, Manuel de. *L'Ecrivain et son langage* (Gallimard, 1960).

Doubrovsky, Serge. *Pourquoi la nouvelle critique?* (Mercure de France, 1966).

Dufrenne, Mikel. "Critique littéraire et phénoménologie," *Revue Internationale de Philosophie*, 68–69 (1964), 193–208.

Fayolle, Roger. *La Critique* (Colin, 1964).

Genette, Gérard. *Figures* (Seuil, 1966).

Girard, René. "Réflexions critiques sur les recherches littéraires," *MLN*, May, 1966, pp. 307–324.

Hell, Henri. "Pourquoi la nouvelle critique?" *La Quinzaine Littéraire*, July 15, 1966, pp. 13–14.

Joncherie, Roger. "A propos d'une critique 'nouvelle'," *La Nouvelle Critique*, November, 1955, pp. 168–180.

Kanters, Robert. "La Querelle des critiques," *La Revue de Paris*, January, 1966, pp. 121–130.

Kanters, Robert. "Critique de la critique," *Le Figaro Littéraire*, September 1, 1966, p. 5.

Moreau, Pierre. *La Critique littéraire en France* (Colin, 1960).

Picard, Raymond. "Critical Trends in France," *The Times Literary Supplement*, September 27, 1963, pp. 719–720.

———. *Nouvelle Critique ou Nouvelle Imposture?* (Pauvert, 1965).

Richard, J. P. "Quelques aspects nouveaux de la critique littéraire en France," *Le Français dans le monde*, March, 1963, pp. 2–9.

Situation de la critique (Syndicat des Critiques Littéraires, 1964).

Starobinski, Jean. "Les Directions nouvelles de la recherche critique," *Preuves*, June, 1965, pp. 23–32.

———. "Psychanalyse et critique littéraire," *Preuves*, March, 1966, pp. 21–32.

Stevens, Linton C. "Major Trends in Postwar French Criticism," *The French Review*, January, 1957, pp. 218–224.

"Pour ou contre la nouvelle critique? Débat entre MM. Pierre de Boisdeffre, Jacques de Bourbon Busset, Charles Dédéyan, Raymond Picard, Jean Sur," *La Table Ronde*, June, 1966, pp. 81–98.

Weber, Jean-Paul. *Néo-critique et Paléo-critique ou Contre Picard* (Pauvert, 1966).

THE CRITICS

GASTON BACHELARD
(1884–1962)

Professor of the history and philosophy of science at the Sorbonne, Gaston Bachelard began his career in 1919 teaching physics and chemistry in the collège of Bar-sur-Aube, his birthplace. He left there in 1930 and, having studied successfully for the agrégation and the doctorat-ès-lettres, accepted a chair in philosophy at Dijon, where he remained until called to Paris. Bachelard must be reckoned as an important influence upon contemporary French philosophers and writers, who followed with keen interest his efforts to establish fruitful relationships between science, psychology, and poetry, and his ultimate recognition of phenomenology as the method par excellence of exploring the human soul. Of primary concern to Bachelard was the poetic image, for him the most exquisite expression of man's soul; his analyses of the imaginal processes that underlie poetry have inspired and oriented the younger critics of today.

This great teacher and prolific writer carried out several important investigations in the field of the poetic imagination, illustrating them by wide literary reference. He began by exploring the significance and the representation in the human mind of natural phenomena associated with the four elements postulated by the ancients: fire, water, air, the earth. The various human responses to fire he distinguished by names inspired by psychoanalysis—the Empedocles complex, the Novalis complex, the Hoffmann complex—and linked them to man's most primitive feelings. Responses to water, air, and the earth he likewise traced back to the earliest movements of consciousness. Although Bachelard sounds in these studies and in his book on Lautréamont like a philosopher turned psychoanalyst, and although his debt to Jung is apparent, he increasingly stressed the differences between his own work and psychoanalysis. In the matter of artistic creation, he pointed out, the psychoanalyst is concerned more with the personality behind the work—explains the rose by the manure—whereas the phenomenologist concentrates upon the poetic act itself. His research convinced him that the poetic image is less a reflection of reality than a sublimation of an archetype and that it often surpasses the intention or even the desire of the poet. In Proust, he announced, Elstir's roses are not a faithful copy of roses but a new variety never existing in nature. In demonstrating that the stuff of art is drawn from revery or the undirected play of the imagination, Bachelard made clear the deep significance of the creative act, to the artist as a means of expressing his fundamental being and to the reader as a means of gratifying his own essential nature. Continuing his studies on the creative imagination in *La Poétique de l'Espace*, Bachelard turned to the various spatial representations that evoke or translate feelings of happiness and discussed such items as the house, the drawer, the nest, the shell, as symbols of security and intimacy. His "phenomenology" of revery (*La Poétique de la Rêverie*), published a year before his death, is a tender evocation of the joys of daydreams—indeed, is a revery of revery—but, in addition, is a vigorous defense of revery as a positive and creative state of mind which links the mature psyche with childhood, art, and the cosmos.

§

One can imagine what readjustment was required of Bachelard when he, a philosopher of science, turned to study the poetic imagination. In explaining how completely, in order to deal with this new subject, he had to break with the modes of thinking most habitual with him—integration, classification, application of causal principles—he suggests not only the reorientation demanded of him but of us all, if we are to comprehend the phenomenon of artistic creativity.

Un philosophe qui a formé toute sa pensée en s'attachant aux thèmes fondamentaux de la philosophie des sciences, qui a suivi, aussi nettement qu'il a pu, l'axe du rationalisme actif, l'axe du rationalisme croissant de la science contemporaine, doit oublier son savoir, rompre avec toutes ses habitudes de recherches philosophiques s'il veut étudier les problèmes posés par l'imagination poétique. Ici, le passé de culture ne compte pas; le long effort de liaisons et de constructions de pensées, effort de la semaine et du mois, est inefficace. Il faut être présent, présent à l'image dans la minute de l'image: s'il y a une philosophie de la poésie, cette philosophie doit naître et renaître à l'occasion d'un vers dominant, dans l'adhésion totale à une image isolée, très précisément dans l'extase même de la nouveauté d'image. L'image poétique est un soudain relief du psychisme, relief mal étudié dans des causalités psychologiques subalternes. Rien non plus de général et de coordonné ne peut servir de base à une philosophie de la poésie. La notion de principe, la notion de "base" serait ici ruineuse. Elle bloquerait l'essentielle actualité, l'essentielle nouveauté psychique du poème. Alors que la réflexion philosophique s'exerçant sur une pensée scientifique longuement travaillée doit demander que la nouvelle idée s'intègre à un corps d'idées éprouvées, même si ce corps d'idées est astreint, par la nouvelle idée, à un remaniement profond, comme c'est le cas dans toutes les révolutions de la science contemporaine, la philosophie de la poésie doit reconnaître que l'acte poétique n'a pas de passé, du moins pas de passé proche le long duquel on pourrait suivre sa préparation et son avènement.

Quand, par la suite, nous aurons à faire mention du rapport d'une image poétique nouvelle et d'un archétype dormant au fond de l'inconscient, il nous faudra faire comprendre que ce rapport n'est pas, à proprement parler, *causal*. L'image poétique n'est pas soumise à une poussée. Elle n'est pas l'écho d'un passé. C'est plutôt l'inverse: par l'éclat d'une image, le passé lointain résonne d'échos et l'on ne voit guère à quelle profondeur ces échos vont se répercuter et s'éteindre. Dans sa nouveauté, dans son activité, l'image poétique a un être propre, un dynamisme propre. Elle relève d'une *ontologie directe.* C'est à cette ontologie que nous voulons travailler.

. . . .

    Dire que l'image poétique échappe à la causalité est, sans doute, une déclaration qui a sa gravité. Mais les causes alléguées par le psychologue et le psychanalyste ne peuvent jamais bien expliquer le caractère vraiment inattendu de l'image nouvelle, non plus que l'adhésion qu'elle suscite dans une âme étrangère au processus de sa création. Le poète ne me confère pas le passé de son image et cependant son image prend tout de suite racine en moi. La communicabilité d'une image singulière est un fait de grande signification ontologique. Nous reviendrons sur cette communion par actes brefs, isolés et actifs. Les images entraînent—après coup—mais elles ne sont pas les phénomènes d'un entraînement. Certes on peut, dans des recherches psychologiques, donner une attention aux méthodes psychanalytiques pour déterminer la personnalité d'un poète, on peut trouver ainsi une mesure des pressions—surtout de l'oppression— qu'un poète a dû subir dans le cours de sa vie, mais l'acte poétique, l'image soudaine, la flambée de l'être dans l'imagination, échappent à de telles enquêtes. Il faut en venir, pour éclairer philosophiquement le problème de l'image poétique, à une phénoménologie de l'imagination. Entendons par là une étude du phénomène de l'image poétique quand l'image émerge dans la conscience comme un produit direct du coeur, de l'âme, de l'être de l'homme saisi dans son actualité.[1]

                        —*La Poétique de l'Espace,* pp.1–2.

Bachelard pursues his discussion of how the phenomenological approach differs from the psychoanalytical:

Peut-être la situation phénoménologique sera-t-elle précisée à l'égard des enquêtes psychanalytiques si nous pouvons dégager, à propos des images poétiques, une sphère de *sublimation pure,* d'une sublimation qui ne sublime rien, qui est délestée de la charge des passions, libérée de la poussée des désirs. En donnant ainsi à l'image poétique de pointe un absolu de sublimation,

---

[1] For a translation of this and the following passages by Bachelard, see Appendix 1.

nous jouons gros jeu sur une simple nuance. Mais il nous semble que la poésie donne des preuves abondantes de cette sublimation absolue. Nous en rencontrerons souvent dans le cours de cet ouvrage. Quand ces preuves leur sont données, le psychologue, le psychanalyste ne voient plus, dans l'image poétique, que simple jeu, jeu éphémère, jeu de totale vanité. Précisément, les images sont alors pour eux sans signification—sans signification passionnelle, sans signification psychologique, sans signification psychanalytique. Il ne leur vient pas à l'esprit que de telles images ont précisément une *signification poétique.* Mais la poésie est là, avec ses milliers d'images de jet, d'images par lesquelles l'imagination créatrice s'installe dans son propre domaine.

Chercher des antécédents à une image, alors qu'on est dans l'existence même de l'image, c'est, pour un phénoménologue, une marque invétérée de *psychologisme.* Prenons, au contraire, l'image poétique en son être. La conscience poétique est si totalement absorbée par l'image qui apparaît sur le langage, au-dessus du langage habituel, elle parle, avec l'image poétique, un langage si nouveau qu'on ne peut plus envisager utilement des corrélations entre le passé et le présent. Nous donnerons par la suite des exemples de telles ruptures de signification, de sensation, de sentimentalité, qu'il faudra bien nous accorder que l'image poétique est sous le signe d'un être nouveau.

Cet être nouveau, c'est l'homme heureux.

Heureux en parole, donc malheureux en fait, objectera tout de suite le psychanalyste. Pour lui, la sublimation n'est qu'une compensation verticale, une fuite vers la hauteur, exactement comme la compensation est une fuite latérale. Et aussitôt, le psychanalyste quitte l'étude ontologique de l'image; il creuse l'histoire d'un homme; il voit, il montre les souffrances secrètes du poète. Il explique la fleur par l'engrais.

Le phénoménologue ne va pas si loin. Pour lui, l'image est là, la parole parle, la parole du poète lui parle. Nul besoin d'avoir vécu les souffrances du poète pour prendre le bonheur de parole offert par le poète—bonheur de parole qui domine le drame même. La sublimation, dans la poésie, surplombe la psychologie de l'âme terrestrement malheureuse. C'est un fait: la poésie a un bonheur qui lui est propre, quelque drame qu'elle soit amenée à illustrer.

La sublimation pure telle que nous l'envisageons pose un

drame de méthode, car bien entendu, le phénoménologue ne saurait méconnaître la réalité psychologique profonde des processus de sublimation si longuement étudiés par la psychanalyse. Mais il s'agit de passer, phénoménologiquement, à des images invécues, à des images que la vie ne prépare pas et que le poète crée. Il s'agit de vivre l'invécu et de s'ouvrir à une ouverture de langage. On trouvera de telles expériences dans de rares poèmes. Tels certains poèmes de Pierre-Jean Jouve. Pas d'œuvre plus nourrie de méditations psychanalytiques que les livres de Pierre-Jean Jouve. Mais, par instant, la poésie chez lui connaît de telles flammes qu'on n'a plus à vivre dans le premier foyer. Ne dit-il pas: "La poésie dépasse constamment ses origines, et pâtissant plus loin dans l'extase ou le chagrin, elle demeure plus libre." (En Miroir, p. 109) Et, page 112: "Plus j'avançais dans le temps et plus la plongée fut maîtrisée, éloignée de la cause occasionnelle, conduite à la pure forme de langage." Pierre-Jean Jouve accepterait-il de compter les "causes" décelées par la psychanalyse comme des causes "occasionnelles"? Je ne le sais. Mais, dans la région de "la pure forme de langage" les causes du psychanalyste ne permettent pas de prédire l'image poétique en sa nouveauté. Elles sont tout au plus des "occasions" de libération. Et c'est en cela que la poésie—dans l'ère poétique où nous sommes—est spécifiquement "surprenante", donc ses images sont imprévisibles. L'ensemble des critiques littéraires ne prennent pas une assez nette conscience de cette imprévisibilité qui, précisément, dérange les plans de l'explication psychologique habituelle.

—*Ibid.*, pp. 12–13.

What Bachelard seems to be taken by is the fact that a poetic image is something more than and something different from the sum total of its explainable causes. This describes the limitations of the psychologist or the "scientific" critic. He does not say that their work is valueless, but that it better serves other objectives than esthetic comprehension. Only the phenomenologist deals directly with the "ontology" of art. One may feel that it is unfortunate that

Bachelard, in an enterprise that is clearly different from psychoanalysis, should use the familiar terminology of psychoanalysis. A sublimation that does not sublimate anything might better be called something else.

In attaching the poetic image to primitive human responses, Bachelard gives the literary critic a touchstone of judgment. An image is true or false, good or bad, depending on whether it has roots in the collective unconscious.

On pourra alors se rendre compte que l'image est une plante qui a besoin de terre et de ciel, de substance et de forme. Les images trouvées par les hommes évoluent lentement, difficilement, et l'on comprend la profonde remarque de Jacques Bousquet: "Une image coûte autant de travail à l'humanité qu'un caractère nouveau à la plante." Bien des images essayées ne peuvent vivre parce qu'elles sont de simples jeux formels, parce qu'elles ne sont pas vraiment adaptées à la matière qu'elles doivent parer.

. . . .

Fort de toutes ces convictions, nous pouvions faire abstraction des connaissances usées, des mythologies formelles et allégoriques qui survivent dans un enseignement sans vie, sans force. Nous pouvions faire aussi abstraction des innombrables poèmes sans sincérité où de plats rimeurs s'acharnent à multiplier les échos les plus divers, les plus brouillés. Quand nous nous sommes appuyés sur des faits mythologiques, c'est que nous avons reconnu en eux une action permanente, une action inconsciente sur les âmes d'aujourd'hui. Une mythologie des eaux, dans son ensemble, ne serait qu'une histoire. Nous avons voulu écrire une psychologie, nous avons voulu relier les images littéraires et les songes.

—*L'Eau et les Rêves*, p. 4.

Like Albert Béguin, Bachelard would stress that revery provides the material of art. Upon the complexes studied by the psychoanalyst there are the grafts of cultural complexes: the study of these latter complexes, manifest in the imagery first of revery and then of art, offers criticism a new approach:

... si nos recherches pouvaient retenir l'attention, elles devraient apporter quelques moyens, quelques instruments pour renouveler la critique littéraire. C'est à cela que tend l'introduction de la notion de *complexe de culture* dans la psychologie littéraire. Nous appelons ainsi des *attitudes irréfléchies* qui commandent le travail même de la réflexion. Ce sont, par exemple, dans le domaine de l'imagination, des images favorites qu'on croit puisées dans les spectacles du monde et qui ne sont que des *projections* d'une âme obscure.

—*Ibid.*, pp. 25–26.

Although the cultural complex may revitalize and rejuvenate a tradition, it usually produces lusterless and meaningless figures of rhetoric. The critic will recognize and condemn this merchandise out of schoolbooks. To show how it is done, Bachelard cites Pierre Louys:

Dans son excès de surcharge mythologique, l'exemple du *cygne* de Pierre Louys peut maintenant faire comprendre le sens précis d'un *complexe de culture*. Le plus souvent le complexe de culture s'attache à une culture scolaire, c'est-à-dire à une culture traditionnelle. ... Pierre Louys s'est adressé à la mythologie scolaire pour écrire sa nouvelle [*Lêda*]. Ne pourront la lire que des "initiés" à la connaissance *scolaire* des mythes. Mais si un tel lecteur est satisfait, sa satisfaction reste impure. Il ne sait pas s'il aime le fond ou s'il aime la forme; il ne sait pas s'il enchaîne des images ou s'il enchaîne des passions. Souvent les symboles sont réunis sans souci de leur évolution symbolique. Qui parle de Lêda doit parler du cygne et de l'œuf. Le même conte réunira les deux histoires, sans pénétrer le caractère mythique de l'œuf. Dans la nouvelle de Pierre Louys l'idée vient même à Lêda qu'elle pourrait "faire cuire l'œuf dans la cendre chaude comme elle avait vu que faisaient les satyres."

—*Ibid.*, pp. 57–58.

SELECTED WORKS

La Psychanalyse du feu (Gallimard, 1938). Translated by Alan C. M. Ross as *Psychoanalysis of Fire* (Boston: Beacon Press, 1964).

Lautréamont (Corti, 1939).

L'Eau et les Rêves (Corti, 1942).

L'Air et les Songes (Corti, 1943).

La Terre et les Rêveries de la Volonté (Corti, 1948).

La Terre et les Rêveries du Repos (Corti, 1948).

La Poétique de l'Espace (Presses Universitaires, 1957). Translated by Maria Jolas as *Poetics of Space* (Orion Press, 1964).

La Poétique de la Rêverie (Presses Universitaires, 1960).

La Flamme d'une Chandelle (Presses Universitaires, 1961).

REFERENCES

"Gaston Bachelard et les poètes," *Cahiers du Sud*, 376 (1964), 179–206.

Christofides, C. G. "Gaston Bachelard's Phenomenology of the Imagination," *The Romantic Review*, February, 1961, pp. 36–47.

Diéguez, Manuel de. *L'Ecrivain et Son Langage* (Gallimard, 1960), "Gaston Bachelard," pp. 221–233.

Faye, Jean-Pierre. "L'Apport de Gaston Bachelard," *Arguments*, Jan.–March, 1959, pp. 41–44.

Quillet, Pierre. *Gaston Bachelard* (Seghers, 1965).

Souriau, Etienne. "L'Esthétique de Gaston Bachelard," *Annales de l'Université de Paris*, Jan.–March, 1963, pp. 11–23.

ROLAND BARTHES

Born in Bayonne in 1915, Roland Barthes received his secondary and university education in Paris. In 1939 he began teaching literature, that year in Biarritz and the next one in Paris. Tuberculosis, which had attacked him once before, in 1933, forced him to give up teaching; he did not go back to teaching until 1948. Then, after one year in Bucharest and one in Alexandria, he apparently decided to try another livelihood. For the next two years he worked for the Cultural Relations Office in Paris. Since then, he has been increasingly taken up by his writing. Besides having published several volumes of critical essays, he edits the magazine *Théâtre populaire* and contributes to *Critique*, which he also serves as a member of the administrative committee. These activities, plus his recent lecturing at the Ecole pratique des Hautes Etudes, have made him one of the most prominent critics in France today. What Robbe-Grillet is to the New Novel, Barthes is to the New Criticism—a leader and the chief target of attack from the opposition.

Histrionics and rhetoric give Barthes' essays a look of originality that they do not always possess. They capture attention by their emphatic style but often add little to what literary historians have already said in studies that maintain better balance and are more wary of specious generalizations. This is already evident in his first work, *Le Degré Zéro de l'Ecriture*, a dazzling piece of argumentation in which he attempts to isolate from language and style a distinct socio-historical aspect that he calls "writing." He pushes his investigation of language problems further in *Mythologies* and takes up the subject of social myths. In the introduction to *Michelet par lui-même* and in the essay on Racine, he tries his hand at literary "psychoanalysis." In his faults and virtues, Barthes typifies the French New Critic. He also offers a fine example of the techniques most in vogue as well as the prejudices and shibboleths that characterize the new school.

Whether his studies take the direction of sociology or psychoanalysis, they depart from the work itself, from the author's writing rather than from his life. Manuel de Diéguez asserts that a Marxist bias keeps Barthes from the crucial problem of stylistic uniqueness. Whatever truth there may be in Diéguez' stricture, it applies only to the sociological interpretations Barthes gives and not to their source. Style is always his point of reference, the subject of his research. As he declares in the introduction to *Michelet par lui-même*, his concern is not with history or biography but only with the work. What he aims to do is to discover in it those basic, recurring themes which may constitute a pattern of obsessions or preoccupations. Thus, in noting Michelet's allusions to qualities, conditions, phenomena, and the like, Barthes hopes to expose Michelet's literary psyche or, as Barthes himself expresses it, arrive at Michelet's basic "coherence." Likewise in his *Racine*, Barthes works exclusively with the texts, but here the results of his analysis have only the most indirect bearing on the personality of the author. Jung rather than Freud (or Marx) seems to guide him as he reduces Racine's theater to archetypal patterns and interprets their significance. The room where the hero is (the site of tragedy) becomes the equivalent of the mythic lair, the antechamber is the place of "transmission," what lies beyond, outside, in the wings, signifies escape or the non-tragic. The plots hark back to folklore or to the primitive psyche—prehistoric tribal struggles between father and sons. For Barthes, Racine's characters are not persons but figures acting out elemental myth material; the interest of his theater is not psychology but the representation of fundamental relationships and conflict between primitive forces.

Included in the volume on Racine is a sort of challenge to

literary historians to renounce the linking of monographs on individual authors and calling the result literary history. What they might better do is investigate the sociology of literature at a given time. But Barthes admits that this sort of literary history would actually be no different from history itself. He nevertheless is dissatisfied with traditional scholarship, considering it superficial and trivial, ridiculous in its scientific pretensions and its fear of systems. He would prefer sociology and psychoanalysis. Barthes' own work, we should note, is, strictly speaking, neither one nor the other. He goes as rhetorician into whatever field he ventures. That is why he always compels our attention and why he often provokes our irritation.

ॐ

Barthes' reading of Racine is extremely stimulating, a tribute to the great dramatist's capacity for limitless interpretation. It is a tribute to the critic, as well, who, by close attention and reflection, can dramatically reinterpret an author enshrined. This does not mean that Barthes' "anthropology" of Racine invalidates other interpretations—even the most conventional—but it does add a dimension, which, although not entirely unperceived by others, had never been presented so completely or with such picturesque vehemence. Who had described the room which the stage represents in such terms as the following: "Le lieu tragique est un lieu stupéfié, saisi entre deux peurs, entre deux fantasmes: celui de l'étendue et celui de la profondeur"? Passionate rhetoric combines with the language of dialectics and erudition to give Barthes' style its particular quality. The following passage from *Sur Racine* will demonstrate more amply:

Le Confident. Entre l'échec et la mauvaise foi, il y a pourtant une issue possible, celle de la dialectique. La tragédie n'ignore pas cette issue; mais elle n'a pu l'admettre qu'à force d'en banaliser la figure fonctionelle: c'est le confident. A l'époque de Racine, la mode du rôle est en train de passer, ce qui accroît peut-être sa signification. Le confident racinien (et cela est conforme à son origine) est lié au héros par une sorte de lien féodal, de *dévotion;* cette liaison désigne en lui un double véritable, probablement délégué à assumer toute la trivialité du conflit et de sa solution, bref à fixer la part non-tragique de la tragédie dans une zone latérale où le langage se discrédite, devient *domestique.** On le sait, au dogmatisme du héros s'oppose continuellement l'empirisme du confident. Il faut rappeler ici ce qu'on a déjà dit à propos de la clôture tragique: pour le confident, le monde existe; sortant de la scène, il peut entrer dans le réel et en revenir: son insignifiance autorise son ubiquité. Le premier résultat de ce *droit de sortie* c'est que pour lui l'univers cesse d'être absolument antinomique:† constituée essentiellement par une construction alternative du monde, l'aliénation cède, dès que le monde devient multiple. Le héros vit dans l'univers des formes, des alternances, des signes; le confident dans celui des contenus, des causalités, des accidents. Sans doute il est la voix de la raison (d'une raison fort sotte, mais qui est tout de même un peu la Raison) contre la voix de la "passion"; mais ceci veut dire surtout qu'il parle le possible contre l'impossible; l'échec constitue le héros, il lui est transcendant; aux yeux du confident, l'échec *touche* le héros, il lui est contingent. D'où le caractère dialectique des solutions qu'il propose (sans succès) et qui consistent toujours à médiatiser l'alternative.

A l'égard du héros, sa médecine est donc apéritive, elle consiste d'abord à ouvrir le secret, à définir dans le héros le point exact de son dilemme; il veut produire un éclaircissement. Sa technique semble grossière, mais elle est éprouvée; il s'agit de provoquer le héros en lui représentant naïvement une hypothèse contraire à son élan, en un mot de "gaffer" (en général, le héros "accuse" le coup, mais il le recouvre rapidement sous un flot de paroles justificatives). Quant aux conduites qu'il recom-

---

* Phèdre charge Oenone de la débarrasser des *tâches* de l'acte, de façon à n'en garder noblement, et enfantinement, que le résultat tragique: "Pour le fléchir enfin tente tous les moyens." (*Phèd.* III, 1.)

† "C'est seulement dans l'existence sociale que les antinomies telles que subjectivisme et objectivisme, spiritualisme et matérialisme, activité et passivité perdent leur caractère antinomique . . ." (Marx, *Manuscrit économico-philosophique.*)

mande face au conflit, elles sont toutes dialectiques, c'est-à-dire subordonnent la fin aux moyens. Voici les plus courantes de ces conduites; *fuir* (qui est l'expression non-tragique de la mort tragique); *attendre* (ce qui revient à opposer au temps-répétition le temps-maturation de la réalité); *vivre* (*vivez*, ce mot de tous les confidents, désigne nommément le dogmatisme tragique comme une volonté d'échec et de mort: il suffirait que le héros fasse de la vie une valeur pour qu'il soit sauvé). Sous ses trois formes, dont la dernière impérative, la viabilité recommandée par le confident est bien la valeur la plus anti-tragique qui soit; le rôle du confident n'est pas seulement de la représenter; il est aussi d'opposer aux alibis dont le héros recouvre sa volonté d'échec une *Ratio* extérieure à la tragédie et qui en quelque sorte l'explique: il *plaint* le héros, c'est-à-dire que d'une certaine manière il atténue sa responsabilité; il le croit libre de se sauver mais non point de faire le mal, *agi* dans l'échec et pourtant disponible à son issue; c'est tout le contraire du héros tragique qui revendique une responsabilité pleine lorsqu'il s'agit d'assumer une faute ancestrale qu'il n'a pas commise, mais se déclare impuissant lorsqu'il s'agit de la dépasser, qui se veut libre, en un mot, d'être esclave mais non point libre d'être libre. Peut-être que dans le confident, bien qu'il soit gauche et souvent très sot, se profile déjà toute cette lignée de valets frondeurs qui opposeront à la régression psychologique du maître et seigneur, une maîtrise souple et heureuse de la réalité.[1]

—*Sur Racine*, pp. 61–63.

Barthes summarizes his views on criticism in two essays that he wrote for Anglo-American readers. "Les Deux Critiques" establishes the distinction between "university" criticism and the new "interpretive" criticism in France. For Barthes, the Sorbonne, still faithful to the Lansonian method postulated upon deterministic concepts of cause and effect, cannot admit a criticism of immanent analysis:

Il semble qu'on approche ici du cœur de la question. Car si l'on se tourne maintenant vers le refus implicite que la critique uni-

[1] For translation, see Appendix 2.

versitaire oppose à l'autre critique, pour en deviner les raisons, on voit tout de suite que ce refus n'est nullement la crainte banale du nouveau; la critique universitaire n'est ni rétrograde ni démodée (un peu lente, peut-être): elle sait parfaitment s'adapter. Ainsi, bien qu'elle ait pratiqué pendant des années une psychologie conformiste de l'homme normal (héritée de Théodule Ribot, contemporain de Lanson), elle vient de "reconnaître" la psychanalyse, en consacrant (par un doctorat particulièrement bien accueilli) la critique de Ch. Mauron, d'obédience strictement freudienne. Mais dans cette consécration même, c'est la ligne de résistance de la critique universitaire qui apparaît à découvert: car la critique psychanalytique est *encore* une psychologie, elle postule un *ailleurs* de l'œuvre (qui est l'enfance de l'écrivain), un secret de l'auteur, une matière à déchiffrer, qui reste bien l'âme humaine, fût-ce au prix d'un vocabulaire nouveau: mieux vaut une psychopathologie de l'écrivain, plutôt que pas de psychologie du tout; en mettant en rapport les détails d'une œuvre et les détails d'une vie, la critique psychanalytique continue à pratiquer une esthétique des motivations fondée tout entière sur le rapport d'extériorité: c'est parce que Racine était lui-même orphelin qu'il y a tant de Pères dans son théâtre: la transcendance biographique est sauve: il y a, il y aura toujours des vies d'écrivains à "fouiller". En somme, ce que la critique universitaire est disposée à admettre (peu à peu et après des résistances successives), c'est paradoxalement le principe même d'une critique d'interprétation, ou si l'on préfère (bien que le mot fasse encore peur), d'une critique idéologique; mais ce qu'elle refuse, c'est que cette interprétation et cette idéologie puissent décider de travailler dans un domaine purement intérieur à l'œuvre; bref, ce qui est récusé, c'est l'*analyse immanente*: tout est acceptable, pourvu que l'œuvre puisse être mise en rapport avec *autre chose* qu'elle-même, c'est-à-dire autre chose que la littérature: l'histoire (même si elle devient marxiste), la psychologie (même si elle se fait psychanalytique), ces *ailleurs* de l'œuvre seront peu à peu admis; ce qui ne le sera pas, c'est un travail qui s'installe *dans* l'œuvre et ne pose son rapport au monde qu'après l'avoir entièrement décrite de l'intérieur, dans ses fonctions, ou, comme on dit aujourd'hui, dans sa structure; ce qui est rejeté, c'est donc en gros la critique phénoménologique (qui *explicite* l'œuvre au lieu de l'expliquer), la critique thématique (qui reconstitue les métaphores intérieures de l'œuvre) et la critique structurale (qui tient l'œuvre pour un système de fonctions).

Pourquoi ce refus de l'immanence (dont le principe est d'ailleurs souvent mal compris)? On ne peut donner pour le moment que des réponses contingentes; peut-être est-ce par soumission obstinée à l'idéologie déterministe, qui veut que l'œuvre soit le "produit" d'une "cause" et que les causes extérieures soient plus "causes" que les autres; peut-être aussi parce que passer d'une critique des déterminations à une critique des fonctions et des significations impliquerait une conversion profonde des normes du savoir, donc de la technique, donc de la profession même de l'universitaire; il ne faut pas oublier que la recherche n'étant pas encore séparée de l'enseignement, l'Université travaille mais aussi elle décerne des diplômes; il lui faut donc une idéologie qui soit articulée sur une technique suffisamment difficile pour constituer un instrument de sélection; le positivisme lui fournit l'obligation d'un savoir vaste, difficile, patient; la critique immanente—du moins lui semble-t-il—ne demande, devant l'œuvre, qu'un pouvoir d'*étonnement*, difficilement mesurable: on comprend qu'elle hésite à convertir ses exigences.

—*Modern Language Notes*, December, 1963, pp. 451–452.

One must say that however accurate Barthes is in describing the traditional concept of scholarship at the Sorbonne, he is unfair to that venerable institution. In the first place, it is far less hostile to new approaches in criticism than he declares. Mauron's psychoanalysis is certainly not strict Freudianism. If this one example does not prove the Sorbonne's broad tolerance, there is that of Jean-Paul Weber and others. In the second place, its stand on documentation and erudition derives less from ideological principles than from pedagogical ones. Knowledge "vast, difficult, and patient" may not justly be equated with a specific nineteenth-century philosophy of life. Finally, in view of the close affiliation of the interpretive critics with universities in the provinces as well as in the capital, the distinction between university and nonuniversity criticism makes little sense today. Some of Barthes' colleagues have chided him for harping on an outmoded distinction; the professors have defended themselves by attacking. Raymond Picard scored Barthes' own critical method in a lengthy article in the *Revue des Sciences Humaines*. Professor Pommier had already commented harshly upon Barthes' study of Michelet; now Professor Picard denounces the subjective and often apparently gratuitous character of Barthes' assertions concerning Racine. Although concentrated upon Barthes, this article constitutes the most serious indictment to date of the assumptions and procedures of all the "new" critics. It has appeared in pamphlet form under the title *Nouvelle Critique ou Nouvelle Imposture?*[2]

"Qu'est-ce que la Critique?" begins with the theme of the first article, "Les Deux Critiques," reiterating that university criticism, in spite of its professed objectivity, is indeed postulated upon an ideology as much as any of the types of interpretive criticism which it accuses of systematic *parti-pris*. Barthes believes there can be no criticism without an implicit ideology. But that does not have much importance in fact, since he considers that criticism, having language rather than the world as its object, is concerned with validities and not with verities. A piece of literature is valid if it constitutes a coherent system of signs. This the critic tests by trying to fit the language of his period (Existentialist, Marxist, Psychoanalytical) to the language of the author in question.

C'est en effet en reconnaissant qu'elle n'est elle-même qu'un langage (ou plus exactement un méta-langage) que la critique peut être contradictoirement mais authentiquement, à la fois objective et subjective, historique et existentielle, totalitaire et

---

[2] Barthes' reply to Picard is *Critique et Vérité* (1966). The Picard-Barthes quarrel received considerable publicity in the press and gave other critics the opportunity of taking sides. Typical "coverage" is the article by Jean-François Revel and that of Lucette Finas, both published in *La Quinzaine Littéraire*, April 15, 1966 (pp. 14–15). Several other discussions have been included in the General References.

libérale. Car d'une part le langage que chaque critique choisit de parler ne lui descend pas du ciel, il est l'un des quelques langages que son époque lui propose, il est objectivement le terme d'un certain mûrissement historique du savoir, des idées, des passions intellectuelles, il est une *nécessité;* et d'autre part, ce langage nécessaire est choisi par chaque critique en fonction d'une certaine organisation existentielle, comme l'*exercice* d'une fonction intellectuelle qui lui appartient en propre, exercice dans lequel il met toute sa "profondeur", c'est-à-dire ses choix, ses plaisirs, ses résistances, ses obsessions. Ainsi peut s'amorcer au sein de l'œuvre critique le dialogue de deux histoires et de deux subjectivités, celles de l'auteur et celles du critique. Mais ce dialogue est égoïstement tout entier déporté vers le présent: la critique n'est pas un "hommage" à la vérité du passé, ou à la vérité de "l'autre", elle est construction de l'intelligible de notre temps.

—*Essais Critiques,* p. 257. First published in English under the title "Criticism as Language," *The Times Literary Supplement,* September 27, 1963, pp. 739–740.

One may applaud the tolerant eclecticism that Barthes' position implies and reflect that indeed, if a piece of literature is to remain meaningful, it must always be capable of translation into contemporary language. This is what we have always meant by the "universality" of great art. One may reflect, nevertheless, that to equate language so exactly with a given ideology is not what we have had in mind and that a Marxist study of Racine or an Existentialist study of Pascal cannot remain on a plane of language but must always slip down to that of verities and the world.

With the collection of articles and prefaces where these two essays figure, the place of Barthes among contemporary French critics becomes quite clear. Definitely aligned with the interpretive group, he has made his own particular business the analysis of literary language from the point of view of history and society. The distinctions of language, writing, and style, which laid the foundation of his work, still support his research, which tends now to broaden out from literature into semantics and structural linguistics.

SELECTED WORKS

Le Degré Zéro de l'Ecriture (Seuil, 1953).

Michelet par lui-même (Seuil, 1954).

Mythologies (Seuil, 1957).

Sur Racine (Seuil, 1963). Translated by Richard Howard as *On Racine* (Hill and Wang, 1964).

"Criticism as Language," *The Times Literary Supplement,* September 27, 1963, pp. 739–740.

"Les Deux Critiques," *Modern Language Notes,* December, 1963, pp. 447–452.

Essais Critiques (Seuil, 1964).

Critique et Vérité (Seuil, 1966).

REFERENCES

Diéguez, Manuel de. *L'Ecrivain et son langage* (Gallimard, 1960), "Roland Barthes," pp. 133–148.

Doubrovsky, Serge. *Pourquoi la nouvelle critique?* (Mercure de France, 1966).

Genette, Gérard. "L'Homme et les signes," *Critique,* February, 1965, pp. 99–114.

Girard, René. "Racine, poète de la gloire," *Critique,* June, 1964, pp. 483–506.

Mauriac, Claude. *L'Alittérature contemporaine* (Albin Michel, 1958), p. 201.

Picard, Raymond. *Nouvelle Critique ou Nouvelle Imposture?* (Pauvert, 1965).

Pingaud, Bernard. *Ecrivains d'aujourd'hui* (Grasset, 1960), "Roland Barthes," pp. 59–64.

Pommier, Jean. "Baudelaire et Michelet devant la jeune critique," *Revue d'Histoire littéraire*, Oct.–Dec., 1957, pp. 544–564.

Weber, Jean-Paul. *Néo-critique et Paléo-critique ou contre Picard* (Pauvert, 1966).

ALBERT BÉGUIN
(1901–1957)

At the time of his sudden death, Albert Béguin was one of the leading literary editors and scholars in Paris. He was of Swiss origin and had received his education at the Faculté des Lettres of Geneva and at the Sorbonne (doctorat ès lettres). A sojourn of five years at the University of Halle (1929–1934) gave him direct contact with the culture which attracted him by its Romantic Movement. Béguin's monumental thesis, *L'Ame romantique et le Rêve*, which stands as one of the most significant books of literary scholarship and intuition of the age, draws enormously on German literature. The year of its publication (1937), Béguin accepted the chair of French literature at Basel left vacant by Marcel Raymond and held it until 1945. Already apparent in his work on the Romantic soul, the interest this critic took in spiritual matters from the oneiric to the mystic becomes increasingly evident in subsequent publications. After his conversion to Catholicism, he devoted himself particularly to the study of Péguy, Bloy, and finally Bernanos. The movement known as Personalism, a philosophical movement basically Christian but with some elements common to Marxism and Existentialism, received his wholehearted support. He worked closely with its founder, Emmanuel Mounier, and upon the latter's death in 1950, took over the direction of his review *Esprit*.

Given to speaking his mind quite bluntly and not always sympathetic towards the efforts of young writers, Albert Béguin had, however, nothing but praise for the young critics such as Roland Barthes and Jean-Pierre Richard who were practicing a new kind of criticism based exclusively on the artistic phenomenon. Too long, Béguin explained in an article in *Esprit* (March, 1955), literary criticism had been deformed to serve history, psychology, or sociology. He even wondered, moreover, if literary history as such were still possible. In a previous article (January, 1955), he had stressed the regrettable tendency of the historical method to turn a work of art into a document. All this he had already stated or implied as early as 1937 in the introduction to his *L'Ame romantique*. His distrust of conventional scholarly techniques is demonstrated by remarks such as "l'erreur qui consiste à croire que dépister les 'sources' et suivre le cheminement des influences équivaut à expliquer la vie de l'esprit." (p. xiii) It is understandable that Béguin, himself a pioneer in textual analysis and chiefly interested in studying the processes of the creative imagination, should approve only that critical approach which limits itself to the work itself. Béguin hailed Marcel Raymond, Gaston Bachelard, and Georges Poulet as the leaders of a long-awaited revolution in French literary analysis. His own name should join the others, for Béguin's soundings into the artistic soul, his establishment of the artist's personal mythology and imagery have been an inspiration to all the new critics.

§

Typical of his critical approach is his work on Balzac. The result is a picture quite different from the old textbook image of the father of French realism. The Balzac that we see today, the viable and meaningful Balzac, derives from Béguin's interpretation.

Il y eut, sans événement qui puisse porter une date, une véritable conversion de Balzac. Conversion à la vie—s'il est possible de penser qu'un homme qui portait en lui la vie elle-même eût besoin de la découvrir. A ne considérer que les œuvres brèves de la *Comédie Humaine*, ou les contes dispersés dans les périodiques, on voit déjà que l'imagination balzacienne possède deux registres à la fois très différents et liés entre eux par une analogie à peu près parfaite. D'une part, ce sont les contemplations, les visions autonomes, où la pureté appartient à des anges, le mal à Satan et à ses suppôts, les événements se déroulant dans un univers qui ne ressemble que de loin à notre monde temporel. Mais d'autre part, des nouvelles plus dramatiques que fantastiques mettent sous nos yeux de simples aventures humaines, comme dans l'*Auberge rouge* par exemple, ou dans la terrible histoire de la *Grande Bretèche*, qui est un hallucinant chef-d'œuvre. Et pourtant, ces œuvres situées dans un temps absolument 'normal', loin des frontières où les lois du temporel allègent leur tyrannie, ne sont pas exemptes de mystérieuses présences, diaboliques ou divines. Les influences surnaturelles, pour n'emprunter aucune des apparences de la légende, n'y sont pas moins sensibles. Point de Satan en personne, ni de démons subalternes, mais dans le cœur des hommes les insinuations de la passion, la folie de l'or, du pouvoir, les penchants criminels. Point d'ange Séraphitus-Séraphita, mais l'amour et ses espérances lumineuses, les mystères de la sympathie, le mariage silencieux des âmes à travers la distance. Par-dessus tout, le règne terrestre de la douleur, des échecs, des catastrophes. Tout cela n'existe, n'a de sens, que par rapport à un ciel et à un enfer, qui ne sont pas explicitement évoqués, mais qui orientent tous les destins, partagés entre leurs appels contraires.

Le monde des nouvelles balzaciennes propose à la méditation du lecteur, dans des drames d'une intensité prodigieuse, une constante interrogation sur la nature humaine, ou plutôt encore sur les limites de la personne. Ce n'est pas en vain que tout y est expliqué par le magnétisme, la sympathie des âmes, l'influence sourde des images et des couleurs. La grande question de Balzac est toujours la même: où sont nos frontières? qu'est-ce qui est moi? à quoi suis-je exposé, de quelles communications avec autrui, de quels échanges avec tout ce qui m'entoure dois-je faire dépendre mes actes et mon destin? Le conte fantastique évoque les présences sensibles de Satan et de Dieu, exerçant leur influence, intervenant dans nos actes, guidant notre sort, et déjà la personne y apparaît non pas comme un être clos, qui se déterminerait lui-même, mais comme ouverte à des forces surnaturelles. Le conte dramatique, à son tour, décèle d'autres échanges, d'autres intrusions: le pressentiment maternel, dans le *Réquisitionnaire*, témoigne qu'un être aimé mène à **la fois**

sa vie hors de nous et une seconde vie, ou la même, en nous, si
bien que la mère peut lire dans son propre cœur ce qui advient
à son fils. Dans l'*Auberge rouge*, la velléité criminelle de l'un des
deux amis suscite mystérieusement le crime de l'autre, et toute
l'anxiété panique qui règne dans ce conte vient de cette effray-
ante pensée: nous pouvons obéir à une volonté qui est non pas
en nous-même mais dans un autre être.

L'homme, donc, se situe à l'entre-croisement d'influences diverses, et sa vraie personnalité, à chaque instant, est constituée
par la mécanique vivante de ces forces dont il n'est pas le maître.
Balzac traduit ainsi la peur qu'il avait lui-même d'être envahi,
de céder à la pression trop forte de la nature ou d'un monde
des esprits animé de pouvoirs agressifs. Quelle résistance opposer
à cette invasion, comment échapper à l'abîme de la démence
menaçante? Les contes qui ont pour héros des songeurs, des
chercheurs d'absolu, donnent la réponse balzacienne à cette
question: l'homme a, pour se défendre, le pouvoir de son intelligence, les dons qui le mettent en mesure de comprendre,
d'ordonner autour de lui les forces amies ou ennemies. Déchiffrer le réel, en lire les signes, c'est aussi se donner les moyens de
le dominer. Sans doute Balthasar Claes et Frenhofer, en se
proposant pour objet de leur pensée ou de leur art la découverte
d'une formule magique ou d'un pouvoir sans limites, se con-
damnent-ils à la catastrophe. Mais, si la conclusion de la *Recherche de l'Absolu* ou du *Chef-d'œuvre inconnu* est tragique,
si le peintre qui ambitionne la perfection divine aboutit au
néant, et si Claes ne peut crier *Eurêka* avant l'heure de sa mort,
ils sont tout de même des héros, et leur quête est une noble
quête. Qui a raison, se demande-t-on, de Balthasar Claes qui
sacrifie le bonheur des siens à l'effort de la pensée, ou de
Marguerite, sa femme, qui défend sa vie pied à pied contre
cette folle destruction? Ils ont raison tous les deux, car Balzac
ne choisit pas ici des responsabilités; l'affrontement tragique
des deux époux symbolise une lutte qui ne s'est apaisée dans
la conscience de Balzac lui-même, et qui, à ses yeux, se poursuit
éternellement en tout être humain. Cette lutte est la loi de la
vie, partagée entre le désir du bonheur et l'ambition de la
connaissance ou du pouvoir, déchirée par les vœux contradic-
toires de la tranquillité temporelle et des triomphes de l'esprit.
L'esprit est meurtrier pour qui suit son impérieuse exigence, il
use la vie, il lui tourne le dos et la nie; mais pour autant il n'est

pas question de refuser la vocation spirituelle au profit de la vie. Le paradoxe demeure insoluble, l'éternité ne peut être possédée ni par la résignation à l'humble bonheur humain, ni par la conquête héroïque de l'intelligence. Elle est au delà de la mort.

Parvenu à ce terme, Balzac est au moment de découvrir la beauté de la vie, de comprendre que c'est une beauté dans l'imparfait et dans l'insatisfaction. De la plongée dans le mystère qu'il vient d'opérer en écrivant ses nouvelles, il rapporte, en outre, ce sentiment que la personne est ouverte de toutes parts et composée de bien plus de choses que nous ne le savons d'ordinaire. Mais, instruit par l'expérience même de ses visions fantastiques, il va s'apercevoir que cette ouverture et cette complexité des êtres, cette constitution de chaque destinée par la rencontre d'influences multiples, peuvent se lire et se déchiffrer sans recours explicite au surnaturel. C'est ainsi qu'il devient définitivement romancier.[1]

—*Balzac Visionnaire*, pp. 199–204.

In pronouncing a eulogy for Albert Béguin in a commemorative issue of the *Cahiers du Sud*, Georges Poulet defines a critic as "un être apte à se glisser dans la pensée d'autrui, voire dans son corps, dans ses sens, et surtout dans son regard" and declares that such a definition fits Béguin exactly. Jean Rousset, in the *Mercure de France* (July, 1963), describes Marcel Raymond in similar terms. Criticism as communion or identification with an author, usually spoken of in connection with Charles du Bos, is regarded with favor by the new critics, doubtless because it is obviously something different from the scholarly, objective method. What it is exactly is hard to define. In the case of Albert Béguin it is not a mimetic aptitude at all but an attraction to authors in whom he can project his own preoccupations. He does not identify with them so much as they with him, as is illustrated by what he makes of Balzac in the foregoing passage. In the introduction to *L'Ame romantique et le Rêve*, which could

[1] For translation, see Appendix 3.

in many respects serve as a manifesto for the New Critics, Béguin's very personal involvement in his subject is avowed:

C'est donc "notre" expérience,—s'il est vrai que celle des poètes que nous adoptons s'assimile à notre essence personnelle pour ... l'aider dans sa confrontation avec l'angoisse profonde, —c'est notre expérience que je pensais retrouver dans l'étude que j'entrepris. Et je n'ai renoncé ni à cet espoir ni à cette orientation de mon enquête.

. . . .

Ce livre ne se propose donc pas de réduire à un système claire-ment analysable les ambitions et les œuvres d'une "école" poé-tique. Pareil propos me semble inintelligible. Consacrer son effort à la définition d'une réalité historique, sans se donner d'autre but, est une entreprise singulière et peut-être désespé-rée. L'objectivité, qui peut, et doit sans doute, être la loi des sciences descriptives, ne saurait régir fructueusement les sciences de l'esprit. Toute activité "désintéressée" dans ce sens-là exige une impardonnable trahison vis-à-vis de soi-même et vis-à-vis de l'"objet" étudié. L'œuvre d'art et de pensée intéresse, en effet, comme la reminiscence et le rêve, cette partie la plus secrète de nous-mêmes où, détachés de notre apparente individualité, mais orientés vers notre personalité réelle, nous n'avons plus qu'un souci: un souci qui est de nous ouvrir aux avertissements, aux signes, et de connaître par là la stupeur qu'inspire la condition humaine, contemplée un instant dans toute son étrangeté, avec ses risques, son anxiété entière, sa beauté et ses décevantes limites.

. . . .

Le besoin de l'histoire est pour l'humanité cette même re-cherche de sa propre mélodie, à laquelle se livre l'individu. C'est pourquoi une œuvre historique, et singulièrement un essai d'histoire spirituelle, interdit à son auteur de faire abstraction de lui-même. Cela ne veut pas dire, bien entendu, qu'il lui soit loisible de faire fi de la vérité des faits ou d'en disposer à sa guise. Mais cette honnêteté de l'information est une insuffisante vertu, simple condition préalable d'une recherche où l'on aime à sentir la présence d'une interrogation personnelle et inéluctable.

. . . .

Qu'était-ce que ce romantisme allemand vers lequel m'attiraient tant de séduisants appels? Si je voulais saisir le sens de ses démarches spirituelles, préciser en quoi il nous concernait, nous hommes de ce temps-ci, il fallait passer de la lecture enchantée des œuvres à leur étude, tracer des limites, chercher des traits qui fussent communs à tous les visages romantiques. Longtemps je marchai de déconvenue en déconvenue: j'avais commencé par recourir aux ouvrages innombrables où la critique allemande, depuis quelques années, s'épuise à donner une formule du romantisme. Bien des analyses et des vues, profondes, vivantes, perspicaces, se trouvent aux pages de ces livres. Mais la synthèse souveraine, qui définirait sans réserves l'esprit romantique, semble se dérober à toutes les tentatives.

. . . .

Je pris mon parti de l'incertitude des classifications, et je me décidai à choisir d'instinct *mes* romantiques ...

. . . .

C'est à ces principes romantiques que j'ai tenté de conformer les démarches de mon enquête, convaincu que j'étais, avec mes poètes et mes philosophes, qu'on ne connaît que ce que l'on porte en soi, et qu'on ne peut que romantiquement parler du romantisme. L'échec de trop de critiques, empressés à juger d'un point de vue goethéen les contemporains de Goethe, eût suffi d'ailleurs à me mettre en garde contre toute autre méthode que celle de la sympathie.

—*L'Ame romantique et le Rêve* (Cahiers du Sud), pp. xvi–xxii.

SELECTED WORKS

L'Ame romantique et le Rêve (Cahiers du Sud, 1937; Corti, 1946).

La Prière de Péguy (La Baconnière, 1944).

Léon Bloy l'impatient (Egloff, 1944).

Gérard de Nerval (Stock, 1945).

Balzac visionnaire (Skira, 1946).

Léon Bloy, mystique de la douleur (Labergerie, 1948). Translated as *Léon Bloy* (Sheed and Ward, 1948).

Patience de Ramus (La Baconnière, 1950).

Pascal par lui-même (Seuil, 1952).

Bernanos par lui-même (Seuil, 1954).

Poésie de la présence (Seuil, 1957).

Balzac lu et relu (Seuil, 1965).

REFERENCES

Diéguez, Manuel de. *L'Ecrivain et son langage* (Gallimard, 1960), "Albert Béguin," pp. 204–220.

Les Cahiers du Rhône, December, 1957. Number devoted to Béguin.

Revue des Belles-Lettres, Nov.–Dec., 1958. Number devoted to Béguin.

Poulet, Georges. "La pensée critique d'Albert Béguin," *Cahiers du Sud,* 360 (1961), 177–198.

Rustan, Marie-Josèphe. "Albert Béguin et la tradition romantique," *Cahiers du Sud,* 351 (1959), 247–259.

MAURICE BLANCHOT

Maurice Blanchot, born September 22, 1907, in Quaint (Saône-et-Loire), is generally considered one of the greatest of living French literary critics. He is an essayist, actually, rather than a critic in any limited sense—a philosopher, for whom a literary text is only a point of departure for rumination over the nature of literature and language. Although he often appears in the role of reviewer or columnist writing on current books, he tells us little about them, never discussing the conventional matters of form and content or passing any judgments. He cares nothing about a work as an individual accomplishment or as the product of one personality but only as a specimen of verbal creation, the phenomenon which never ceases to fascinate Blanchot, for in it he reads the riddle of art, life and the world—a riddle of antinomies: speech and silence, presence and absence, life and death.

The basis for Blanchot's endless lucubrations may be found in Hegel—sometimes in the very chapter headings of the *Phenomenology of Mind*. Along with Sartre, Blanchot has transplanted into France a German philosophy of art which goes back through Heiddeger and Husserl to Hegel. Two of the master's sententious utterances have been particularly influential upon Blanchot—first, that art is a thing of the past, and, second, that to name a thing is to destroy it. The first, implying that the movement towards the fusion of the real and the ideal which is the course of civilization makes art more and more obsolete, explains Blanchot's (and Sartre's) interest in the "authenticity" of literature at a given historical moment and his conviction that literature is moving towards its death. Blanchot's criticism may be thought of as a doctor's periodic checking of the failing health of a patient. The second utterance, often repeated by Existential philosophers, refers to the human faculty of symbolizing and abstracting. To know a thing is to replace it by a sign, "annihilate" it by naming it. Equating language (symbols and signs) with abstractions creates the basic dichotomy between literature and life which provides Blanchot with an inexhaustible theme.

Like his basic assumptions, Blanchot's method derives from Hegel. The familiar thesis and antithesis take the form of a paradox from which Blanchot proceeds in dialectical fashion until by successive affirmations and negations he has reached a resolution in the complete fusion of the antinomies. His essays follow a set formula: statement of paradox, expression of his astonishment before the phenomenon, explanation and resolution, arrival back at point zero. The reader following the cold and grave logic of Blanchot's essays falls easily under his spell. The atmosphere, created by the funereal tempo and the lexicon of the visionary, is so powerful that even Blanchot's commentators tend to speak in his tongue: "Maurice Blanchot, à travers une patiente et systématique destruction du langage, tache de dépeindre la sombre et dévorante absence que révèle et dissimule à la fois le langage."[1] His peers are convinced of his profundity and leave it at that; it is safe to say the general public does not read him at all. Perhaps he deserves the esteem in which other critics hold him, but we suspect that he is the victim of his obsession—language—and that his intuitions are little more than complicated verbal games, where only the metaphorical shadow is grasped and the substance is lost. Nobody ever actually killed a cat just by saying "cat," no matter how solemnly it is said. But a great many critics seem to think so.

One may guess that certain writers have lent themselves better than others to Blanchot's ontological investigations. Kafka, Hölderlin, de Sade, Char have been favorite subjects.

[1] J. Hillis Miller. "La Critique de Georges Poulet," *Mercure de France*, April, 1965, p. 654.

His essays used to appear in *Les Temps Modernes;* they now can be found in *La Nouvelle Revue Française.* Blanchot is also a novelist; he is the author of several weird prose pieces reminiscent of Franz Kafka. As a "new" critic, he differs from the younger thematic critics, primarily in his indifference to the individual writer and his unconscious. He shares with them, however, the inheritance of phenomenology. Blanchot's particular contribution is his systematic application of the teaching of Hegel to the field of literary enquiry.

❧

A master of style, Maurice Blanchot deploys all the resources of eloquence to support his subtle paradoxes. An article on the moralist Joseph Joubert (1754–1824) begins as follows:

Que nous pensions à Joubert comme à un écrivain qui nous est proche, plus proche que les grands noms littéraires dont il fut le contemporain, ce n'est pas seulement à l'obscurité, d'ailleurs distinguée, sous laquelle il vécut, mourut, puis survécut, que nous en sommes redevables. Il ne suffit pas d'être de son vivant un nom faiblement éclairé pour rayonner, comme l'espérait Stendhal, un ou deux siècles plus tard. Il ne suffit même pas à une grande œuvre d'être grande et de s'affirmer à l'écart, pour que la postérité, un jour reconnaissante, la remette dans l'éclat du plein jour. Il se peut que l'humanité un jour connaisse tout, les êtres, les vérités et les mondes, mais il y aura toujours quelque œuvre d'art—peut-être l'art tout entier—pour tomber hors de cette connaissance universelle. C'est là le privilège de l'activité artistique: ce qu'elle produit, même un dieu souvent doit l'ignorer.

Il reste vrai que bien des ouvrages s'épuisent prématurément à être trop admirés. Cette grande flambée de gloire dont les écrivains et les artistes, vieillissants, se réjouissent et qui jette ses derniers feux à leur mort, brûle en eux une substance qui manquera désormais à leur œuvre. Le jeune Valéry cherchait dans tout livre illustre l'erreur qui l'a fait connaître: jugement d'aristo-crate. Mais l'on a souvent l'impression que la mort va apporter enfin le silence et le calme à l'ouvrage laissé à lui-même. Durant sa vie, l'écrivain le plus détaché et le plus négligent combat encore pour ses livres. Il vit, cela suffit; il se tient derrière eux, par cette vie qui lui reste et dont il leur fait présent. Mais sa mort, même inaperçue, rétablit le secret et referme la pensée. Celle-ci va-t-elle, étant seule, se déployer ou se restreindre, se défaire ou s'accomplir, se trouver ou se manquer? Et sera-t-elle jamais seule? Même l'oubli ne récompense pas toujours ceux qui semblent l'avoir mérité par le don de grande discrétion qui a été en eux.

Joubert eut ce don. Il n'écrivit jamais un livre. Il se prépara seulement à en écrire un, cherchant avec résolution les condi-tions justes qui lui permettraient de l'écrire. Puis il oublia même ce dessein. Plus précisément, ce qu'il cherchait, cette source de l'écriture, cet espace où écrire, cette lumière à circonscrire dans l'espace, exigea de lui, affirma en lui des dispositions qui le rendirent impropre à tout travail littéraire ordinaire ou le firent s'en détourner. Il a été, par là, l'un des premiers écrivains tout modernes, préférant le centre à la sphère, sacrifiant les résultats à la découverte de leurs conditions et n'écrivant pas pour ajouter un livre à un autre, mais pour se rendre maître du point d'où lui semblaient sortir tous les livres et qui, une fois trouvé, le dispenserait d'en écrire.[1]

—Le Livre à venir, pp. 63–64.

In the essay entitled "La littérature et le droit à la mort," Blanchot formulates what we might call his ontology of literature. The following passages occur early in the text:

Admettons que la littérature commence au moment où la lit-térature devient une question. ... La question qu'elle renferme ne concerne pas, à proprement parler, sa valeur ou son droit. S'il est si difficile de découvrir le sens de cette question, c'est que celle-ci tend à se transformer en un procès de l'art, de ses pou-voirs et de ses fins. La littérature s'édifie sur ses ruines: ce

---

[1] For translation, see Appendix 4.

paradoxe nous est un lieu commun. Mais encore faudrait-il re-
chercher si cette mise en cause de l'art, que représente la partie
la plus illustre de l'art depuis trente ans, ne suppose pas le
glissement, le déplacement d'une puissance au travail dans le
secret des œuvres et répugnant à venir au grand jour, travail
originellement fort distinct de toute dépréciation de l'activité
ou de la Chose littéraires.

Remarquons que la littérature, comme négation d'elle-même,
n'a jamais signifié la simple dénonciation de l'art ou de l'artiste
comme mystification et tromperie. Que la littérature soit illégitime, qu'il y ait en elle un fond d'imposture, oui, sans doute.
Mais certains ont découvert davantage: la littérature n'est pas
seulement illégitime, mais nulle, et cette nullité constitue peut-
être une force extraordinaire, merveilleuse, à la condition d'être
isolée à l'état pur. Faire en sorte que la littérature devînt la mise
à découvert de ce dedans vide, que tout entière elle s'ouvrît à
sa part de néant, qu'elle réalisât sa propre irréalité, c'est là l'une
des tâches qu'a poursuivies le surréalisme, de telle manière qu'il
est exact de reconnaître en lui un puissant mouvement négateur,
mais qu'il n'est pas moins vrai de lui attribuer la plus grande
ambition créatrice, car que la littérature un instant coïncide
avec rien, et immédiatement elle est tout, le tout commence
d'exister: grande merveille.

Il ne s'agit pas de maltraiter la littérature, mais de chercher à
la comprendre et de voir pourquoi on ne la comprend qu'en la
dépréciant. On a constaté avec surprise que la question: "Qu'est-
ce que la littérature?" n'avait jamais reçu que des réponses
insignifiantes. Mais voici plus étrange: dans la forme d'une
pareille question, quelque chose apparaît qui lui retire tout
sérieux. Demander: qu'est-ce que la poésie? qu'est-ce que l'art?
ou même: qu'est-ce que le roman? on peut le faire et on l'a
fait. Mais la littérature qui est poème et roman, semble l'élément du vide, présent dans toutes ces choses graves, et sur lequel
la réflexion, avec sa propre gravité, ne peut se retourner sans
perdre son sérieux. Si la réflexion imposante s'approche de la
littérature, la littérature devient une force caustique, capable
de détruire ce qui en elle et dans la réflexion pouvait en imposer.
Si la réflexion s'éloigne, alors la littérature redevient, en effet,
quelque chose d'important, d'essentiel, de plus important que
la philosophie, la religion et la vie du monde qu'elle embrasse.
Mais que la réflexion, étonnée de cet empire, revienne sur cette

puissance et lui demande ce qu'elle est, pénétrée aussitôt par un élément corrosif, volatil, elle ne peut que mépriser une Chose aussi vaine, aussi vague et aussi impure et dans ce mépris et cette vanité se consumer à son tour, comme l'a bien montré l'histoire de Monsieur Teste.

L'on se tromperait en rendant les puissants mouvements né-gateurs contemporains responsables de cette force volatilisant et volatile que semble être devenue la littérature. Il y a environ cent cinquante ans, un homme qui avait de l'art la plus haute idée qu'on en puisse former,—puisqu'il voyait comment l'art peut devenir religion et la religion art—, cet homme (appelé Hegel) a décrit tous les mouvements par lesquels celui qui choisit d'être un littérateur se condamne à appartenir au "règne animal de l'esprit". Dès son premier pas, dit à peu près Hegel, l'individu qui veut écrire, est arrêté par une contradiction: pour écrire, il lui faut le talent d'écrire. Mais, en eux-mêmes, les dons ne sont rien. Tant que ne s'étant pas mis à sa table, il n'a pas écrit une œuvre, l'écrivain n'est pas écrivain et il ne sait pas s'il a des capacités pour le devenir. Il n'a du talent qu'après avoir écrit, mais il lui en faut pour écrire.

—*La Part du Feu*, pp. 305–307.

In 1959, the magazine *Arguments*, feeling that literary criti-cism no longer could be defined as representing either the opinion of the average reader or universal taste, opened one of its issues to a forum discussion. Here we find Maurice Blanchot discussing the nature of criticism. He begins by calling criticism the compromise product of journalism and the university, which uses literature as its object but actually serves the two institutions it represents:

Nous parvenons donc à cette idée que la critique est en elle-même presque sans réalité. Idée qui elle aussi est réduite. Il faut y ajouter aussitôt qu'une telle vue dépréciatrice ne choque pas la critique, mais qu'elle l'accueille volontiers, avec une curieuse humilité, comme si cette manière de n'être rien an-nonçait au contraire sa plus profonde vérité. Quand Heidegger commente les poèmes de Hölderlin, il dit (je cite approximativement): quoi que puisse le commentaire, en regard du poème, il doit toujours se tenir pour superflu, et le dernier pas de l'interprétation, le plus difficile, est celui qui l'amène à disparaître devant la pure affirmation du poème. Heidegger se sert encore de cette figure: dans le bruyant tumulte du langage non poétique, les poèmes sont comme une cloche suspendue à l'air libre, et qu'une neige légère, tombant sur elle, suffirait à faire vibrer, heurt insensible, capable pourtant de l'ébranler harmonieusement. Peut-être le commentaire n'est-il qu'un peu de neige faisant vibrer la cloche.

Blanchot has been deeply impressed by Heidegger's conceit to the effect that criticism, in the measure that it realizes itself, must disappear. Since that is so, Blanchot asks, why is the critic necessary at all?

Pourquoi, entre le lecteur et elle, entre l'histoire et elle, devrait venir s'interposer ce méchant hybride de lecture et d'écriture, cet homme bizarrement spécialisé dans la lecture et qui, pourtant, ne sait lire qu'en écrivant, n'écrit que sur ce qu'il lit et doit en même temps donner l'impression, écrivant, lisant, qu'il ne fait rien, rien que laisser parler la profondeur de l'œuvre, ce qui en elle demeure et y demeure toujours plus clairement, plus obscurément?

Apparently Blanchot makes a distinction between the critic and the literary historian, since he insists upon the very limited function of the critic. Criticism, he declares, cannot claim a place among the historical sciences, has no right to place the work under discussion in history; it is entirely restricted to the present and belongs with noises of the market place. Yet its task is more than vulgarization:

Acceptons un instant la délicate image de Heidegger: cette neige qui fait vibrer la cloche, cette blanche motion, impalpable et un peu froide, qui disparaît dans le chaud ébranlement qu'elle suscite. Ici, la parole critique, sans durée, sans réalité, voudrait se dissiper devant l'affirmation créatrice: ce n'est jamais elle qui parle, lorsqu'elle parle; elle n'est rien; remarquable modestie; mais peut-être pas si modeste. Elle n'est rien, mais ce rien est précisément ce en quoi l'œuvre, la silencieuse, l'invisible, se laisse être ce qu'elle est: parole et lumière, affirmation et présence, parlant alors comme d'elle-même, sans s'altérer, dans ce vide de bonne qualité que l'intervention critique a eu pour mission de produire. La parole critique est cet espace de résonance dans lequel, un instant, se transforme et se circonscrit en parole la réalité non parlante, indéfinie, de l'œuvre. Et ainsi, du fait que modestement et obstinément elle prétend n'être rien, la voici qui se donne, ne se distinguant pas d'elle, pour la parole créatrice dont elle est comme l'actualisation nécessaire ou, pour parler métaphoriquement, l'épiphanie.

—*Arguments*, Jan.–March, 1959, pp. 34–36.

The elegance of Blanchot's argument does not hide the fact that its basis is quite arbitrary and that its construction depends upon conceit and proliferation of metaphor.

SELECTED WORKS

Faux Pas (Gallimard, 1943).

Lautréamont et Sade (Minuit, 1949).

La Part du Feu (Gallimard, 1949).

L'Espace littéraire (Gallimard, 1955).

Le Livre à venir (Gallimard, 1959).

"Qu'en est-il de la critique?" *Arguments*, Jan.–March, 1959, pp. 34–37.

REFERENCES

Critique, June, 1966. Number devoted to Blanchot.

Diéguez, Manuel de. *L'Ecrivain et son langage* (Gallimard, 1960). "Maurice Blanchot," pp. 149–172.

Oxenhandler, Neal. "Ontological Criticism in America and France," *Modern Language Review*, January, 1960, pp. 17–23.

―――. "Paradox and Negation in the Criticism of Maurice Blanchot," *Symposium*, Spring, 1962, pp. 36–44.

Picon, Gaëtan. "L'œuvre critique de Maurice Blanchot," *Critique*, August–September, 1956, pp. 675–694; October, 1956, pp. 836–854.

ROBERT CHAMPIGNY

Born in Chatellerault in 1922, Robert Champigny took the licence ès lettres at the University of Poitiers in 1943, studied at the Ecole Normale Supérieure from 1943 to 1947, and passed the agrégation in 1947. In 1956, he obtained the doctorat ès lettres. He is a professor of French at Indiana University, specializing in the modern period.

Professor Champigny's writing reveals a keen interest in Existentialism and the influence of Jean-Paul Sartre. This is already suggested in his first study, *Portrait of a Symbolist Hero*, which is an Existentialist psychoanalysis of Alain-Fournier. Champigny might have substituted "esthetic" for "symbolist" in his title, for the study has little to do with definition of a literary school and a great deal to do with the Kierkegaardian distinctions separating the ethical, esthetic, and religious as its author seeks for the real face of Fournier behind the masks of the characters in *Le Grand Meaulnes*. His next work, *Stages on Sartre's Way*, traces the development of Sartre's thought through his literary works. Of incidental but noteworthy interest is a brief excursion into Bachelardian analysis to show that Sartre's imagery is of the "earth" type. In *Sur un héros païen*, Greek words replace the more usual Sartrian phraseology, but the concepts do not seem to differ radically as Champigny defines Meursault, the hero of *L'Etranger* by Camus, in terms of *phusis* and *antiphusis*. The analysis here is conducted with the rigorous order of a lesson or demonstration. This is the technique Champigny employs in the next three studies, designed specifically for university courses. *Le Genre romanesque, Le Genre poétique,* and *Le Genre dramatique* are essays in literary science, attempts to arrive at a clear concept of genre. The undertaking is somewhat like describing the ideal violet, which never exists in nature.

❦

Champigny makes an extremely interesting application of Bachelard's mythology as he relates Sartre's metaphors to his thought:

Let us try to define the purpose inherent in Sartre's metaphors.

The symbolism of liquid and solid and the emphasis on the clogged and slimy conditions are used to depreciate the morals of being and orient the reader toward the morals of doing.

.   .   .   .

The man who adopts the morals of being tries to attain the solidity of the stone, to coincide fully with himself, to expel nothingness, hence consciousness, hence conscience. Both *La Nausée* and *L'Etre et le néant* criticize this project in the abstract, and they also depreciate it by the use of concrete epithets which are intended to provoke disgust: what the adept of the morals of being can reach, in fact, is a clogged or slimy state.

The desire to *be* is the fundamental temptation of the Sartrean man. *La Nausée* and *L'Etre et le néant* are mainly concerned with breaking its spell. It is only when the Sartrean man has forsaken his instinctive project to *be* that he has to overcome a second temptation: the desire not to be, the desire to become pure, elusive water or air. This desire will concern the second phase of the Sartrean campaign: the stress will be placed on commitment.

We shall deal with this phase when we study *Les Mouches* and *Le Diable et le bon Dieu*. Actually, by pointing out that freedom and situation define each other, Sartre has already, in *L'Etre et le néant*, warned against the morals of non-being. The reader is already oriented toward the morals of doing, toward commitment. Will this commitment stress the physical or the social situation? In the first case, we should progress toward the morals of making, toward what we have called poetic morals; in the second case, toward ethics, toward the interhuman aspect of morals.

An orientation toward the morals of making should broaden the concrete symbolism. Water should appear from now on powerful as well as elusive and transparent, and its dynamics should be supplemented with the dynamics of air and fire. Substantially and symbolically, it is by appropriating the powers of fire, air, and water that man triumphs over the opaque recalcitrance of the solid, of the earth.

—*Stages on Sartre's Way*, pp. 61–62.

In studying *L'Etranger*, Champigny places himself within the book in order to examine Meursault as if he were a real person. The artifice can be cumbersome: it takes the first twenty-eight pages to say that up to the time of the shooting, Meursault was not considered odd by his associates and might be considered so only by the reader:

Pourtant, dès le début, Meursault peut apparaître comme un étranger à une personne: le lecteur du livre. L'étude que j'ai entreprise concerne Meursault et n'envisage le livre intitulé *L'Etranger* que comme document, seul document que je possède sur Meursault. Autrement dit, au lieu de considérer Meursault comme un personnage de roman, je me place à l'intérieur de la fiction selon laquelle le récit a été écrit par Meursault. En quoi ce que Meursault raconte sur lui-même peut-il le faire apparaître comme un étranger?

Ce que j'ai dit jusqu'à présent est fondé sur une lecture du livre. Or, il m'est apparu que, dans la première partie, Meursault ne se sentait aucunement étranger et que les autres personnages ne le considéraient pas comme un étranger. Comment, dans ces conditions, pourrait-il apparaître comme un étranger au lecteur? Je ne veux sans doute pas affirmer que Meursault apparaîtra nécessairement au lecteur comme un étranger: divers lecteurs réagiront diversement, le même lecteur peut varier sa réaction. Mais je dis du moins que Meursault *peut*, dès le départ, apparaître au lecteur comme un étranger, bien qu'il n'apparaisse étranger ni à lui-même ni aux autres personnes.[1]

—*Sur un héros païen*, pp. 24–25.

The slow, deliberate manner, with repetitions and heavy underscoring, is fatiguing; one is not unrewarded for one's pains, however, for Champigny's minute scrutiny exposes very interesting aspects of Camus' hero. His analysis of Meursault's language seems particularly worthwhile:

Meursault apparaîtra ainsi, au long de son récit, soucieux de ne pas dire ce qu'il ne sait pas, même à propos de détails qui peuvent nous sembler négligeables. Car il n'est pas négligeable pour lui de marquer les limites de ce qu'il sait. Quant à la notation des faits eux-mêmes, il essaie d'être aussi complet que possible. Mais quand les souvenirs lui manquent, il le dit: il ne romance pas. Il dit de même qu'il ne comprend pas, s'il ne comprend pas ...

Une expression revient dans le récit de Meursault, qui marque bien son souci pointilleux de justesse. C'est l'expression "dans un sens," expression familière sans doute, mais que Meursault rehausse par l'usage qu'il en fait à des moments assez inattendus. En voici des exemples:

"Il a remarqué que le temps passait vite et, dans un sens, c'était vrai. ... Dans un sens, cela me déséquilibrait. Mais, dans un autre, cela tuait le temps... Dans un sens, c'était un avantage ... Dans un sens, cela m'intéressait de voir un procès ... Par suite, ce qu'il y avait d'ennuyeux, c'est qu'il fallait que le condamné souhaitât le bon fonctionnement de la machine. Je dis que c'est le côté défectueux. Cela est vrai, dans un sens. Mais dans un autre sens, j'étais obligé de reconnaître que tout le secret d'une bonne organisation était là. En somme, le condamné était obligé de collaborer moralement."

—*Ibid.*, pp. 80–82.

In his latest three books, Champigny sets himself to the task of forming and analyzing a concept of genres. Perhaps here

[1] For translation, see Appendix 5.

we can see most clearly the qualities of this brilliant young professor—wide erudition and rigor of method. These qualities, excessively exploited, may become the faults of pedantry and intellectual games. More what one might call a scholastic than a thematic critic, Champigny shares, however, with other young French critics their lofty dedication, their tendency to treat literature in the context of philosophy, and their subjective approach. Yet it is to be noted that Champigny's analysis of a work on the basis of genre seems intended to serve as a basis for judging the work, an aspect of criticism generally ignored by the new school:

Lorsqu'il s'agit de traiter des sujets tels que celui qui est ici en question, on peut faire trois choses: rationaliser ses goûts, rationaliser les goûts des autres, ou rationaliser dans le vide. Mes goûts, plutôt que ceux des autres, peuvent fournir une base à l'essai que j'écris: car je ne connais les goûts des autres que très partiellement et douteusement: par ouï-dire. Cela ne signifie pas que tous mes goûts, quels qu'ils soient, doivent être justifiés coûte que coûte: la rationalité exclut la démesure rationaliste. Il s'agit d'expliciter la cohérence que j'éprouve entre certains de mes goûts. L'explication correcte de cette cohérence est ce qui guide et peut justifier cet essai. Comme à la démesure du rationalisme, ma méthode s'oppose donc, non aux impressions, mais à l'impressionnisme, que cet impressionnisme se présente comme "subjectif" (personnel) ou "objectif" (collectif).

Pour pouvoir, en matière de critique littéraire, se parer des plumes de "l'objectivité," il faut apparemment s'abstenir de juger (de critiquer), ou faire semblant de s'abstenir, ou encore s'arranger pour que le jugement soit assez vague pour faire écho à la moyenne des jugements précédemment formulés. Or, si le langage d'un essai sur la poésie doit en quelque manière ressembler à celui d'un traité scientifique, ce n'est pas par son "objectivité," par sa recherche de l'universalité, c'est par sa cohérence. La recherche de l'universalité, dans un essai comme celui-ci, rapprocherait le discours, non pas de la prose scientifique, mais de la prose électorale; elle consisterait à ménager la chèvre et le chou. En science, universalité et cohérence vont de pair; dans

un essai critique tel que celui-ci, elles sont incompatibles.
—*Le Genre poétique*, pp. 26–27.

It would be wrong, however, to insist too much on the part reserved for judgment in Champigny's criticism. Whatever implications the above remarks—and his method as such—may have for an ultimate goal of value judgment, one must say that his work on genre deals principally with definition and propriety of terms.

SELECTED WORKS

Portrait of a Symbolist Hero (Bloomington: Indiana University Press, 1954).

Stages on Sartre's Way (Bloomington: Indiana University Press, 1959).

Sur un héros païen (Gallimard, 1959).

Le Genre romanesque (Monte-Carlo: Regain, 1963).

Le Genre poétique (Monte-Carlo: Regain, 1964).

Le Genre dramatique (Monte-Carlo: Regain, 1965).

REFERENCES

Borel, Jacques. "Nature et histoire chez Albert Camus," *Critique*, June, 1961, pp. 507–521.

Cruickshank, John. "*Sur un héros païen*," *French Studies*, April, 1961, pp. 193–194.

Grimsley, Ronald. "*Stages on Sartre's Way*," *French Studies*, July, 1960, pp. 281–282.

Lindsay, Marshall. "*Le Genre poétique*," *The Romanic Review*, October, 1965, pp. 235–236.

MANUEL DE DIÉGUEZ

Born in 1922, Manuel de Diéguez completed his studies in letters, law, and political science towards the end of World War II and then began to publish. Three political and philosophical essays, two stories, and one play comprise his work before 1960, the year he entered the field of literary criticism with an essay on Rabelais and a treatise on theory.

Diéguez is a vociferous advocate of an "existential psychoanalytical" approach to literature. He exhorts critics to concentrate their attention on style, the uniqueness of each author's expression. A young modernist who does not hesitate to dismiss the efforts of his elders in brusque fashion, he finds little value in the historical, biographical, or any conventional academic approach to art. History (which he likes to capitalize) is his *bête noire*. He would discredit it even in its own field, insisting upon the unavoidable subjectivity and inconstancy of any picture of the past. In the field of art, he cites again the mischief of "Historicism" in reducing a work of art to a document and points out that even critics who, in principle, do not accept this reduction, often still maintain the methodology of historicism. In other words, Diéguez has no use for erudition with or without ideological bias. Impenitent historical (we should say, scientific) criticism lingers today in Marxism, which Diéguez calls "une sorte de sociologie où les événements seraient définitivement commis dans leur signification finale,"[1] and in Freudian psychoanalysis.

Concerning the critics who have abandoned the method of Taine and have correctly oriented their work towards the existential level, Diéguez' approval is not without reserves. Sartre and Barthes have not extricated themselves from historicism, Béguin slips into religious apologetics, Blanchot and Poulet are too much involved in philosophy. And Diéguez

[1] *Rabelais par lui-même*, p. 137.

explains: "Il y a un divorce fondamental entre la philosophie et l'esthétique: une philosophie ne constituera jamais un fondement valable de l'esthétique littéraire, parce que la philosophie est de l'ordre de la connaissance et la littérature de l'ordre de la résonance."[2] Only Bachelard seems free of extraneous entanglement, but then he too is limited. Diéguez may leave us quite perplexed and frustrated. His thought seems as complicated as his language is tempestuous and pedantic. We follow him in his insistence on the importance of studying the creative processes but cannot keep up in his explanation of the Existential context into which he would place such study. Moreover, his own demonstration of Existential psychoanalysis of style fails to elucidate. What he offers as a sample in *L'Ecrivain et son langage* seems only a piece of bravura on the trite theme of Montherlant's "classic" style. With the uncomfortable feeling of being blockheads or dupes, we may decide just to watch the show put on by this verbal prestidigitator who can build, out of an intuition or a wild notion, a marvelous house of cards.

The major spectacle he has offered to date is *Chateaubriand ou le poète face à l'histoire*. In very prosy terms, the subject is the theme of death in the works of Chateaubriand. But such a statement gives little idea of the dialectical drama which Diéguez creates by imagining Chateaubriand torn between the two antagonistic forces of poetry and history. Poetry is what gives meaning to life; history is the record of apparently meaningless killings. How can a poet treat history? Out of this purely verbal dilemma, Diéguez constructs a great Orphic myth, in which History serves as Eurydice's cadaver.

č

Already in his study of Rabelais, we may see in Diéguez the ardent champion of an "Existential" method, liberated

---

[2] *L'Ecrivain et son langage*, p. 160.

from historicism. He makes it clear from the outset that, in sketching Rabelais' life, he will not be the traditional biographer who counts the socks his subject owns, his mistresses, and so on. The significant biography of the great writer is inseparable from the mythology of his creation, Diéguez declares—he lives in the verbal universe he creates.

Mais l'œuvre de Rabelais, comme toute grande œuvre, est une ville construite par un seul homme, une ville usée au jour le jour par le pas de cet homme, que ne pouvait trouver autrement *guide de Dieu et compaignie.* Si nous nous interrogeons sur la provenance de ces pierres et sur la manière d'en desceller quelques-unes pour construire ou reconstruire nos propres cités, nous ne sommes que des barbares. Pour comprendre avec qui et de quoi cet homme parle à travers les pierres, il ne faut pas lire les inscriptions sur les façades, il faut scruter l'insolite démarche elle-même de qui se retire au désert pour arracher sa ville au silence. La critique d'aujourd'hui sur Rabelais veut interroger ce mystère spirituel qu'on appelle l'art et qui donne des voix à une nuit immense. Alors apparaît le Rabelais le plus intérieur, celui qui questionne, et dont l'œuvre débouche sur une solitude, celui qui combat pied à pied pour ancrer son ordre (le vrai, l'imaginaire) dans le chaos de l'autre cité; celui qui, transporté par son mythe, s'y accroche, s'y use, s'y détruit.[3]
—*Rabelais par lui-même,* pp. 130–131.

Assuming that Diéguez refers to himself as one who "interrogates that spiritual mystery that is called art," we may wonder what "inner" Rabelais he has called forth. Throughout his study he has spoken of Rabelais' verbal exuberance and in general has emphasized what conventional criticism terms the "universe" of the author. But Diéguez' practice falls short of his preaching; lively and interesting as his discussion is, it does not really add any new dimension to our picture of Rabelais.

[3] For translation, see Appendix 6.

Mais dans le *Prologue* [to the Tiers Livre], on voit bien que Rabelais a livré son secret d'écrivain, la forme de son défi au monde par le style: une sorte de rivalité prestigieuse des mots avec l'univers entier. On sent que Rabelais répond au silence, hors de tout système philosophique, en grand écrivain, c'est-à-dire par une certaine écriture calquée sur son comportement le plus profond, qui est de relever le défi de la matière, de lui opposer une masse équivalente, de substituer un verbe à toute chair. Dans ce *Prologue*, l'épaisseur et la durée sont saisissantes —un torrent verbal a submergé le réel. Mais, comme chez Balzac, c'est par une insurrection spirituelle que la chair se fait verbe: les mots ne rivalisent pas avec la léthargie du monde et sa grisaille, comme chez Flaubert, ils sont une victoire sur la léthargie de la matière. Il y a donc un souffle rabelaisien sans lequel la masse des mots ne détruirait pas l'angoisse et n'égalerait pas la création.

—*Ibid.*, p. 85.

The following gives an idea of the critical method Diéguez proposes. One will notice how he seizes the text, so to speak, and carries it up to the heights of his own purple eloquence. Whether Pascal is panting like an exhausted runner is not sure. But Diéguez most certainly is as he pursues his frantic course through argumentation and affirmation:

Chateaubriand et Bossuet témoignent d'une même hantise de l'abîme, de l'immensité, du silence. Mais Pascal seul maintient le pur vertige. Que donnerait enfin une psychanalyse existentielle du style de Pascal? Nous ne pouvons que l'esquisser ici.

"Je ne sais qui m'a mis au monde, ni ce que c'est que le monde, ni que moi-même, je suis dans une ignorance terrible de toutes choses; je ne sais ce que c'est que mon corps, que mes sens, que mon âme et cette partie même de moi qui pense ce que je dis, qui fait réflexion sur tout et sur elle-même et ne se connaît non plus que le reste. Je vois les effroyables espaces de l'univers qui m'enferment et je me trouve attaché à un coin de cette vaste étendue sans que je sache pourquoi je suis

plutôt placé en ce lieu qu'en un autre, ni pourquoi ce
peu de temps qui m'est donné à vivre m'est assigné à
ce point plutôt qu'à un autre de toute l'éternité qui m'a
précédé et de toute celle qui me suit. Je ne vois que
des infinités de toutes parts, qui m'enferment comme
un atome et comme une ombre qui ne dure qu'un
instant sans retour. Tout ce que je connais est que je
dois bientôt mourir; mais ce que j'ignore le plus est
cette mort même que je ne saurais éviter."

Cette fusion haletante de la logique avec le vertige, cette
respiration comme exténuée d'un esprit qui va pourtant toujours
jusqu'au bout de sa course, ce style comme armé d'un dernier
souffle et qui murmure, pressant, des constats sans recours, tout
cela n'est pas "pure mélodie." Nous l'avons vu, à propos de
Sartre, l'intuition originelle du néant chez Pascal, sa vision de
l'homme "étranger" au monde, son regard moderne sur la
vanité du savoir scientifique et sur la mort, sa liberté liée à
l'angoisse en font le plus existentialiste des grands écrivains, et
il se trouve que cet existentialiste échappe complètement à une
psychanalyse existentielle du style selon la méthode de Sartre.
Pourquoi cela? C'est que pour Sartre l'homme est *signifiant*,
alors que la démarche de Pascal vise justement à pulvériser les
significations humaines, à les réduire à une absurdité tragique
par un pur regard organisant l'effroi. Et c'est pourquoi Pascal ne
peut être saisi qu'à partir d'une psychanalyse du pur regard—
c'est ce regard qui est au centre et qui s'exerce au foudroiement,
au désordre et à la terreur, par la logique la plus irréfutable.
Parfois, la gloire habite ce cerveau étonné; l'orgueil alors l'emporte sur la stupeur de se voir ainsi, jeté parmi les choses. Mais
presque toujours cet esprit hors du monde vient chercher des
indices, quelques traces ou vestiges de son inexplicable aventure,
et quelque espoir d'un destin échappant à l'absurde. Personne
ne s'est arrêté comme cela sur le chemin de l'abîme, avec ce
regard égaré et tout-puissant, nourri d'un vertige à même le
monde physique, avec cette fermeté terrible du murmure, et
dans ce rythme expirant qui efface la chair par la seule raison:
de sorte que le verbe naît miraculeusement de la chair qu'il
efface aussitôt.

Or, une telle entreprise du langage exige justement le refus
d'organiser le monde par la parole, de combler le vide où nous
sommes jetés par les splendeurs et la parure de Chateaubriand;

et même de le combler par la phrase en voûte de la grande éloquence cosmique, celle de Bossuet. D'où ce rythme toujours brisé, ce souffle sur le point de s'éteindre et qui se prolonge par-delà le souffle. Il s'agit de maintenir le vide pur, et l'angoisse de ce vide, par une phrase qui ne se laisse enfermer dans aucune structure, et qui soit toujours ce pur suspens. "La vraie éloquence se moque ..." C'est que toute éloquence, par le seul fait qu'elle propose une architecture de la phrase, échappe au néant, et modèle l'univers sur une forme qui fera figure de réponse. Tout ordre remplit le vide. Par contre un style du pur effroi et du pur constat refuse tout mode d'organisation du verbe, donc de l'être, qui jetterait sur le vide quelque voile ou quelque armure, quelque panoplie, quelque laconisme dédaigneux, quelque minutieux réseau d'équivalences. Pascal éprouve pour tout *procédé* une horreur qui va par-delà le mépris de la rhétorique: il sait bien qu'un *procédé* est un alibi ontologique, et qu'un tissu de procédés suffit à aveugler les hommes en comblant les abîmes.

—*L'Ecrivain et son langage*, pp. 304–307.

SELECTED WORKS

De l'Absurde (Triolet, 1948).

Rabelais par lui-même (Seuil, 1960).

L'Ecrivain et son langage (Gallimard, 1960).

Chateaubriand ou le poète face à l'histoire (Plon, 1963).

REFERENCES

Albérès, R.-M. "La nouvelle critique," *Les Nouvelles Littéraires*, August 22, 1963, p. 5.

Bastaire, Jean. "*L'Ecrivain et son langage*," *Esprit*, December, 1960, pp. 2142–2143.

Guillaume, J. "*Chateaubriand*," *Les Etudes Classiques*, October, 1963, p. 435.

Spens, Willy De. "*Chateaubriand*," *La Table Ronde*, July–Aug., 1963, pp. 128–129.

MICHEL FOUCAULT

Michel Foucault, born in 1926, an agrégé in philosophy and author of works on psychopathology, teaches at Clermont-Ferrand. Along with Roland Barthes, he is a member of the editorial board of the magazine *Critique*, which counts Maurice Blanchot on its advisory committee and several other critics associated with the New Criticism as its contributors. In a recent (June, 1966) number dedicated entirely to Blanchot, Foucault contributed a long and important article. In considering these critics as a group, as with any artistic school or movement, we bear in mind that the spiritual affiliation is often seconded by a social and professional association. Kindred spirits are often colleagues of the university or of the editorial office. Without knowing more of Foucault's associations, we can say that his essay on Raymond Roussel exhibits a wholehearted commitment to the principles of the New Criticism and an especial affinity to Maurice Blanchot. What concerns Foucault in this work is primarily language: his thesis is that, despite the opinions of André Breton concerning the possibility of ulterior significance in Roussel's strange verbal inventions, there is nothing either in the poems or the plays that goes beyond language itself. It was language, Foucault believes, that fascinated Roussel—language and its disturbing ambiguity.

❧

In explicating the texts of the enigmatic punster-poet, Foucault uses the rhetorical style that has become conventional among French critics today, who revel in erudite words and luxuriant metaphorical expression. Foucault reminds one very much of Maurice Blanchot, not only in style but also in subject matter. The ruminations over the nature of language that accompany his textual analyses, his allusions to death, destruction, and chance are all highly reminiscent:

Ramené à cette destruction de soi qui est aussi bien son hasard de naissance, le langage aléatoire et nécessaire de Roussel dessine une figure étrange: comme tout langage littéraire il est destruction violente du ressassement quotidien, mais il se maintient indéfiniment dans le geste hiératique de ce meurtre; comme le langage quotidien, il répète sans trêve, mais cette répétition n'a pas pour sens de recueillir et de continuer; elle garde ce qu'elle répète dans l'abolition d'un silence qui projette un écho nécessairement inaudible. Le langage de Roussel s'ouvre d'entrée de jeu au déjà dit qu'il accueille sous la forme la plus déréglée du hasard: non pas pour dire mieux ce qui s'y trouve dit mais pour en soumettre la forme au second aléa d'une destruction explosive et, de ces morceaux épars, inertes, informes, faire naître en les laissant en place la plus inouïe des significations. Loin d'être un langage qui cherche à commencer, il est la figure seconde de mots déjà parlés: c'est le langage de toujours travaillé par la destruction et la mort. C'est pourquoi son refus d'être original lui est essentiel. Il ne cherche pas à trouver, mais, par-delà la mort, à retrouver ce langage même qu'il vient de massacrer, à le retrouver identique et entier. De nature, il est répétitif. Parlant, pour la première fois, d'objets jamais vus, de machines jamais conçues, de plantes monstrueuses, d'infirmes dont Goya n'aurait pas rêvé, de méduses crucifiées, d'adolescents au sang glauque, ce langage cache soigneusement qu'il ne dit que ce qui a été dit. Ou plutôt, il l'a révélé au dernier moment dans la déclaration posthume, ouvrant ainsi par la mort volontaire une dimension intérieure au langage qui est celle de la mise à mort du langage par lui-même, et de sa résurrection à partir des splendeurs pulvérisées de son cadavre. C'est ce vide soudain de la mort dans le langage de toujours, et aussitôt la naissance d'étoiles, qui définissent la distance de la poésie.[1]
—*Raymond Roussel*, pp. 61–62.

Where Foucault joins the structuralist group is in his reduction of Roussel's verbal pranks to phenomenal patterns. The

[1] For translation, see Appendix 7.

play of identities, doubles, disguises, masks suggest to Foucault basic obsessions of a man forever in anguish because things and their names—the signified and the signifiers—are imperfectly coordinated:

Si le langage était aussi riche que l'être, il serait le double inutile et muet des choses; il n'existerait pas. Et pourtant sans nom pour les nommer, les choses resteraient dans la nuit. Cette lacune illuminante du langage, Roussel l'a éprouvée jusqu'à l'angoisse, jusqu'à l'obsession, si l'on veut ...

—*Ibid.*, p. 208.

SELECTED WORKS

Histoire de la folie à l'âge classique (Plon, 1961). Translated by R. Howard as *Madness and Civilization* (Pantheon, 1965).

Raymond Roussel (Gallimard, 1963).

Les Mots et les Choses (Gallimard, 1966).

REFERENCES

Bertherat, Y. "*Raymond Roussel*," *Esprit*, January, 1965, p. 286.

Sollers, Philippe. "Logicus Solus," *Tel Quel*, 14 (Summer, 1963), 46–50.

Sorin, Raphaël. "Le pendule de Foucault ... ," *Bizarre*, 1964, pp. 75–76. Special number on Raymond Roussel.

FRANÇOIS GERMAIN

A student at the Ecole Normale Supérieure, agrégé in letters, professor at the Lycée of Cannes, now at the University of Dijon, François Germain began by writing a number of texts designed to aid the candidate for the baccalauréat: *L'Art de commenter* (une tragédie, une comédie, un texte littéraire, etc.). What interests us here is his doctoral thesis, *L'Imagination d'Alfred de Vigny* (1961), which demonstrates the impact of the New Criticism even upon the most traditional French literary institutions. The work was directed by Professor Pierre Moreau, who, in his *Histoire de la Critique française*, published the year before the thesis, had voiced definite reservations on the subject of the new tendencies in criticism. But here, in a work written for a university degree, the debt to Gaston Bachelard, to Poulet, and to the psychoanalysts is clearly evident. In outward aspect, this study presents no striking change from the conventional thesis. It has the usual bulk and heavy machinery: introductions, definitions, historical surveys, recapitulations, notes, references, bibliography. Its language, too, has the sobriety of the scholarly work in contrast with the rhetoric adopted by the new structuralists. Yet the aim to bring to light the creative processes of an author is the same as theirs, and the investigation procedures indicate commitment to the same fundamental assumptions.

❦

Germain first studies Vigny's imagery—the primary material of his poetry—to show what were his sensorial awarenesses, his sensitivities. Then he studies themes and motifs to establish what were the symbolic structures of his mind, his characteristic patterns. He arrives at what he refers to as the "topography" of Vigny's imagination—his heaven and his hell—making a spatial representation of Vigny's attitude towards himself and the world. This he further elaborates through a study of the poet's complexes, conflicts, and ideas. Germain calls the subject of his study the imagination of Vigny. Another critic might have called it a phenomenological portrait, for it equates the poetic production entirely with the personality. Such a work, combining, as it does, the old and the new, makes the distinction between New Criticism and university criticism, never quite literally true, now definitely obsolete.

Logiquement liés par une dialectique de compensation, le Paradis et l'Enfer composent, dans le domaine des images, une figure d'ensemble qui est, à proprement parler, l'univers de Vigny. Nous abordons ainsi une structure globale, très simple, celle du cercle, et quelquefois de la sphère. A la fin du xviii° siècle, le mot "cercle" a connu les faveurs de la mode. Il ne désigne pas seulement une réunion mondaine, mais un domaine, un milieu, une zone d'activité, et dans une acception qui peut être très abstraite. Cette inflation de sens, au moment où la littérature se plaît à décrire, a naturellement favorisé l'apparition de tableaux circulaires: "Au levant les fleurs du printemps, au midi les fruits de l'automne, au nord les glaces de l'hiver" (Rousseau, N.H., t.I, p. 52); "Un horizon immense s'étendait en cercle autour de nous," écrit Chateaubriand. "On découvrait, à l'Orient, les sommets d'Horeb et de Sinaï, le désert de Sur et la mer Rouge; au midi les chaînes de montagne de la Thébaïde, au nord les plaines stériles où Pharaon poursuivit les Hébreux; et à l'occident, par-delà les sables où je m'étais égaré, la vallée féconde de l'Egypte" (Martyrs, t.II, p. 19). Mme de Staël décrit peu de paysages, sans doute, mais dans les tableaux mondains qu'elle imagine, le personnage principal, Delphine dans son salon, Corinne au Capitole ou au Cap Misène, est toujours au centre d'un cercle d'admirateurs (Delphine, t.I, p. 195; Corinne, t.I, p. 93; t.II, p. 137, 164, 228), et cette composition n'est pas seulement pittoresque: "Je me sentais hors de l'ordre, à l'extrémité du cercle de l'existence; mais rentrée dans la morale je suis au centre de la vie, et loin d'être agitée par le mouvement universel, je le vois tourner autour de moi" (*Delphine*, t.III, p. 122). Vigny s'est largement inspiré de ces modèles, mais il va plus loin qu'eux. Le cercle et la sphère, dans leur nudité géométrique, finissent par représenter l'œuvre d'art et le génie même qui la crée.[1]

—*L'Imagination d'Alfred de Vigny*, pp. 226–227.

SELECTED WORKS

L'Art de commenter une tragédie (Foucher, 1956). Two vols.

L'Art de commenter une comédie (Foucher, 1957).

L'Imagination d'Alfred de Vigny (Corti, 1961).

REFERENCES

Fellows, Otis. "*L'Imagination d'Alfred de Vigny*," *The Romanic Review*, April, 1965, pp. 157–158.

Moreau, Pierre. "Récentes études sur Alfred de Vigny," *Revue de Littérature Comparée*, Jan.–March, 1963, pp. 105–110.

[1] For translation, see Appendix 8.

RENÉ GIRARD

Born in Avignon in 1923, René Girard studied at the Ecole des Chartes and at Indiana University, where he obtained the Ph.D. degree. He taught French in that institution and at Bryn Mawr before moving to Johns Hopkins in 1957. He is editor of *Modern Language Notes*.

Professor Girard joined the ranks of structural critics with his *Mensonge romantique et vérité romanesque* (1961), in which he expounds, with the subtle argumentation and diction characteristic of the young French philosopher-critics, his theory of "mediation" in the novel. Beginning with the assumption that the modern work of fiction is chiefly the story of a person's desire—desire, which, since Romanticism, has been considered some sort of spontaneous manifestation—Girard would demonstrate that the line of desire between hero and object is rarely direct, but rather deflected through another person, the "mediator" of desire. In other words, the hero desires what he imagines another person desires, models himself on someone else. This gives a novel a basic triangular design: hero→ mediator→ object of desire.

This mediator may be outside the novel, such as Amadis of Gaul, who functions for Don Quixote, or as the heroines of Romantic fiction, who function for Madame Bovary; he may be inside, as in the novels of Proust and Dostoevsky. Sometimes there are both internal and external mediators, as in *Le Rouge et le noir*, where Julien's desire is guided by his image of Napoleon and also, depending upon the moment, by characters within the novel. Except in a work like Cervantes', the triangle never appears simple. A hero may find a mediator in a rival and at the same time in the person loved; he wins his suit and he becomes mediator in turn. We have reciprocal mediation, double mediation, even chain mediation. Girard does not concern himself with examples of simple external mediation or of internal mediation where the author does not recognize the mechanics of his hero's desire. The latter sort demonstrates the "romantic lie" of the book's title; the guilty authors, referred to as Romantics and neo-Romantics, are summarily dismissed. What Girard focuses on in this work are the authors who make their hero's motives clear, who illustrate "fictional truth." Such authors are Stendhal, Proust, and Dostoevsky.

Twisted and turned to explain all the vagaries of desire and fluctuating relationships which these writers present, the schematic device of the triangle becomes too complicated to follow easily, and the word "mediator" becomes quite vague as to meaning. Its inadequacy was apparent from the outset. Don Quixote's delusions, Julien Sorel's ambitions (in the critic's words, the ascetic instinct of internal mediation), Madame Bovary's daydreams, the anguish and hatred of Dostoevsky's characters, the snobbery of Proust's, the psychology of love and of hypocrisy constitute far too much material to be reduced to any precise formula. And even with the most discreet application, it can scarcely represent a concept which will furnish a new interpretation of literature or a new insight into human nature. The mechanics of desire in Stendhal and Proust have been explained many times. "Triangular desire" is a banality of psychology, in and out of novels; for imitation, hero worship, concern with one's image are in themselves too general and normal phenomena to be treated as manifestations of an "ontological malady."

Professor Girard's second work is on Dostoevsky alone. Although not patently a demonstration of "mediation," but rather a broad "psycho-portrait," the emphasis given to Dostoevsky's "mediators," particularly to the critic Bielinski, who "l'avait arraché à son affreuse adolescence,"[1] is evidence

---

[1] *Dostoïevski* (Plon, 1963), p. 66.

that the subject has not faded from his mind. What Girard claims actually to be doing in this study is to be showing the evolution of the writer, whose each successive volume exorcised another one of his demons, killed a self now surpassed. He uses the novels to explain the man, with the idea, no doubt, that light shed upon the man will refract to illuminate the novels. He shows Dostoevsky's ambivalent feelings towards his father, his timidity in the presence of women, his pride, his humility, and other features of his sadomasochistic personality as they reveal themselves progressively in his works. Recurrent themes and characteristic structures furnish the proof: the number of triangle situations in which the lover accepts the role of best friend indicates Dostoevsky's latent voyeurism, the number of parricides points to his guilt complexes. By working on a level of consciousness below that of the author's intention, the critic is able to solve some of the apparent inconsistencies and contradictions that have puzzled critics before him. Altogether he would show how Dostoevsky ultimately achieved unity in his personality—from the "descente aux enfers," the title of Chapter I, to the heights described in the last chapter as "résurrection."

§

Girard's triangle theory of fiction involves him constantly in philosophy and psychology. It would seem to permit him even to compensate for the shortcomings of the professionals. Psychiatrists, for example, seem to have misunderstood the phenomenon of masochism:

Le masochiste est plus lucide, et plus aveugle, à la fois, que les autres victimes du désir métaphysique. Il est plus lucide, de cette lucidité toujours plus répandue de nos jours, parce que, seul de tous les sujets désirants, il perçoit le lien entre la médiation interne et l'obstacle; il est plus aveugle parce que, au lieu de pousser cette prise de conscience jusqu'aux conclusions qu'elle réclame, au lieu, en d'autres termes, de fuir la transcendance déviée, il s'efforce paradoxalement de satisfaire son désir en se précipitant sur l'obstacle, en se vouant au malheur et à l'échec.

La source de cette lucidité néfaste qui caractérise les stades ultimes du mal ontologique n'est pas difficile à déceler. C'est le rapprochement du médiateur. L'esclavage est toujours le terme du désir mais ce terme est d'abord très lointain et le sujet désirant ne peut pas le percevoir. Ce terme se fait de plus en plus visible car, à mesure que la distance diminue entre médiateur et sujet, les phases du processus métaphysique s'accélèrent. Tout désir métaphysique tend donc au masochisme car le médiateur se rapproche toujours et la lumière qu'il apporte avec lui est incapable, à elle seule, de guérir le mal ontologique; elle fournit seulement à la victime le moyen de précipiter l'évolution fatale. Tout désir métaphysique marche vers sa propre vérité et vers la prise de conscience de cette vérité par le sujet désirant; il y a masochisme lorsque le sujet entre lui-même dans la lumière de cette vérité et collabore avec ardeur à son avènement.

.   .   .   .

Le masochisme révèle pleinement la contradiction qui fonde le désir métaphysique. Le passionné recherche le divin à travers l'obstacle infranchissable, à travers ce qui, par définition, ne se laisse pas traverser. C'est ce sens métaphysique qui échappe à la plupart des psychologues et psychiatres. Leurs analyses se situent donc à un niveau d'intuition très inférieur. On affirme, par exemple, que le sujet désire, tout simplement, la honte, l'humiliation et la souffrance. Personne n'a jamais désiré de telles choses. Toutes les victimes du désir métaphysique, y compris les masochistes, convoitent la divinité du médiateur et c'est pour cette divinité qu'elles accepteront, s'il le faut,—et il le faut toujours—ou même qu'elles rechercheront, la honte, l'humiliation et la souffrance. Le malheur doit révéler à ces victimes l'être dont l'imitation leur paraît la plus susceptible de les soustraire à leur misérable condition. Mais jamais ces consciences malheureuses ne désirent, purement et simplement, la honte, l'humiliation et la souffrance. On ne comprend pas le masochiste tant qu'on ne perçoit pas la nature triangulaire de son désir. On imagine un désir linéaire et on trace, à partir du sujet, la sempiternelle ligne droite; cette ligne aboutit toujours aux désagréments que l'on sait. On croit alors tenir l'*objet* même du désir; on affirme que le masochiste désire cet objet, qu'il désire, en somme, ce que nous autres ne désirons jamais.[1]

—*Mensonge romantique et vérité romanesque*, pp. 184–187.

SELECTED WORKS

Mensonge romantique et vérité romanesque (Grasset, 1961). Translated by Y. Freccero as *Deceit, Desire, and the Novel* (Johns Hopkins Press, 1965).

Dostoïevski (Plon, 1963).

REFERENCES

Albérès, R.-M. "Les grandes études littéraires," *La Table Ronde,* November, 1961, pp. 100–110.

Deguy, Michel. "Destin du désir et roman," *Critique,* January, 1962, pp. 19–31.

Giraud, Raymond. "*Mensonge romantique et vérité romanesque*," *MLN,* December, 1962, pp. 537–541.

Goldmann, Lucien. "Marx, Lukàcs, Girard et la sociologie du roman," *Médiations,* II (1961), 143–153.

[1] For translation, see Appendix 9.

LUCIEN GOLDMANN

Born in Roumania in 1913, Lucien Goldmann studied law and letters at the Universities of Bucharest, Vienna, Zurich, and Paris. He holds the doctorat ès lettres from the Sorbonne. From 1946 to 1959 he worked at the Centre National de la Recherche Scientifique. Since 1959 he has been at the Ecole Pratique des Hautes Etudes as a professor in the fields of sociology, literature, and philosophy. In 1961 Goldmann was asked to direct research in the sociology of literature at the University of Brussels.

Goldmann is a Marxist critic, strongly influenced by Georg Lukàcs, whose work he has translated into French. He claims, however, independence from Stalinism and party commitment. In an article published in *Arguments*, he explicitly states what he owes to Marxism in providing him with working principles for his criticism: (1) the concept of meaningful structure in the comprehension of history, the world, and creations of the mind; (2) the concept of social realism; (3) the concept of unity of content and form in works of art. Applied to the study of literary texts, all these concepts contribute to an understanding of the social and historical reality which has produced such texts. For Goldmann, therefore, the work of art is just a means to an end. However, because he feels that a serious and rigorous science of creative activity is necessary to make a work of art serve his end, he looks with favorable eye upon the techniques of the New Critics. In fact, two out of his three Marxist concepts point directly to the phenomenological and structural approach. By adding to such criticism the dimension of society and its dialectical evolution, Goldmann has what he considers the supremely valid method for investigation in all the humane sciences—he gives this method the name genetic-structural analysis.

※

All Goldmann's criticism involves sociology and history. In studying Racine, he finds the explanation of problems of dramaturgy in the context of the social reality of the times:

La solitude du héros tragique, l'abîme qui le sépare et du monde et de Dieu, a d'autre part posé à la tragédie racinienne un autre problème de composition, celui du *chœur*. Racine, comme probablement tous les écrivains tragiques modernes, en a été continuellement préoccupé. Il a toujours cherché une possibilité d'introduire, comme l'ont fait les tragiques de l'antiquité, le chœur dans les pièces qu'il écrivait. Mais le problème était et reste insoluble. Le chœur a une signification précise. Il est *la voix de la communauté humaine* et par cela même la voix des dieux. La tragédie grecque racontait la destinée d'un héros qui, dans un univers homogène, régi par l'accord de la communauté et de la divinité, venant de briser par son "hybris" l'ordre traditionnel, en quittant l'une et en irritant l'autre, avait ainsi attiré sur soi la colère et la vengeance des dieux.

Dans la tragédie racinienne—et dans toute grande tragédie moderne—la communauté authentique des hommes a par contre depuis longtemps disparu; au point qu'il n'en subsiste aucun souvenir. Le monde, qui n'est plus lié au héros, est une jungle d'égoïsmes rapaces et de victimes inconscientes, il est ce monde dont Pascal disait qu'il écrase l'homme, mais un homme plus grand que lui, parce qu'il sait qu'il est écrasé alors que le monde l'ignore. C'est pourquoi il ne saurait plus être le témoin effrayé ou même impassible des événements.[1]

—*Jean Racine, dramaturge*, pp. 27–28.

For Goldmann, Racine and Pascal represent Jansenism, which was trying to stem the tide of rationalism and restore

[1] For translation, see Appendix 10.

the moral values that had been swept away. God was no
longer visible, yet he was felt to be still there: "Deus abscon-
ditus." The tragic vision of Racine and Pascal is a product of
this sense of an alienated world experienced most keenly by
the Jansenist thinkers:

Or, c'est en face de ce développement ascendant du rationalisme
(développement qui s'est continué en France jusqu'au XX⁰
siècle, mais qui se trouvait au XVII⁰ siècle *à un tournant quali-*
tatif puisqu'il venait de constituer avec les œuvres de Descartes
et de Galilée un système philosophique cohérent et une physique mathématique incomparablement supérieure à l'ancienne
physique aristotélicienne) que, grâce à un concours de circonstances que nous examinerons plus loin, se développe la pensée
janséniste qui trouvera son expression la plus cohérente dans
les deux grandes œuvres tragiques de Pascal et de Racine.
   On peut caractériser la conscience tragique à cette époque
par la compréhension rigoureuse et précise du monde nouveau
créé par l'individualisme rationaliste, avec tout ce qu'il contenait
de positif, de précieux et surtout de définitivement acquis pour
la pensée et la conscience humaines, mais en même temps par
le refus radical d'accepter ce monde comme seule chance et
seule perspective de l'homme.
   La raison est un facteur important de la vie humaine, un
facteur dont l'homme est à juste titre fier et qu'il ne pourra
plus jamais abandonner, mais elle *n'est pas tout l'homme* et
surtout *elle ne doit et ne peut pas suffire* à la vie humaine; et
cela sur aucun plan, pas même celui qui lui semble particulièrement propre de la recherche de la vérité scientifique.
   C'est pourquoi la vision tragique est, après la période amorale
et areligieuse de l'empirisme et du rationalisme, un retour à la
morale et à la *religion*, à condition de prendre ce dernier mot
dans son sens le plus vaste de *foi* en un ensemble de valeurs qui
transcendent l'individu. Il ne s'agit cependant pas encore d'une
pensée et d'un art qui pourraient remplacer le monde atomiste
et mécaniste de la raison individuelle par une *nouvelle com-*
munauté et un nouvel *univers.*
   Envisagée *dans une perspective historique,* la vision tragique
n'est qu'une position de *passage* précisément parce qu'elle admet
comme définitif et inchangeable le monde, en apparence clair

mais pour elle en réalité confus et ambigu de la pensée rationaliste et de la sensation empirique, et qu'elle lui oppose seulement une nouvelle exigence et une nouvelle échelle de valeurs.
—*Le Dieu caché*, pp. 42–43.

Goldmann's method is already apparent in his works on
Racine and Pascal. Its most strict application, however, can
be seen in his study of Malraux's novels. First they are
examined in chronological order for the ideas, the prejudices,
the values they express—the "structures," which an old-fashioned critic might have called "philosophy," "universe," or
"Weltanschauung." Once defined, they are linked with the
period of history to which they belong:

En étudiant l'œuvre de Malraux, un premier fait frappe tout
d'abord: entre ses premiers écrits: *Royaume Farfelu, Lunes en
Papier, la Tentation de l'Occident,* qui affirment la mort des
Dieux et la décomposition universelle des valeurs, et les écrits
suivants: *Les Conquérants, la Voie royale, la Condition humaine,* il y a non seulement une différence de contenu mais
aussi une différence *de forme.* Bien qu'il s'agisse, en effet, dans
les deux cas, d'œuvres de fiction, seuls les seconds créent un
univers à intention réaliste constitué d'êtres, imaginaires sans
doute mais individuels et vivants, et ont par cela même un
caractère romanesque, alors que les premiers sont, soit ... des
essais ... soit des histoires fantastiques et allégoriques ...
  Si nous constatons en outre que tous les romans ultérieurs
de Malraux créeront des univers régis par des valeurs positives
et universelles, et que le premier écrit, qui indique une nouvelle
crise: *la Lutte avec l'Ange,* sera à la fois le dernier et le moins
romanesque, le plus intellectuel des écrits de fiction de Malraux,
il nous semble qu'on pourrait formuler une première hypothèse:
*Dans cette œuvre dominée par la crise des valeurs qui caractéri-
sait l'Europe occidentale à l'époque où elle a été élaborée, la
création proprement romanesque correspond à la période dans
laquelle l'écrivain a cru pouvoir, envers et contre tout, sauve-
garder l'existence de certaines valeurs universelles authentiques.*
—*Pour une sociologie du roman*, pp. 41–42.

By developing the sociological implications of their theories, Goldmann can turn the work of other structuralist critics to account. Thus with René Girard's triangle scheme, the "referred good" is equated with a social ideal: the values represented by Amadis of Gaul which Don Quixote borrows and those which Madame Bovary attributed to the society of the château constitute a collective good. Of course this makes Girard's theory say no more than that the individual's values reflect those of his time or something just as obvious. Goldmann discusses what he feels is Girard's contribution to the sociology of the novel:

Or, le problème d'une sociologie du roman a toujours préoccupé les sociologues de la littérature sans que jusqu'ici ils aient fait, nous semble-t-il, un pas décisif dans la voie de son élucidation. Au fond, le roman étant, pendant tout la première partie de son histoire, une biographie et une chronique sociale, on a toujours pu montrer que la chronique sociale reflétait plus ou moins la société de l'époque, constatation pour laquelle il n'est vraiment pas besoin d'être sociologue.

D'autre part, on a aussi mis en relation la transformation du roman depuis Kafka et les analyses marxistes de la réification. Là aussi, il faut dire que les sociologues sérieux auraient dû voir un problème plutôt qu'une explication. S'il est évident que le monde absurde de Kafka, de l'Etranger de Camus, ou le monde composé d'objets relativement autonomes de Robbe-Grillet, correspondent à l'analyse de la réification telle qu'elle a été développée par Marx et les marxistes ultérieurs, le problème se pose de savoir pourquoi, alors que cette analyse était élaborée dans la seconde moitié du XIX⁰ siècle et qu'elle concernait un phénomène dont l'apparition se situe bien auparavant, ce même phénomène ne s'est manifesté dans le roman qu'à partir de la fin de la première guerre mondiale.

Bref toutes ces analyses portaient sur la relation de certains éléments du *contenu* de la littérature romanesque et de l'existence d'une réalité sociale qu'ils reflétaient presque sans transposition ou à l'aide d'une transposition plus ou moins transparente.

Or, le tout premier problème qu'aurait dû aborder une sociologie du roman est celui de la relation entre la *forme romanesque* elle-même et la *structure* du milieu social à l'intérieur duquel elle s'est développée, c'est-à-dire du roman comme genre littéraire et de la société individualiste moderne.

Il nous semble aujourd'hui que la réunion des analyses de Lukàcs et de Girard, bien qu'elles aient été élaborées l'une et l'autre sans préoccupations spécifiquement sociologiques, permet, sinon d'élucider entièrement ce problème, du moins de faire un pas décisif vers son élucidation.

—*Ibid.*, pp. 22–23.

In those critical approaches where there seems no possibility of involving society and its dialectical evolution, Goldmann shows far less interest. Freudian psychoanalysis, for example, is far too anchored in the individual to be of value for cultural analysis:

Malheureusement, en tant que structuralisme génétique, la psychanalyse, tout au moins telle que Freud l'a élaborée, n'est pas suffisamment conséquente et se trouve beaucoup trop entachée du scientisme qui dominait la vie universitaire de la fin du XIX⁰ siècle et du début du XX⁰. Cela se manifeste notamment sur deux points capitaux.

Premièrement, dans les explications freudiennes, la dimension temporelle de l'avenir manque complètement et de manière radicale. Subissant en cela l'influence du scientisme déterministe de son temps, Freud néglige entièrement les forces positives d'équilibration qui agissent dans toute structure humaine, individuelle ou collective; expliquer, c'est pour lui revenir aux expériences de l'enfance, aux forces instinctives refoulées ou opprimées, alors qu'il néglige entièrement la fonction positive que pourraient avoir la conscience et la relation avec la réalité.

Deuxièmement, l'individu est, pour Freud, un sujet absolu pour lequel les autres hommes ne peuvent être que des *objets* de satisfaction ou de frustration; ce fait est peut-être le fondement de l'absence d'avenir que nous venons de mentionner.

Sans doute serait-il faux de réduire, d'une manière trop étroite, la libido freudienne au domaine sexuel; il n'en reste pas moins qu'elle est toujours *individuelle* et que, dans la vision freudienne de l'humanité, le sujet collectif et la satisfaction qu'une action collective peut apporter à l'individu font entièrement défaut.

. . . .

L'intégration des œuvres dans la biographie individuelle ne saurait en effet révéler que leur signification individuelle et leur relation avec les problèmes biographiques et psychiques de l'auteur. C'est dire que, quelles que soient la validité et la rigueur scientifique des recherches de ce type, elles doivent nécessairement situer l'œuvre en dehors de son contexte culturel et esthétique propre, pour la mettre au même niveau que tous les symptômes individuels de tel ou tel malade soigné par le psychanalyste.

—*Ibid.*, pp. 225–227.

SELECTED WORKS

Le Dieu caché (Gallimard, 1955). Translated by Philip Thody as *The Hidden God* (Humanities, 1964).

Jean Racine, dramaturge (L'Arche, 1956).

"L'Apport de la pensée marxiste à la critique littéraire," *Arguments*, Jan.–March, 1959, pp. 44–46.

Pour une sociologie du roman (Gallimard, 1964).

REFERENCES

Albérès, R.-M. "Sur le méta-roman," *Les Nouvelles Littéraires*, December 19, 1963, p. 5.

Alquié, Ferdinand. "Pascal et la critique contemporaine," *Critique*, November, 1957, pp. 953–967.

Brereton, Geoffrey. "New views of the old Masters," *The New Statesman and Nation*, September, 1956, pp. 248–249.

Girard, René. "Racine, poète de la gloire," *Critique*, June, 1964, pp. 483–506.

CHARLES MAURON

Born in 1899, Charles Mauron is a professor at the University of Aix-en-Provence.[1] He came to literature somewhat late in life—after pursuing a career as an engineer. His degree in letters was awarded by Aix-en-Provence for a thesis on Racine. Professor Mauron is one of the pioneers in psychoanalytical criticism.

Charles Mauron's early essay on esthetics and psychology already shows the direction he will subsequently take. In it he treats esthetics as a branch of psychology; and although disclaiming any professional qualifications himself and preferring Roger Fry and other experimental psychologists to psychoanalysts, he seems already committed to a study of the subconscious. The object of his first formal investigation is Mallarmé: the death of the poet's sister as an unconscious *leitmotif* in his work. This study is followed by one on Racine, in which Mauron shows the effect of the dramatist's orphaned condition. Both studies are meticulous expositions of the thesis. If they do not elicit great admiration, it is because they make quite tedious reading and, whether false or true, the thesis does not seem to merit all the labor.

こ

The same may be said of the monumental *Des Métaphores obsédantes au mythe personnel,* which represents a definitive formulation of Mauron's method. He calls it psychocriticism and demonstrates step by step its empirical procedures. The basic technique is the superimposing of texts

---

[1] Announcement of Professor Mauron's death was made while this book was already in galley proof, late in 1966.

to bring to light facts and relationships produced by the author's subconscious—patterns that lie deep below the conscious patterns of the works. What distinguishes psychocriticism from thematic criticism is its concentration on the subconscious and its frame of psychoanalytical reference. Thus, while admittedly no more than partial criticism, it claims to make a unique contribution to our knowledge of literary works and of their genesis. Mauron uncovers in Mallarmé the obsession of a female figure; in Baudelaire he finds recurring images of weight which impede forward movement; in Nerval he notes a type-situation involving a young wife and an older husband. He plots the appearances and disappearances of these patterns, their developments and ramifications, to show that underneath each poet's work there is a supporting architecture unknown to the author and reader alike.

L'expérience ainsi tentée sur des textes de Mallarmé donne-t-elle des résultats comparables si l'on superpose d'autres textes d'un poète différent? Par exemple Baudelaire. Je commencerai par quelques poèmes en prose.

Le premier est *Un Hémisphère dans une Chevelure.* Il fourmille de thèmes baudelairiens: invitation au voyage, beau navire, paresse et parfum des pays chauds, etc. Ni ses sources extérieures, ni sa signification ne font le moindre doute. Partons de la dernière phrase de ce texte: "Laisse-moi mordre longtemps tes tresses lourdes et noires. Quand je mordille tes cheveux élastiques et rebelles, il me semble que je mange des souvenirs."

Nos analyses de Baudelaire et Mallarmé auront ainsi des points de départ comparables. Mais elles vont aussitôt diverger. Dans le texte du poème en prose, l'adjectif "lourdes" appliqué à une chevelure féminine constitue à coup sûr un leit-motif baudelairien: "Longtemps! toujours! ma main dans ta crinière lourde ... " (*La Chevelure*) " ... ses cheveux qui pendaient dans son dos, épais comme une crinière ... " (*Les Vocations*). Nous ne serons pas étonnés de trouver dans un autre poème en prose, *La Belle Dorothée,* évidemment relié par son sujet au précédent, la phrase suivante: " ... Le poids de son énorme chevelure presque bleue tire en arrière sa tête délicate ... " La lourdeur s'est accusée: elle tire la tête en arrière. Rien ne nous autorise, cependant, à voir là autre chose qu'un trait dessinant de façon charmante le port d'une jeune fille. Mais ce texte en évoque aussitôt un autre, non moins familier et pourtant bien différent. Il s'agit de la lettre adressée par Baudelaire à Asselineau le 13 mars 1856 et dans laquelle le poète raconte à son ami un de ses rêves. Voici l'épisode qui nous intéresse: le poète aperçoit un monstre, juché sur un piédestal où il s'ennuie mortellement. Cet être fantastique doit, dans une certaine mesure, représenter le rêveur lui-même, puisque Baudelaire avoue s'être réveillé dans la posture qu'il attribuait au monstre. Or ce dernier porte, enroulé autour du corps, un appendice qui lui part de la tête: " ... quelque chose d'élastique comme du caoutchouc, et si long, si long que, s'il le roulait sur sa tête comme une queue de cheveux, cela serait beaucoup trop lourd, et absolument impossible à porter." Revoici donc à la fois le chignon trop pesant qui tirerait la tête en arrière (*La Belle Dorothée*) en même temps que la lourdeur élastique des tresses de Jeanne Duval (*Un Hémisphère dans une Chevelure*).

Cependant le rêve précise l'embarras du monstre: " ... S'il le laissait traîner par terre, cela lui renverserait la tête en arrière" ... le soir, " ... il est obligé ... de marcher en chancelant, avec son appendice de caoutchouc, jusqu'à la salle du souper ... " Cette démarche comique et piteuse, embarrassée par quelque chose qui traîne à terre, n'évoque-t-elle pas à son tour un poème fameux des *Fleurs du Mal*: *l'Albatros?*

> A peine les ont-ils déposés sur les planches,
> Que ces rois de l'azur, maladroits et honteux,
> Laissent piteusement leurs grandes ailes blanches
> Comme des avirons traîner à côté d'eux.

Hésiterons-nous devant ce rapprochement? Par son sujet même, *l'Albatros* est lié aux thèmes du navire, du voyage, donc de la chevelure. L'Albatros représente le poète:

> Le Poëte est pareil au prince des nuées.

Mais nous avons vu que le monstre, dans une grotesque déformation onirique, le représentait aussi (plein d'ennui, immobilisé sur son piédestal, ridicule quand il marche, tandis que des hommes circulent autour de lui). D'ailleurs dans les *Fleurs du Mal*, nous glisserons sans la moindre difficulté de l'Albatros au Cygne, et du Cygne à la Malabaraise, qui nous ramène aussitôt à la belle Dorothée des Poèmes en Prose. Le réseau d'associations ainsi dessiné renforce, par sa cohérence totale, la probabilité de chaque liaison. De la belle Dorothée, en passant par le rêve du monstre (et incidemment l'Albatros), nous sommes donc conduits à un autre poème en prose: *Chacun sa Chimère*, où nous retrouverons la même marche de plus en plus alourdie.

Chacun d'eux portait sur son dos une énorme Chimère, aussi lourde qu'un sac de farine ou de charbon, ou le fourniment d'un fantassin romain.

Mais la monstrueuse bête ... enveloppait et opprimait l'homme de ses muscles élastiques et puissants; elle s'agrafait avec ses deux vastes griffes à la poitrine de sa monture; et sa tête fabuleuse surmontait le front de l'homme, comme un de ces casques horribles par lesquels les anciens guerriers espéraient ajouter à la terreur de l'ennemi.

Le casque rappelle la chevelure (Mallarmé, dans l'un de nos trois poèmes, avait repris la métaphore, et Valéry la reprendra à son tour). Mais la Chimère, pesant sur la nuque et le dos, ceinturant le torse, est comparée aussi à un fardeau de débardeur (sac de charbon, sac militaire). Elle n'en reste pas moins la Chimère, le Rêve, exigence de voyage plutôt qu'invitation, vers la mort, à travers l'ennui d'une terre qui ressemble à un terrain vague. De ces tristes errants que leur fantastique fardeau coiffe et harasse, nous passerons sans difficulté à la figure du *Mauvais Vitrier*. Courbé sous une charge accrochée comme un sac de soldat et dépassant normalement la tête, il déambule par les quartiers pauvres, s'accroche maladroitement dans l'escalier qu'on lui fait monter, et ploie sous le faix de ses vitres qui devraient être magiquement colorées pour faire voir la vie en beau:

... —Comment? vous n'avez pas de verres de couleur? des verres roses, rouges, bleus, des vitres magiques, des vitres de paradis? Impudent que vous êtes! vous **osez** vous promener dans des quartiers pauvres, et vous n'avez pas même de vitres qui fassent voir la vie en beau!

Et je le poussai vivement vers l'escalier, où il trébucha en grognant.

Je m'approchai du balcon et je me saisis d'un petit pot de fleurs, et, quand l'homme reparut au débouché de la porte, je laissai tomber perpendiculairement mon engin de guerre sur le rebord postérieur de ses crochets; et, le choc le renversant, il acheva de briser sous son dos toute sa pauvre fortune ambulatoire qui rendit le bruit éclatant d'un palais de cristal crevé par la foudre.

Ainsi tiré en arrière, le porteur de fausses chimères s'écroule.

A la marche embarrassée succède la chute. Et si l'on veut apprécier le sens cruel de cette catastrophe, (qui atteint, nous le soupçonnons, plutôt qu'un vitrier, le poète dont il est l'image comme l'Albatros), il faudra glisser de ce poème en prose à un autre: *Une Mort héroïque.*

Le Mauvais Vitrier et *Une Mort héroïque* se superposent très exactement. Les deux poèmes décrivent la tension croissante puis la brusque décharge d'une pulsion agressive perverse. Le prince, d'un coup de sifflet, fait s'écrouler le comédien comme le poète fait du vitrier. Les deux personnages agressifs coïncident. Ce sont des artistes, pleins d'ennui et de perversité—l'une des images que Baudelaire se faisait de lui-même et à l'égard de qui il affecte une attitude de médecin, moraliste et théologien. Les deux agressions présentent les mêmes caractéristiques: cruauté, violence inattendue, exécution calculée, tir bien ajusté, rire. Les deux victimes sont des êtres accablés par la vie, contraints de dispenser une beauté chimérique et succombant sous la charge—évidemment une autre image que Baudelaire se faisait de soi. Une pensée préconsciente, en Baudelaire, réunit donc cette série d'images: Fancioulle—le mauvais vitrier—le monstre du rêve—l'albatros—le cygne—Andromaque—la Malabaraise—la belle Dorothée. Bien d'autres figures pourraient s'ajouter à cette liste. Mais nous sentons assez déjà que le réseau existe et qu'il intéresse profondément la personalité de Baudelaire. Ce qui lui tenait le plus à cœur, sa destinée poétique, est en cause. Je me bornerai à citer encore deux poèmes.

Dans *le Fou et la Vénus,* nous trouvons une image infantile du bouffon, qui se situe entre Fancioulle et le monstre du rêve:

... Aux pieds d'une colossale Vénus, un de ces fous
artificiels, un de ces bouffons volontaires chargés de
faire rire les rois quand le Remords ou l'Ennui les ob-
sède, affublé d'un costume éclatant et ridicule, coiffé
de cornes et de sonnettes, tout ramassé contre le piédestal, lève des yeux pleins de larmes vers l'immortelle
Déesse.

Cette Vénus trop grande, inébranlable, rêvant à autre chose,
hors d'atteinte, rappelle à la fois la *Géante* et la *Beauté*:

J'eusse aimé vivre auprès d'une jeune géante,
Comme aux pieds d'une reine un chat voluptueux ...

... Parcourir à loisir ses magnifiques formes;
Ramper sur le versant de ses genoux énormes ...

et:

Je suis belle, ô mortels! comme un rêve de pierre

. . . .

Les poëtes, devant mes grandes attitudes,
Que j'ai l'air d'emprunter aux plus fiers monuments,
Consumeront leurs jours en d'austères études ...

Des humiliations et des hontes d'adulte réévoquent certaine-
ment, par analogie (comme dans le rêve) des situations infan-
tiles. Mais surtout, la Chimère est devenue trop pesante, froide
et pétrifiée. Le poète ressent le mépris accablant de sa propre
conscience esthétique. La Chimère s'est détachée de lui et s'est
unie au Prince pour lui marquer une froideur d'autant plus
cruelle que l'atmosphère est plus ardente. "Tous connaissent
l'amour, semble dire le Fou, monstre ou poète, sauf moi, des-
cendu de mon piédestal."

Cet accablement se distingue de la chute, comme l'ennui de
la crise dépressive aiguë. Mais leur résultante est le sentiment
de guignon:

Pour soulever un poids si lourd,
Sisyphe, il faudrait ton courage!
Bien qu'on ait du coeur à l'ouvrage,
L'art est long et le Temps est court.

Et nous voici dans les régions funèbres du spleen baudelairien:

Loin des sépultures célèbres,
Vers un cimetière isolé,
Mon coeur, comme un tambour voilé,
Va battant des marches funèbres.

Sous l'effet de la dépression, le poids de la chevelure, puis de la Chimère, devient celui du Destin et, enfin, du tombeau.[1]
—*Des Métaphores obsédantes au Mythe personnel*, pp. 58–63.

In his recent work, *Psychocritique du genre comique*, Mauron applies his technique to a whole literary genre. His previous investigations required the careful identification and elimination of the factors of period and genre if they were to isolate the personal myth of the writer. Now Mauron turns to these factors, taking his departure from the study of Molière that he had made for *Des Métaphores obsédantes*. His method is the same as before: the search for common, basic situations or motifs. The obvious explanation of an artistic tradition is brushed aside as superficial. Mauron would dig more deeply, discover why a situation could be used again and again to appeal to audiences of different time and place. For, he says, if writers consciously copy one another, audiences do not. We might think that even the most impenitent of the source-hunters would grant that if a plot is passed down through the ages, its audience appeal is definitely a contributing factor. But it is interesting to see that in this book Mauron shifts his attention from author to audience and offers as reason for the perennial popularity of certain situations in classic comedy their association with Freudian complexes. Whereas formerly he psychoanalyzed the writer, now he psychoanalyzes the public.

SELECTED WORKS

Aesthetics and Psychology (Hogarth, 1935).

Mallarmé l'obscur (Denoël, 1941).

[1] For translation, see Appendix 11.

Sagesse de l'Eau (Laffont, 1945).

Introduction à la psychanalyse de Mallarmé (La Baconnière, 1950). Translated by Will McLendon and Archibald Henderson, Jr. as *Introduction to the Psychoanalysis of Mallarmé* (University of California, 1963).

L'Inconscient dans l'œuvre et la vie de Racine (Ophrys, 1957).

"La psychocritique et sa méthode," *Théories et Problèmes*. Supplementum II, *Orbis Litterarum* (Munksgaard, 1958), p. 104.

"L'Art et la psychanalyse," *Psyché*, January, 1962, pp. 24–36.

Des Métaphores obsédantes au mythe personnel (Corti, 1963).

Mallarmé par lui-même (Seuil, 1964).

Psychocritique du genre comique (Corti, 1964).

Le Dernier Baudelaire (Corti, 1966).

REFERENCES

Autrand, Michel. "*Psychocritique du genre comique*," *Revue d'Histoire Littéraire*, Oct.–Dec., 1965, pp. 725–727.

Bertherat, Yves. "Le Secret des poètes," *Esprit*, January, 1964, pp. 104–109.

Cohn, Robert Greer. "Mauron on Mallarmé," *MLN*, December, 1963, pp. 520–526.

Durry, Marie-Jeanne. "Charles Mauron ou la critique par rapprochement," *Le Figaro Littéraire*, January 27, 1963, p. 5.

Genette, Gérard. "Psycholectures," *Critique*, October, 1963, pp. 868–872.

GEORGES POULET

Born in Belgium in 1902, Georges Poulet is the brother of the journalist and critic Robert Poulet. After his studies in law and letters at the University of Liége, Georges Poulet became a professor. For many years he taught French literature at the University of Edinburgh (1927–1952), then at Johns Hopkins (1952–1957), then at Zurich, where he is still teaching. While in Scotland he brought out his first collection of studies on time in literature. Republished a year later (1950) by Plon, it captured wide critical attention and received the Prix Sainte-Beuve. A second volume appeared in 1952 and was awarded the Prix de la Critique of that year. Subsequent publications have each been greeted with acclaim, and it seems likely that Poulet will continue to exploit the same rich critical vein for the rest of his career.

Georges Poulet is generally accorded a very high place among the critics of today. His essays are held up as examples of the new type of serious and significant criticism as opposed to the external trivialities of the literary historians or the subjective judgments of the reviewers. In choosing to explore the subject of time in literature, he hit upon an approach that seemed to give philosophic dignity to criticism. To be sure, some critics have questioned whether his essays do not belong to philosophy rather than to criticism, but most, more than content to share their berth with philosophers, psychoanalysts, and even "scientists," do not let the question worry them.

Actually, Poulet's work does not qualify as philosophy in the sense of an exposition of a philosophical position. Its declared aim, as stated in the preface to his first volume, is to study "human time" in the works of a number of French authors more or less representative of their period. Thus, for

Montaigne, time is the fleeting present; for Corneille, it is an act of will realized in a present lifted out of duration, and so on. In the second volume, the "internal distance" (the space between the thinking me and the object which is thought) adds a spatial consideration to the problem of human time. But the terms may be misleading, for along with individual authors' conceptual idiosyncracies in regard to time and space, Poulet seems to be grouping quite loosely general attitudes towards life, themes of imagery, characteristic allusions and phraseology. What philosophical insight such a gigantic undertaking yields may seem a paltry return for Poulet's effort and that of his reader. The same might be said of esthetic, psychological, or literary insight. But whatever misgivings we may feel about it, Poulet's work is indeed representative of the new tendency in French literary criticism, one which started with Albert Béguin and Marcel Raymond, Poulet's avowed masters.

ॐ

To understand Poulet's method, let us follow him through his essay on Flaubert.[1] It is typical and will demonstrate the oversubtle quality of Poulet's argument, often constructed upon questionable distinctions, affirmations, and suppositions. He begins by quoting from the Correspondence a passage in which Flaubert speaks of moments of enthusiasm as his "grands jours de soleil." Poulet says he thus appears as a Romantic, not because of love for the picturesque but because of the consciousness of an exceptional inner experience. (One may interject here that artists of all times have given similar testimony of experiencing states of euphoria, usually equated with states of "inspiration." There is nothing remarkable about it.) Poulet then proceeds to separate

[1] *Etudes sur le temps humain*, Chapître XV: "Flaubert" (University of Edinburgh Press, 1949), pp. 322–333.

Flaubert from the Romantics on the grounds that such a mood does not prompt him to turn inwards towards his own being but rather towards the external world. Poulet cites passages from widely different places in the Correspondence in which Flaubert speaks of perceiving, gives examples of his talent and fondness for perception and of the importance he attaches to modes of perception. All this is proof of a remarkable peculiarity in Flaubert: he has full self-awareness only when perceiving, when he is fusing himself with an object. Objectivity is therefore no acquired discipline for Flaubert but an instinct. In privileged moments he succeeds in bridging the gap between subject and object, attains "integral phenomenalism." Soul and nature become one, one becomes nature. Poulet offers evidence of this pantheistic ecstasy in Flaubert from a number of works. By now we infer what the theme of this essay is—what we might call Flaubert's solidarity with the concrete world. In itself it is a basic characteristic of all artistic temperaments, and all Poulet's quotations and rhetoric do not establish anything really unusual about Flaubert's. But if we accept what he says, we may still ask, "What has it to do with Flaubert's notion of time?" His answer eventually comes forth: in Flaubert's moments of felicity, the sense of living intensely and of blending with the cosmos implies the experience of duration. Here is a quote from *Madame Bovary*:

> "Le silence était partout; quelque chose de doux semblait sortir des arbres; elle sentait son cœur, dont les battements recommençaient, et le sang circuler dans sa chair comme un fleuve de lait. Alors, elle entendit tout au loin, au delà du bois, sur les autres collines, un cri vague et prolongé, une voix qui se traînait, et elle l'écoutait silencieusement, se mêlant comme une musique aux dernières vibrations de ses nerfs émus."[2]

[2] For translation, see Appendix 12.

Poulet declares that this passage possesses a spatial and temporal density so particular that the moment appears to belong to a duration of a kind quite different from that of ordinary days:

C'est comme si le temps, telle une brise qui passe, pouvait être senti dans les battements de cœur qui recommencent, dans le sang qui circule ainsi qu'un fleuve de lait. Ce n'est plus la conscience amère d'un intervalle qui se creuse, il n'y a plus d'intervalle, il n'y a plus qu'un glissement général à la fois des choses et de l'être sentant, avec le sentiment d'une homogénéité absolue entre les différents éléments qui composent ce moment. L'être sentant, et son corps, et le paysage, et la nature, et la vie, tout participe au même moment du même devenir.

Poulet sounds as moved as Emma, but however vivid Flaubert's metaphor is, it simply conveys a sensation of excited heartbeats and nothing at all really about duration.

Poulet admits that the state of mind described by Flaubert on his "grands jours de soleil" is the same as experienced by all nature mystics—ego blending into the universe and sentiment of timelessness. But, Poulet insists, with the difference that with Flaubert this state can only be glimpsed. His thought cannot get into it or isolate it. It is only the culminating point of a temporal line, of a movement of thought. The same is true whether the stimulus is sensorial or one of memory:

Il y a, chez Flaubert, d'autres grands jours de soleil, où l'âme n'est plus ouverte au soleil présent, mais à la "vapeur d'or" qui émane encore des soleils révolus. Il y a chez lui un présent qui est le lieu d'aboutissement des images-souvenirs, comme il y a un présent qui est le lieu d'aboutissement des images-sensations.

In other words, Flaubert has sense experiences and memories. Flaubert prefers the latter, Poulet declares, and for the reason that when sensation appears as memory it is an internal phenomenon, and that is more intimate:

Toute distance alors est abolie comme dans la plus rare et la plus parfaite union sensible. La reviviscence est une pure viviscence. Elle a la même intensité, la même richesse, elle aboutit à la même synthèse de l'objet et du moi.

Memory with Flaubert is activated by the awareness of some object. Once activated, it brings up a whole series of things—plurality is the most striking feature of Flaubert's memory. This leads him deeper and deeper into the depths of duration. In the moment of revelation he encompasses in one sweeping glance all that memory has evoked. What we make out to be Poulet's point here is that Flaubert's "mystic" experience may excite memory processes or that memory processes may bring on the "mystic moment"—whichever way it is, during such an experience, the consciousness is flooded with images from the past.

After the exaltation of the "moment éternel," anguish. The gap between present and past opens again and Flaubert cannot bridge it. He has no sense of continuous identity: the past is beyond reach, the future empty, the present a prison. Duration has become stagnant water. The sense of human duration with Flaubert threatens to dissolve in a general sense of illusion and wearing out. But Flaubert is saved by the faculty of turning sentiments into ideas. Through a methodical use of the reconstructive power of thought, Flaubert can link his memories and disparate perceptions. Differing from Balzac, who first establishes a law-power and then observes its application in the concrete, Flaubert reaches the law through gradual steps in the concrete. The law is a summit of synthesis and, having reached it, Flaubert begins the journey back down:

Le mouvement descendant de la pensée de Flaubert prend alors l'aspect d'une représentation prospective de la vie qui, du passé, se ramène par une série d'états jusqu'au présent et y aboutit, en lui donnant pour signification d'être un effet conséquent à tout un vaste travail génétique perceptible en l'espace et la durée—perspective semblable à celle que l'on a, quand, du rivage, l'on reporte lentement les yeux jusqu'à la pleine mer, pour suivre de là une vague qui se rapproche et qu'on voit finale-ment mourir à ses pieds; —expérience que l'on a encore toutes les fois qu'en écrivant une phrase périodique—une phrase à la Flaubert—on trouve que de la protase à l'apodose les différents éléments se composent en une synthèse montante et descend-ante qui, en s'achevant, permet de découvrir en la phrase une unité indissoluble où tout *devient* présent. Dès lors le problème du temps n'est plus qu'un problème de style.
—*Etudes sur le temps humain*, pp. 322–333.

In retrospect, we may feel that, in this essay, to get to the subject of time Poulet has led us along a very twisting path. And we are not sure we ever reached it. We conclude that the subject of time is just a thematic device and that the brilliance of an essay by Georges Poulet, with its superb imagery and impeccable construction, is lyrical and rhetorical in nature, not philosophical or even critical in the ordinary sense of the word.

As we take up the second volume of *Etudes sur le temps humain*, *La Distance intérieure*, we anticipate that the word "space" will give us as much trouble as the word "time." The expression "distance intérieure" in itself suggests a figure of speech, but one that has something to do with the subject's concept of space. It seems, however, only to derive from the critic's private mythology. We read in the introduction:

Ma pensée est un espace où ont lieu, où ont leur lieu mes pensées. Les voici qui arrivent, passent, s'écartent ou s'enfoncent, et je les distingue à des distances spatiales ou temporelles qui ne cessent de varier. Ma pensée n'est pas faite seulement de mes pensées; elle est faite encore, et bien plus peut-être, de toute la *distance intérieure* qui me sépare ou me rapproche de ce que je puis penser. Car tout ce que je pense, c'est en moi que je le pense. La distance n'est pas seulement un intervalle, elle est un milieu ambiant, un champ d'union.

So what Poulet is actually doing is not seeking his subject's notions of space but translating his characteristics as a writer into spatial terms. Everyone knows about Mallarmé's "sterility"—Poulet opens his discussion of Mallarmé with this topic, which he treats entirely in images of motion. Note how they lead him to the spatial figure:

Dès le début la pensée mallarméenne se trouve donc comme frappée de paralysie. Elle ne part pas. Elle ne prend son essor ni spontanément comme la poésie de Lamartine ou de Vigny, ni même artificiellement comme la poésie de Baudelaire. Et si rêver, c'est imaginer, elle ne rêve même pas. Elle situe à une distance infinie un idéal dont elle ignore tout, sinon qu'il dépend de son rêve et qu'elle ne peut le rêver. Alors elle attend de pouvoir rêver. A la place d'un point de départ il n'y a chez Mallarmé qu'immobilité et attente:

> J'attends en m'abîmant que mon ennui s'élève ...

Point donc de mouvement initial. Rien qu'un état négatif qui peut se prolonger indéfiniment, éternellement, comme un temps vide.

Mais pourtant, s'il n'y a pas de mouvement initial, il y a cette situation initiale. En l'absence de tout mouvement et de toute durée positive, il y a tout de même quelque chose qui existe ou qui existerait s'il pouvait être rêvé. Il y a, si l'on veut, non pas encore une poésie, mais l'espèce de vacance que forment en le ciel de la pensée, l'oubli des choses du monde et la simple attente de ce qui n'a pas encore eu lieu. Il y a déjà le lieu de ce qui pourrait avoir lieu.

La poésie de Mallarmé a donc, malgré tout, une espèce de commencement. Ce n'est ni un point ni un mouvement, c'est un espace initial.

Having thus stated his theme, Poulet goes on to execute some dazzling improvisations involving an imagery of spatial relationships and rhetorical antitheses:

Espace absolument vierge et comparable d'une part à la blancheur de la feuille où l'on écrira, comparable de l'autre à l'uniformité du ciel bleu. Parmi les poèmes de jeunesse de Mallarmé il n'en est peut-être pas un seul qui n'ait pour thème l'Azur. Mais il n'en est peut-être pas non plus un seul qui s'efforce d'en faire une description directe ou d'en saisir la signification positive. L'Azur est le symbole ou la présence d'une réalité intérieure, indéfinie, qui ne peut s'exprimer que sous la forme déjà négative de l'espace ou du ciel. Présence ineffable, indescriptible, qui semble se mirer en la pensée, comme le ciel dans une pièce d'eau:

... un grand jet d'eau soupire vers l'Azur!
—Vers l'Azur attendri d'Octobre pâle et pur
Qui mire aux grands bassins sa langueur infinie ...

C'est à peine si une ombre de mouvement est esquissée. Sans doute le jet d'eau s'élève, mais ce mouvement d'ascension tout de suite s'épuise, il n'a que la valeur d'un soupir, d'un soupir *vers* l'azur. Tout n'existe que dans la relation presque purement statique d'un espace à une pensée, et d'une pensée à cet espace. Mais du fait même qu'il y a cette relation, l'indétermination initiale prend une signification nouvelle. Ce n'est plus simplement un espace, c'est l'espace *vers lequel* il y a ce soupir. C'est un espace positif, le lieu d'un désir. De plus, entre ce désir et ce lieu il y a un autre espace, un espace négatif, un vide, une distance. L'Azur est donc ce qui se présente au-delà de son absence, ce qui s'affirme au-delà de ce qui le dénie, ce qui existe au-delà de ce qui n'existe pas. Il est une présence mais à dis-

tance. Tel un objet entr'aperçu au travers d'une vitre, tel un reflet dans un miroir. C'est dans son absence que transparaît sa présence; c'est dans le vide que se mire sa plénitude.
—*Etudes sur le temps humain*, II: *La Distance Intérieure*, pp. 299–301.

SELECTED WORKS

Etudes sur le temps humain (University of Edinburgh Press, 1949; Plon, 1950). Translated as *Studies in Human Time* by Elliott Coleman (Johns Hopkins Press, 1956).

Etudes sur le temps humain, II: *La Distance intérieure* (Plon, 1952). Translated by Elliott Coleman as *Interior Distance* (Johns Hopkins Press, 1959).

Les Métamorphoses du cercle (Plon, 1961).

L'Espace proustien (Gallimard, 1963).

Etudes sur le temps humain, III: *Le Point de départ* (Plon, 1964).

Trois Essais de Mythologie romantique (Corti, 1966).

REFERENCES

Diéguez, Manuel de. *L'Ecrivain et son langage* (Gallimard, 1960), "Georges Poulet," pp. 173–203.

Jonchérie, Roger. "A propos d'une critique nouvelle," *La Nouvelle Critique*, November, 1955, pp. 168–180.

Miller, J. Hillis. "The Literary Criticism of Georges Poulet," *MLN*, December, 1963, pp. 471–488.

———. "La Critique de Georges Poulet," *Mercure de France*, April, 1965, pp. 652–669.

MARCEL RAYMOND

Marcel Raymond was born in Geneva in 1897 and educated at the Sorbonne, where he received the doctorat ès lettres in 1927. After teaching at the University of Basel, he went, in 1936, to the University of Geneva. He occupied the chair of French literature there until his retirement in 1963.

A professor, translator, and literary historian, Raymond is best known for a single work, *De Baudelaire au Surréalisme*, which is esteemed as one of the classics of contemporary criticism. It traces the history of modern poetry from Baudelaire, who is the first to illustrate the modern concepts of the poet as artist and as seer. Of particular interest is Raymond's declared intention in this work not to be concerned with what he calls external features—specific influences, derivations, debts—but to pursue the history of modern poetry along the lines of inner affiliations or affinities. The artistic line beginning with Baudelaire passes through Mallarmé to Valéry; the line of seers through Rimbaud to the Surrealists. Perhaps long familiarity with the work, although in no way affecting our impression of its authority, blinds us to its originality. It is not without surprise that we note how often Raymond is treated by the New Critics as a revered ancestor. Like Charles DuBos, he is said to have the power of communing with an author, of penetrating directly to the heart of a work and viewing it with the inner eye. His art is described therefore as criticism from the inside or criticism of participation. Unless a critic is obviously imitating an author—which Raymond is not doing—these figurative terms do not seem appropriate. Raymond appears to us simply as an excellent professor and literary historian who, although eschewing Lansonian techniques of scholarship, traces literary history and analyzes writers in a way commonly practiced in the lecture hall. His study of Paul Valéry, done during World War II and inspired, according to his own statement, by "ontological preoccupations,"[1] is no exception. Valéry's lifelong struggle between the pull of pure spirit and the pull of the flesh is in the order of conventional themes for academic disquisitions; and although Raymond was obviously affected by Sartre and Existentialism coming into vogue at the moment of writing, he could have done the same job without having read *L'Etre et le Néant*.

As a professor of French, Raymond was always interested in new literary trends and concepts. One of his later works, *Baroque et Renaissance poétique*, is made up of comments, in the main, on recent interpretations of a period in which he had worked thirty years before as a doctoral candidate. Jean Rousset's exploration of the French literary baroque and H. Woefflin's investigations in art history doubtless inspire the essay on the baroque; the brilliant lessons on Ronsard and Malherbe, which fill out the small volume, are in the tradition of the best academic *exposés*. In sum, Marcel Raymond merits our attention rather as a sound and erudite scholar who has written very well, if not very much, rather than as a great initiator.

❦

Raymond's style is easy and colorful; his views are clear and helpful, and as he surveys literary history, it is with a very sure hand that he arranges and groups according to significant characteristics and tendencies:

Dans l'introduction au florilège de poésies "fantaisistes" publié en octobre 1913 par *Vers et Prose*, Francis Carco, après s'être incliné devant Paul Fort, fixait la position de ses amis et la

---

[1] *Paul Valéry et la tentation de l'esprit*, avant-propos, p. 7.

sienne, à la droite d'André Salmon, d'Apollinaire, de Max Jacob, d'Henri Hertz, dans le voisinage de Toulet et de Tristan Klingsor, "qui ont donné à la fantaisie, disait-il, un caractère moins disparate." Le groupe d'Apollinaire doit être mis à part, aile avancée, aile marchante, qui a orienté la poésie vers un certain cubisme littéraire, lequel a préparé à son tour les manifestations d'avant-garde des années d'après-guerre. En revanche, on a pu regarder comme un néo-classique Jean-Marc Bernard, qui figure parmi les fantaisistes dans *Vers et Prose*, et l'on ferait sans peine de Vincent Muselli et Léon Vérane des poètes néo-romans. Le mouvement s'étend donc sur un large front; c'est autour de P.-J. Toulet, pour garder sa mémoire, plus précisément, que les poétes du groupe se sont retrouvés, après l'Armistice, pendant quelques saisons.

Mais quels que soient les maîtres qu'ils se sont choisis et les sources variées de leur poésie, les fantaisistes, par l'esprit, sont des modernes. Ils ont dit adieu aux légendes; les regrets, les plaisirs, les tristesses de leur vie, comment les oublier? A peine leurs rêves essayent-ils de s'envoler qu'ils sont pris dans l'atmosphère trouble, dans l'odeur amère et forte qui s'accumule au-dessus des paysages de notre temps. Cette existence du XXe siècle, il faut bien l'accepter telle qu'elle est; la poésie, peut-elle se nourrir d'autre chose que de sensations, d'émotions vraies? Impressionnistes en cela, ces poètes s'apparentent à Jammes, à Verlaine, à Laforgue, à Corbière même et au Rimbaud des premiers vers; aux décadents, en somme, plutôt qu'aux symbolistes.

Ils sont les libertins de la bohème moderne; bohème de la province, où s'ennuie dans de pauvres fêtes ce jeune homme, fonctionnaire ou soldat, qui n'aime rien tant que la poésie et rien moins que son métier; bohème de Paris, qui gravita d'abord autour du *Lapin agile*, à Montmartre, avant d'établir, vers 1910, ses quartiers, à Montparnasse. L'étrange déesse Fantaisie, oscillant entre le réalisme et la chimère, s'est éveillée au cours d'une nuit blanche ou sous la lumière rose et grise d'un de ces crépuscules du matin immortalisés par Baudelaire. Cette bohème contemporaine rappelle par plusieurs traits celle de Baudelaire et de Banville comme celle des Jeune-France; mais les fantaisistes d'aujourd'hui, si quelque chose subsiste en eux de la sentimentalité romantique, ont décidé d'être sans illusion. Les hommes ne sont point bons, ils le savent. Ils ne songent pas à soutenir à leur profit les droits de l'art, ou ceux de la passion ou de la justice. Aimant sans croire à l'amour, sans croire au bonheur, la pudeur, le souvenir d'anciennes larmes, un certain détachement à l'égard de soi-même les invitent à ne se confesser qu'avec ironie.

En cet humour, moins naturel que voulu, ou naturel seulement par l'effet d'une coutume délibérément adoptée, humour qui va fournir un instant au poète le moyen d'échapper au poids de sa vie, d'en percer l'illusion, de la juger et de retrouver, en marge du réel opprimant, une possibilité de jeu, de liberté, réside peut-être le seul caractère commun à des esprits par ailleurs bien différents. C'est Laforgue sans doute, plus que tout autre, qui leur a donné l'exemple de cette attitude "spectaculaire" ... [2]

—*De Baudelaire au Surréalisme,* Corti, 1947, pp. 137–139.

To whatever subject he treats, Raymond brings the perspective of a broad humanistic culture. Knowledge never gets in his way, however, and he knows how to choose the telling example, establish the right parallel, put his finger on the distinguishing feature. From his introduction to Rousseau's *Confessions,* we read:

Saint Augustin, bien avant lui, avait écrit des *Confessions.* Comme saint Augustin, Jean-Jacques aurait pu dire: j'aimais à aimer (*amabam amare*). Mais ces formules, sous la plume de l'Eveque d'Hippone, ne s'appliquent qu'à sa jeunesse. Se confesser, pour lui, c'est se placer dans sa condition de créature pécheresse, mais pardonnée, tournée toute vers Dieu, non plus vers soi, plus assoiffée de connaître Dieu que de se connaître. Chez les Grecs déjà la connaissance de soi ne pouvait être une fin. Le but, c'est la sagesse (la philosophie), le but est de se faire "le démiurge de soi-même," sachant ce que l'on veut être.

Le prédécesseur immédiat de Rousseau, c'est Montaigne, "notre maître à tous," dira-t-il. Montaigne, comme les Anciens, désire la sagesse, mais se persuadant peu à peu qu'il n'y a de sagesse vivante qu'à la mesure de chacun, il aboutit à la peinture de soi. Rousseau, d'entrée de jeu, décide de tout dire,

[2] For translation, see Appendix 13.

sans quoi son livre ne serait pas ce livre unique qu'il entend faire, quitte à divulguer chemin faisant quelques secrets de sagesse, ou plutôt de bonheur. C'est après avoir écrit les *Essais* que Montaigne murmurera: "J'ai tout dit." Non! proteste Rousseau, Montaigne s'est peint de profil. Mais il concédera dans la quatrième *Rêverie* que lui aussi, "sans y songer" (là serait toute la différence) s'est peint de profil. Au surplus, l'homme que décrivent les *Confessions* n'est pas sans rappeler celui dont les *Essais* font la peinture: muable, dissemblable toujours à ce qu'il était la minute précédente, toujours en contradiction avec soi. Nul, avant Rousseau, ne s'était complu en soi-même comme Montaigne. Bien peu avaient été plus vulnérables: "Chacun est heurté [par l'imagination], mais aucuns en sont renversés. Son impression me perce." De plus, Montaigne comme Rousseau accorde un privilège extraordinaire au sujet se connaissant: "Il n'y a que vous qui sache si vous êtes tendre ou cruel." La conscience subjective est seule dans l'axe de la vérité, elle ne consent pas à tenir pour valable le jugement qu'autrui, bien ou mal intentionné, porterait sur elle. La conscience de soi est conscience de son intériorité et, déjà, de son isolement dans le monde.

Mais le climat spirituel de l'autobiographie, chez Rousseau, est si différent, tellement plus orageux! C'est que la hantise de soi y tourne à la fascination. L'amour de soi, lié à la conscience, y devient passion et souffrance.

Tourmenté de s'aimer, tourmenté de se voir,

tel est l'homme, selon le poète de *La Maison du Berger*, telle est sa punition. Et un autre poète nous montre Psyché poursuivant son ombre autour d'elle, tourbillonnante. Mais cette conscience finit par être épuisante. N'est-ce pas là le destin de l'homme moderne, le destin qui suit son cours à travers le romantisme et l'existentialisme, depuis les *Confessions?* L'homme de l'âge baroque se plaisait entre l'être et le paraître, mettant à l'un le masque de l'autre. Rousseau, au contraire, se fait un devoir de ne paraître que ce qu'il est, il veut obéir à une vocation de sincérité sans alibi, maintenir son cœur en état d'absolue transparence. Mais cette voie est celle de l'orgueil, la bonne intention n'y est pas récompensée: on risque de s'y perdre, d'être réduit à mentir, d'épouser les ténèbres. D'où la soif lancinante d'une disculpation, qui va de pair avec l'affirmation de l'innocence. Car cette affirmation est pénétrée d'angoisse, bien qu'elle s'appuie sur la persuasion que le *moi*, s'aimant lui-même sans esprit de concurrence, participe à l'innocence de la nature. Le sentiment de la faute, nié toujours, mais partout diffus, se fixe ici ou là suivant les circonstances; à chaque instant débusqué par la conscience, mais se reformant toujours au zénith comme un point noir. Rousseau est dans la situation d'un chrétien qui se déroberait à l'action de la grâce (trop humiliante), mais qui demanderait que sa non-culpabilité foncière fût proclamée au siècle des siècles. Il interjette appel devant l'Etre éternel, il consent à reconnaître ses indignités et ses misères; mais c'est pour que les autres en gémissent, en rougissent à sa place. Peut-être que la faute est précisément de se croire sans faute, peut-être que le mal est de se juger incapable d'un mal qui serait spontané. Il est de fait que la délivrance n'est possible, dans le cas de Rousseau, ou le sursis, que par l'oubli, ou par une occultation provisoire d'un *moi* qui ne se sent plus exister que par ses sensations.

    —*Œuvres complètes de Jean-Jacques Rousseau*, Gallimard, 1959, I, xii–xiv.

All Raymond's writing reveals the qualities of a great teacher. His erudition, perspicacity, and talent for clear but colorful exposition are complemented by a gift for fine literary analysis. Below is an example of Raymond's explication of a text. We quote only the first paragraphs:

"On s'inquiète de ce que j'ai voulu *dire*, c'est ce que j'ai voulu *faire* qui importe ... " Mais presque partout le dire et le faire sont étroitement impliqués l'un dans l'autre. Il n'est donc pas illégitime d'indiquer la place d'un poème dans le champ de la pensée de Valéry, et d'en éclairer la signification.

    La Jeune Parque est un drame, on l'a dit trop rarement. Le débat métaphysique qui en forme le sujet est chargé d'un haut potentiel humain, et même tragique. Est tragique, ce qui est extrême, irréparable. Tout le poème développe les conséquences d'un événement de ce genre, d'une catastrophe métaphysique.

L'action nous est présentée ou suggérée par une pantomime ardente, qui a l'aspect d'un récitatif extraordinairement modulé, coupé par des blancs, et où le *pathos* l'emporte sur l'*ethos*— l'héroïne souffre son destin.

Elle est seule, dans ce poème de la solitude intérieure et de l'être divisé; monologue du *moi*, dialogue du *moi* avec lui-même. La pensée de l'autre ne fait que s'y profiler en un ou deux passages, et seulement par réfraction. Quant à l'esprit du serpent, il s'est inoculé au *moi* comme un venin: il est devenu sa conscience. Sa morsure faite, son crime accompli, il disparaît.

> Quel crime par moi-même ou sur moi consommé?

demande la Jeune Parque: le serpent n'est donc pas un autre qu'elle-même, c'est par elle que le mal est venu au monde.

Ce poème, disait Albert Thibaudet de *La Jeune Parque*, passe pour le plus difficile de la littérature. Réputation tout à fait imméritée.

S'il est "l'histoire d'une conscience pendant la durée d'une nuit," comme a déclaré Valéry, son obscurité est celle d'une nuit toute traversée d'éclairs. Si l'obscurité, en quelques vers, une douzaine peut-être, s'accumule, c'est par excès de clartés superposées, entrecroisées. Mais le sens général s'impose plus nettement à chaque lecture. Sens universel, et spécifiquement valéryen: la Jeune Parque est partagée, une double tentation l'assaille, celle de la conscience négative—volonté implacable de lucidité, de pureté, qui fait que tout lui devient étranger—et tentation de la vie, ou de la volonté de vivre, qui est opposée à la conscience, mais qui est celle du monde, auquel l'homme appartient par tout ce qui en lui n'est pas son *moi pur.*

—*Paul Valéry et la tentation de l'esprit,* pp. 129–130.

SELECTED WORKS

L'Influence de Ronsard sur la poésie française (Champion, 1927).

Bibliographie critique de Ronsard en France (Droz, 1927).

De Baudelaire au Surréalisme (Corrêa, 1933; Corti, 1947).

Translated as *From Baudelaire to Surrealism* (London: Peter Owen, 1961).

Henri Ghéon (Montreal: Ed. du Cep, 1939).

Génies de France (Neuchâtel: La Baconnière, 1942).

Paul Valéry et la tentation de l'esprit (La Baconnière, 1944).

Anthologie de la nouvelle française (Lausanne: Guilde du Livre, 1950).

Baroque et Renaissance poétique (Corti, 1955).

Jean-Jacques Rousseau (Corti, 1962).

REFERENCES

Lespire, Roger. "Réflexions sur la critique de Marcel Raymond," *Les Cahiers du Nord*, 90–91 (1950–1951), 365–374.

Poulet, Georges. "La pensée critique de Marcel Raymond," *Saggi e ricerche di letteratura francese* (Milano: Fentrinelli, 1963), pp. 203–229.

Rousset, Jean. "L'œuvre de Marcel Raymond et la nouvelle critique," *Mercure de France*, July, 1963, pp. 462–470.

JEAN-PIERRE RICHARD

Jean-Pierre Richard was born in Marseilles in 1922. He prepared for a teaching career at the Ecole Normale and is an agrégé and a docteur ès lettres. He has taught literature at the French Institute in London and at present is at the French Institute in Madrid. Acknowledging the inspiration of Gaston Bachelard and Georges Poulet, this critic devotes himself to an analysis of the poetic imagination based on Existentialist assumptions. Sartre has declared that consciousness is consciousness of something. Interpreting this something to mean the external world, Richard aims his study at the level of sensorial awareness and primary reactions—at the level, he says, of pure sensation and raw sentiment. Richard believes that these primary contacts, interiorized and prolonged by revery, determine the poetic image and indeed the whole personal "mythology" of the artist. The Existentialist dictum that man can be defined only by his manner of grasping the universe and himself in relation to it is here applied specifically to the artist. By scrutinizing the artist's work for basic patterns of sensation and sentiment, the critic can discover the internal coherence of the work and the particularity of the artist's personality. Richard's ambition in criticism is to define the consciousness of the artist.

Richard tends to present the basic patterns of the authors he studies in terms of ambivalences. Some of the ambivalences are merely the commonplaces of literary manuals reaffirmed and put in a psychoanalytical frame of reference. Thus the romantic and unromantic tendencies in Stendhal he sees as constituting a basic duality in the writer's make-up and as coexisting in all his experiences. He argues that throughout his life and his works, Stendhal moved back and forth, drawn now to logic and order, now to daydreaming and confusion. Stendhal loved clarity but also mystery, common sense but also tender reveries. The conflict that divided Stendhal manifests itself symbolically in his work: geographical opposites, social opposites, air and water, echoes, altitudes and valleys. As for Flaubert, Richard contends that the famous self-discipline of this writer is not a matter of submission to an external artistic ideal but a manifestation of his basic personality. His writings, full of gluttony and *gourmandise*, indicate the voracious appetite of a giant. Flaubert had a voracious appetite for food—food of the senses, of the heart, and of the mind. Yet his stomach was weak, and the man who longed for exotic dishes could relish in fact only the plain fare of Croisset. Moments of temptation to surrender to his softness, abandon himself to the warm bath, alternate with moments of strength and will power— Flaubert's inner tension comes out in his work in the profusion of tactile imagery dealing with softness and hardness and in water symbolism involving drowning or semi-drowning, swimming with or against the current. Failure to solve inner conflicts did not prevent Stendhal or Flaubert from becoming great artists. Indeed their tension may have helped them. But Fromentin and the Goncourt brothers failed in their art as well as in their lives, for Fromentin found nothing better than academicism to oppose to an excessive sensitivity, and the Goncourts, "epidermic" writers *par excellence*, spent themselves in running hither and yon over the surface of things.

We may see from the above how Richard's criticism differs from a conventional analysis of theme and image. The data obtained from an author's work are subjected to an Existentialist psychoanalytical interpretation and offered as a picture of a creative consciousness. From the above, we may see how effective his method is in restoring life and color to the commonplaces of literary history, and also how fraught it is with the dangers of subjectivity and disproportionate emphasis.

The volume of essays entitled *Poésie et Profondeur* likewise deals with themes and images. The four poets examined have in common, according to Richard, "une certaine expérience de l'abîme, abîme de l'objet, de la conscience, d'autrui, du sentiment ou du langage."[1] Nerval tried to reconcile coming forth ("surgissement") and depth, Baudelaire and Rimbaud wished to deny depth, Verlaine turned it into diffused breadth. Richard's method is to survey each author's thematic material and tie it in somehow to a depth obsession. His thought is extremely subtle; but, interesting though the material is, it could be questioned whether much of it has the significance Richard attributes to it or anything really to do with depth. Doubtless, part of our distrust is based on the difficulty of following a discussion so dependent upon the critic's own rhetorical figures and so lacking in the conventional signposts of expository writing. The "Géographie magique de Nerval" deals with Nerval's fondness for labyrinths, volcanoes, verdure, blond hair, and other items of sensual charm or symbolic fascination. The "Profondeur de Baudelaire" presents the abyss as one of Baudelaire's themes but only as one among many. The "Fadeur de Verlaine" deals exclusively with the poet's well-known predilection for soft colors, wistful sentiments and all else that the critic's ingenuity can relate to the notion of faded. "Rimbaud ou la Poésie du Devenir" represents Rimbaud as the poet of the "jet ascensionnel." The reading is hard going. In spite of the title, the word "depth" is scarcely mentioned in this book, and there are only the curious varieties of a common "expérience de l'abîme," as stated in the introduction, to remind us what the author is talking about. If it is hard to remember them, it is harder still to accept them as valid—to accept, say, that Verlaine's "fadeur" could be equated in any sense other than

[1] Introduction, p. 10.

the most whimsical with "largeur diffuse" or that in turn
with a basic mental structure involving depth.

To introduce his *Univers imaginaire de Mallarmé*, Richard
restates, at length and in somewhat more explicit terms than
previously, his concept of criticism—find the inner coherence, relate the apparently disparate parts, by studying the
work on the level of sensation, sentiment, and revery. He
discusses his methodology: pick out themes, symbols, and
images; evaluate them as parts of the unique structure that
the work possesses. Frequency of occurrence is of course a
primary criterion but not an infallible one, since purely statis-
tical compilations do not allow for complexities of meaning
and intentionality. The manner in which themes organize
themselves may be more significant. They tend to form
ensembles, and the principle of equilibrium applies in literature as well as in physics. Antithetical pairs, for example,
seem a common pattern, one which, we remember, Richard
has already made a great deal of. Anticipating certain objections to his work, Richard has several things to say in his
defense. He acknowledges its subjectivity and provisory character but deems it inevitable: "La critique ne peut être
aujourd'hui que partielle, hypothétique et provisoire."[2] If this
is so, some may feel that the return on all the pains it takes
to read it is not a very rich one. Richard dismisses as irrelevant the possibility that he may often confuse archetypal
myth or patently borrowed image with a personal structure.
Such a possibility, on the contrary, seems quite relevant.
Concerning possible indignation—particularly of Anglo-
American critics—at the destruction of a work's formal pattern that his method implies, he may be unduly concerned.
But other critics have raised objections that he does not
anticipate. For instance, that thematic criticism risks wander-
ing off into nonliterary domains (Diéguez) or that, refusing

[2] p. 37.

real psychoanalysis, it accepts a bogus variety (Mauron, *Des Métaphores obsédantes*, introduction, p. 30).

ℰ

The following discussion of blood as a theme in Baudelaire gives an idea of the sharp intuitiveness of Richard as a critic and of his virtuosity:

Ce feu, il flambe aussi dans notre corps: c'est lui qui assure matériellement le rayonnement personnel, et qui permet la relation humaine. Ce soleil charnel, ce sera le *sang*. Le sang a chaleur, souplesse, plénitude, continuité; il fait glisser jusque dans les parties les plus reculées de l'être le secret liquide de la vie. Il illumine, il brûle; la flamme rougeoyante d'un foyer peut "inonder de sang une peau couleur d'ambre." Et tout soleil ressemble inversement à une plaie sanglante. Surtout le sang féconde, il apaise la soif; lui aussi est un "père nourricier"; ainsi le sang perdu de *La Fontaine de Sang* s'en va "transformant les pavés en îlots," "désaltérant la soif de chaque créature"; de façon plus troublante encore le cadavre sadiquement décapité d'*Une Martyre*

> ... épanche comme un fleuve
> Sur l'oreiller désaltéré
> Un sang rouge et vivant dont la toile s'abreuve
> Avec l'avidité d'un pré ...

Boire le sang tout chaud, c'est boire aux sources de la vie. Le sang sera donc le signe même de l'expansion, l'antithèse vivante de toutes les paralysies.

Pourtant il reste lui-même exposé à la paralysie: qu'il se ralentisse, se refroidisse, et le voici devenu sang figé. La coagulation est une pétrification sanguine: c'est pourquoi le soleil couchant ou hivernal, le soleil mourant, apparaît si souvent à Baudelaire sous les espèces d'une sorte de caillot gelé. Mais cette malédiction de l'immobile, le sang peut aussi la rencontrer par de toutes autres voies: celles, par exemple, d'un pourrissement interne. Dans l'échelle de vie et de mort, le sang corrompu ne

vaut guère mieux que le sang coagulé; tous deux signifient stagnation, impuissance, et tous deux se retrouvent en effet dans le
sang engourdi du spleenétique. Car s'il est vrai, comme l'écrit
Baudelaire dans son étude sur Poe, "que notre destinée circule
dans (nos) artéres avec chacun de (nos) globules sanguins,"
il est normal que le signe d'une destinée dès le départ brisée,—
brisée par le péché originel, brisée par le mouvement même de la
conscience,—que le symbole d'une âme fêlée soit un sang lui
aussi divisé, en lutte contre lui-même, donc sans élan, et privé
de cette chaleur expansive que Baudelaire nomme la *curiosité*.
Le spleen est le lieu même de l'incuriosité: ce qui coule dans les
veines du spleenétique, c'est en effet un liquide de mort, "au
lieu de sang l'eau verte du Léthé."

Quelle joie en revanche que de voir couler un sang bien frais!
"La volupté surnaturelle que l'homme peut éprouver à voir
couler son sang" s'explique par la jouissance d'une vie jusque-là
protégée, mystérieuse, et devenue soudain présente, merveilleuse-
ment et dangereusement tangible. Notre réalité la plus loin-
taine, non pas vraiment notre nature, mais ce que Baudelaire
nomme *surnature*, s'étale avec lui au grand jour. Et ce qui rend
cette révélation spécialement bouleversante c'est qu'elle représente en même temps une atteinte à cette surnature; un sacré
s'y trahit et y meurt. La grandeur de l'hémorragie lui vient ainsi
de réunir en elle une évidence de vie et une fatalité de mort;
l'homme ne s'y découvre existant et puissant qu'à travers la
montée d'une faiblesse. Le cauchemar de la source tarie, ou du
soleil éteint va donc se retrouver dans le monde de l'épanche-
ment sanglant: le rêve d'hémophilie que nous décrit *La Fontaine de Sang* traduit admirablement cette hantise d'une vie
saignée à blanc.

Cette saignée ne postule d'ailleurs aucune blessure: la vapori-
sation sanglante qu'est l'hémorragie s'aggrave encore de toute
la porosité des corps; la chair se laisse ici traverser en tous sens
par la circulation sanguine. Pour saigner, elle n'a pas même
besoin d'être entamée, incisée. Tout filtre à travers l'épiderme;
c'est comme si la peau n'existait pas:

> Il me semble parfois que mon sang coule à flots
> Ainsi qu'une fontaine aux rythmiques sanglots.
> Je l'entends bien qui coule avec un long murmure,
> Mais je me tâte en vain pour trouver la blessure ...

Cette même perméabilité épidermique, si douloureuse quand Baudelaire l'éprouve sur son propre corps, lui devient en revanche infiniment précieuse lorsqu'il la découvre en autrui. Elle lui signale alors une chance d'accueil, une possibilité d'ouverture. Elle lui est le symbole charnel d'une transparence spirituelle. Sous cette peau qui est à peine une barrière, il peut voir battre le sang comme on écoute palpiter une âme; il le regarde perler sur l'épiderme; il arrive presque à en ressentir, du dehors, la tiédeur agitée; ainsi, dans la Chair de Rubens

> ... où la vie afflue et s'agite sans cesse
> Comme l'air dans le ciel et la mer dans la mer.

il peut saisir presque directement le battement biologique d'une existence étrangère. Mieux encore; supprimant l'obstacle de la peau, il réussit parfois à recueillir l'immédiate émanation du sang d'autrui. Dans Le Balcon, admirable symphonie de flamme et d'ombre, chaque détail du décor renvoie à la splendeur d'un feu caché dans les ténèbres, à la tendresse fécondante d'un soleil noir: du charbon rougeoie dans la cheminée, le soleil éclaire un crépuscule en train de s'assombrir, deux prunelles brillent dans la pénombre. Sous le voile d'une peau noire, on devine alors la présence d'un sang fort et chaud comme une haleine, vers lequel l'amant peut s'incliner, et dont il parvient à saisir la vapeur, à respirer l'odeur:

> Je croyais respirer le parfum de ton sang ...

Mais la peau peut aussi se durcir, se faire métal ou pierre; le sang s'enfuit alors, il se retire dans les profondeurs charnelles. La femme froide, œil d'acier, chair de marbre, réussit à suggérer qu'elle ne recèle plus ni vie ni sang, et qu'en sa profondeur tout comme en sa surface s'étend le même désert stérile:

> J'unis un cœur de neige à la blancheur des cygnes ...

L'épiderme glacé ne cache plus aucun en-deçà chaleureux: c'est le triomphe du dandysme, le malheur de la communication rompue.

Malheur à double face: car Baudelaire aime cette stérilité qui le protège des atteintes de l'autre, qui le rassure contre tout empiètement. Mais elle protège aussi l'autre contre sa propre atteinte, à chaque mouvement de son désir elle oppose une indifférence, une fin de non-recevoir.

Tout glisse et tout s'émousse au granit de sa peau.

Et Baudelaire de ressentir alors, avec une fureur montante, le besoin de briser ce granit, de violer cette passivité. Il voudra faire fondre la neige de ce cœur, pour atteindre, sous la surface pétrifiée de l'autre, la chaleur d'un sang, le signe d'une vie. Il est prêt au besoin à inciser, à déchirer ce corps refusé pour aller trouver en lui la source sanglante. Le rêve de la plaie infligée traduit ainsi le désir de forcer une intimité rebelle; car toute blessure est un viol, un moyen d'obliger autrui à s'avouer. Contre le dandysme de l'autre, la meilleure arme de Baudelaire, c'est encore son sadisme.[3]

—*Poésie et Profondeur*, pp. 118–121.

SELECTED WORKS

Littérature et Sensation (Seuil, 1954).

Poésie et Profondeur (Seuil, 1955).

L'Univers imaginaire de Mallarmé (Seuil, 1961).

Stéphane Mallarmé et son fils Anatole (Abbeville: Impr. Paillart, 1961).

"Quelques aspects nouveaux de la critique littéraire en France," *Le Français dans le Monde*, March, 1963, pp. 2–9.

Onze études sur la poésie (Seuil, 1964).

REFERENCES

Diéguez, Manuel de. "Jean-Pierre Richard et la critique thématique," *Critique*, June, 1963, pp. 517–535.

[3] For translation, see Appendix 14.

Hahn, Otto. "L'Illusion thématique," *Les Temps modernes*, May, 1963, pp. 2086–2096.

Magowan, Robbin. "Criticism of Sensation," *Criticism*, Spring, 1964, pp. 156–164.

Man, Paul de. "Impasses de la critique formaliste," *Critique*, June, 1956, pp. 483–500.

JEAN ROUSSET

Born in 1910 in Geneva, Jean Rousset is a professor at the university of that city, which is one of the centers for the French New Criticism. He was already known for his studies on the baroque when he joined the group of the New Critics in 1962 with a series of essays entitled *Forme et Signification*. The volume is dedicated to Georges Poulet, to whose work Rousset frequently acknowledges his indebtedness during the course of his own investigations. He is lavish in his praise of the author of *Le Temps humain* as well as of several other avant-garde critics—from his preliminary remarks in this volume, it is clear that he endorses without reserve the new platform for criticism. Concentrating on the work itself, the critic should, Rousset asserts, relive the adventure of creation, then try to grasp it in its totality by uncovering its basic design. He should see art as a universe in itself, a meaningful reconstruction of the real. For the artist, a work is a means of investigation rather than the result of a preconceived idea; his vision comes only as he creates form—the significance of a work is bound up in its structural patterns. This is what Rousset wishes to demonstrate in masterpieces of French literature which range from Corneille to Claudel. With Corneille, he would show the geometrical patterns of *Polyeucte*; with Mme de Lafayette, the function of digressions in *La Princesse de Clèves*. Moving along chronologically, he takes up in turn Marivaux's "double register," the aims and processes of the epistolary novel, Flaubert's "point-of-view," Proust's architectural design, and Claudel's repeated motifs or type-situations.

Jean Rousset's work inspires admiration and respect. He has read his authors closely and has documented himself with thoroughness. His acquaintance with structural criticism extends to the Anglo-American, to the German, and to the Russian, and his knowledge of scholarship devoted to the authors he is treating is equally comprehensive. A sound background combined with real intuitive gifts produces essays capable of setting old subjects in new and interesting light. As demonstrations of Rousset's thesis, however, they are not wholly satisfactory: if the morphology of the works discussed comes out clearly, meaning and its connection with form do not. Obviously it is easier to analyze form than to show that form and meaning are the same. That Rousset's thesis is too simple to embrace the whole truth is apparent when he discusses Marivaux. Marivaux's structural patterns are not necessarily the result of anything that belongs particularly to Marivaux. Minor characters have frequently functioned as the Greek chorus in pointing out the exact state of affairs to the audience, and the dénouement of many plays involves a demasking. We should not be bedazzled by Rousset's brilliant metaphor which actually depicts nothing unique in Marivaux: "Toute pièce de Marivaux pourrait se définir: un organisme à double palier dont les deux plans se rapprochent graduellement jusqu'à leur complète jonction. La pièce est finie quand les deux paliers se confondent, c'est-à-dire quand le groupe des héros regardés se voit comme les voyaient les personnages spectateurs."[1] The only originality here is in the image. Let us say, however, that although Rousset is given in general to a somewhat heightened language, he does not soar so high as some of his colleagues.

❦

The following extract taken from the Introduction to *Forme et Signification* is not only typical of Rousset's style but is clearly indicative of his position as a critic:

[1] *Forme et Signification*, p. 58.

Si l'œuvre est principe d'exploration et agent d'organisation, elle pourra utiliser et recomposer toute espèce d'éléments empruntés à la réalité ou au souvenir, elle le fera toujours en fonction de ses exigences et de sa vie propre; elle est cause avant d'être effet, produit ou reflet, ainsi que Valéry aimait à le rappeler; aussi l'analyse portera-t-elle sur l'œuvre seule, dans sa solitude incomparable, telle qu'elle est issue des "espaces intérieurs où l'artiste s'est abstrait pour créer." (Proust) Et s'il n'y a d'œuvre que dans la symbiose d'une forme et d'un songe, notre lecture s'appliquera à les lire conjointement en saisissant le songe à travers la forme.

Mais comment saisir la forme? à quoi la reconnaître? Tenons tout d'abord pour assuré qu'elle n'est pas toujours où on s'imagine la voir, qu'étant jaillissement des profondeurs et révélation sensible de l'œuvre à elle-même, elle ne sera ni une surface, ni un moulage, ni un contenant, qu'elle n'est pas plus la technique que l'art de composer et qu'elle ne se confond pas nécessairement avec la recherche de la forme, ni avec l'équilibre voulu des parties, ni avec la beauté des éléments. Principe actif et imprévu de révélations et d'apparition, elle déborde les règles et les artifices, elle ne saurait se réduire ni à un plan ou à un schéma, ni à un corps de procédés et de moyens. Toute œuvre est forme, dans la mesure où elle est œuvre. La forme en ce sens est partout, même chez les poètes qui se moquent de la forme ou visent à la détruire. Il y a une forme de Montaigne et une forme de Breton, il y a une forme de l'informe ou de la volonté iconoclaste comme il y a une forme de la rêverie intime ou de l'explosion lyrique. Et l'artiste qui prétend aller au-delà des formes le fera par les formes—s'il est artiste. "A chaque œuvre sa forme," le mot de Balzac prend ici tout son sens.

Mais il n'y a de forme saisissable que là où se dessine un accord ou un rapport, une ligne de forces, une figure obsédante, une trame de présences ou d'échos, un réseau de convergences; j'appellerai "structures" ces constantes formelles, ces liaisons qui trahissent un univers mental et que chaque artiste réinvente selon ses besoins.

Convergences, liaisons, ordonnances; mais on évitera de tout ramener aux seules vertus de proportion et d'harmonie. C'est une habitude ancienne, une habitude "classique" et qui survit chez un Valéry, de définir la forme comme relation des parties au tout. Sans doute, il en est souvent ainsi, et je recourrai à ce principe dans mon analyse du roman de Proust; l'auteur lui-même m'y invitait expressément. Ce n'est pourtant qu'un critère parmi d'autres. Balzac a raison: "à chaque œuvre sa forme." Ni l'auteur ni le critique ne savent à l'avance ce qu'ils trouveront au terme de l'opération. L'instrument critique ne doit pas préexister à l'analyse. Le lecteur demeurera disponible, mais toujours sensible et aux aguets, jusqu'au moment où surgira le signal stylistique, le fait de structure imprévu et révélateur. Dans le cas des œuvres étudiées ici, ce sera une certaine alternance caractérisant la *Princesse de Clèves*, ou, chez Marivaux, une distribution particulière des fonctions actives et passives, tandis que le Flaubert de *Madame Bovary* appelle une analyse du point de vue. Les voies d'approche sont aussi libres et diverses que peut l'être l'invention de l'écrivain.

Il n'en reste pas moins vrai que, même si elle se manifeste de façon très variable, la tendance à l'unité, à ce que Proust nomme la "complexité ordonnée," marque la plupart des œuvres; il arrivera souvent que l'un des faits de composition à retenir soit un fait de relation interne. L'œuvre est une totalité et elle gagne toujours à être éprouvée comme telle. La lecture féconde devrait être une lecture globale, sensible aux identités et aux correspondances, aux similitudes et aux oppositions, aux reprises et aux variations, ainsi qu'à ces nœuds et à ces carrefours où la texture se concentre ou se déploie.

De toute façon, la lecture, qui se développe dans la durée, devra pour être globale se rendre l'œuvre simultanément présente en toutes ses parties. Delacroix fait observer que si le tableau s'offre tout entier au regard, il n'en est pas de même du livre: le livre, semblable à un "tableau en mouvement," ne se découvre que par fragments successifs. La tâche du lecteur exigeant consiste à renverser cette tendance naturelle du livre de manière que celui-ci se présente tout entier au regard de l'esprit. Il n'y a de lecture complète que celle qui transforme le livre en un réseau simultané de relations réciproques; c'est alors que jaillissent les surprises heureuses et que l'ouvrage émerge sous nos yeux, parce que nous sommes en mesure d'exécuter avec justesse une sonate de mots, de figures et de pensées.[2]

—*Forme et Signification*, pp. x–xiii.

[2] For translation, see Appendix 15.

SELECTED WORK

Forme et Signification. Essai sur les structures littéraires (Corti, 1962).

REFERENCES

Albérès, R.-M. "La nouvelle critique," *Les Nouvelles Littéraires,* August 22, 1963, p. 5.

Brereton, Geoffrey. "New Views of the Old Masters," *The New Statesman and Nation,* September, 1956, pp. 248–249.

Sayce, R. A. *"Forme et Signification,"* French Studies, July, 1964, pp. 290–291.

JEAN-PAUL SARTRE

Born in Paris in 1905, Jean-Paul Sartre took his lycée training in La Rochelle and in Paris (Lycée Henri IV). He went on with his studies at the Ecole Normale. A brilliant student, in 1929 he was received first at the agrégation de philosophie. During the 1930's he taught in several lycées, first in Le Havre, then in Laon, finally in Paris at the Lycée Pasteur. In 1933–1934 Sartre spent a year at the French Institute of Berlin, a highly significant year for him, for it brought him under the direct influence of Heidegger and Husserl. His contact with German phenomenology bore fruit in the essay he wrote on the imagination (1936) and in an essay on the theory of emotions (1939). Prior to the war he had begun his career in fiction and in literary criticism as well as in philosophy. Sartre's notoriety, however, dates from the Occupation years. Conscripted, captured in June of 1940, released in April of the following year, Sartre returned to teaching but the classroom would not hold him for long. L'Etre et le Néant (1943) made him the leading philosopher for the new generation of intellectuals, and his plays brought his name to the masses. After the Liberation, his fame spread throughout the world. In the Existentialism he popularized, the mood of the postwar period found articulate expression.

For more than twenty years now Sartre has remained one of the intellectual forces of the world. His every utterance and action has been the subject of passionate interest. The year he definitively abandoned his career as a professor (1945) he founded the Temps Modernes, a magazine more political in intent than literary. His revolutionary ambition in founding this periodical is reported by Simone de Beauvoir, his colleague and companion, in Les Mandarins. His subsequent disappointments, his political oscillations, his ideological quarrels with associates and friends like Merleau-Ponty and Albert Camus have been amply reported throughout the worldwide press. His refusal of the Nobel Prize in 1964 marks the most newsworthy point to date in an extremely newsworthy career.

In the diversity of his writing during the 1950's and 1960's the creative sort seems least important. His cyclic novel, *Les Chemins de la liberté*, still remains unfinished, and his recent plays add more to his luster as a polemicist than as a dramatist. On the other hand, he has produced a major philosophical work, *Critique de la raison dialectique*, a major study on a literary subject, *Saint-Genet*, a great deal of political writing, and an autobiography. The direction his writing has taken is not surprising. Sartre's creative work was never more than a vehicle for his ideas, and perhaps ideological questions, which concern him increasingly, lend themselves less well to indirect expression than ontological matters, which were the subject of his early plays and novels.

Sartre's first essays tore down the literary gods of the 1930's and set up new ones whose works mirrored a universe more compatible to his way of thinking. To replace Mauriac and his Christian universe and Giraudoux and his world of Aristotelian essences, Sartre proposed American neo-realists like Dos Passos, in whose work he saw a chaotic and contradictory universe where characters create their own destiny even though it be foreordained. By the late 1940's and early 1950's, critics examined literature almost solely for pictures of the moral man, of mankind in the world; the essays of Albérès, Boisdeffre, or Pierre-Henri Simon repeatedly traced the features of the Existentialist hero as he appeared in fiction and in drama. At the same time, young novelists of the future were building a new esthetic upon the literary principles to which Sartre had been led by his philosophical thesis. To reflect an Existentialist universe in the novel, drastic changes had to be made in structure, dialogue, point of view, and tense. These problems, raised first by Sartre, are still the basic concern of French technicians and theorists of fiction. Phenomenology, which the new generations encountered through Sartre's popularization of Existentialism, has been exploited by both novelists and critics, who conceive of their arts in terms of phenomenological description. Sartre himself, in his essays on Baudelaire and Jean Genet, showed the new critics how phenomenology could be combined with psychological analysis in order to investigate a writer and his work. These latter works show an increasing sociological concern, however, not often shared by his followers. Young Manuel de Diéguez laments the emphasis Sartre has put on sociological matters, declaring that Marxism has spelled the doom of Sartre as a literary critic.

Of course Sartre has often been repudiated in whole or in part since the heyday of Existentialism. Traditional critics have always questioned whether Sartre's essays should be called criticism at all, since they have so little to do with esthetic matters; critics have pointed out how little the essay on Baudelaire had to do with poetry and how much more Sartre's concern was with Baudelaire the social misfit than with Baudelaire the poet. Sartre's own disciples have always differed from him on certain fundamental assumptions. These differences have been various; only concerning "engagement" have most of the young theorists and critics opposed Sartre *en bloc*. It is possible that the rift will widen. Sartre's projected work on Flaubert may be more political even than his *Genet*, and the young critics may move farther up in their ivory tower. They must, in any event, recognize their common debt to the pioneer of the New Criticism in France.

č

In his critical essays, Sartre's style is a curious mixture of philosophical loftiness and polemical vulgarity. Relating a fictional technique to a metaphysical attitude, he lambasts

François Mauriac for playing God in the universe of the novel:

Voilà bien ce qui le perd. Il a écrit un jour que le romancier était pour ses créatures comme Dieu pour les siennes, et toutes les bizarreries de sa technique s'expliquent par ce qu'il prend le point de vue de Dieu sur ses personnages: Dieu voit le dedans et le dehors, le fond des âmes et les corps, tout l'univers à la fois. De la même façon, M. Mauriac a l'omniscience pour tout ce qui touche à son petit monde; ce qu'il dit sur ses personnages est parole d'Evangile, il les explique, les classe, les condamne sans appel. Si on lui demandait: "D'où savez-vous que Thérèse est une désespérée prudente?", il serait sans doute fort étonné, il répondrait: "Ne l'ai-je point faite?"

Eh bien non! Il est temps de le dire: le romancier n'est point Dieu. Rappelez-vous plutôt les précautions que prend Conrad pour nous suggérer que Lord Jim est peut-être "un romanesque." Il se garde bien de l'affirmer lui-même, il place le mot dans la bouche d'une de ses créatures, d'un être faillible, qui le prononce en hésitant. Ce terme si clair de "romanesque" y gagne du relief, du pathétique, je ne sais quel mystère. Avec M. Mauriac, rien de tel: "désespérée prudente" n'est pas une hypothèse, c'est une clarté qui nous vient d'en haut. L'auteur, impatient de nous faire saisir le caractère de son héroïne, nous en livre soudain la clé. Mais, précisément, je soutiens qu'il n'a pas le droit de porter ces jugements absolus. Un roman est une action racontée de différents points de vue. Et M. Mauriac le sait bien, qui écrit justement dans *La Fin de la Nuit*: "... les jugements les plus opposés sur une même créature sont justes, c'est une affaire d'éclairage, aucun éclairage n'est plus révélateur qu'un autre ..." Mais chacune de ces interprétations doit être en mouvement, c'est-à-dire entraînée par l'action même qu'elle interprète. En un mot, c'est le témoignage d'un acteur et elle doit révéler l'homme qui témoigne aussi bien que l'événement dont il est témoigné; elle doit susciter notre impatience (sera-t-elle confirmée, ou démentie par les événements?) et par là nous faire sentir la résistance du temps: chaque point de vue est donc relatif et le meilleur sera tel que le temps offre au lecteur la plus grande résistance. Les interprétations, les explications données par les acteurs seront toutes conjecturales: peut-être le lecteur, par delà ces conjectures, pressentira-t-il une réalité absolue de l'événement, mais c'est à lui seul de la rétablir, s'il a du goût pour cet exercice, et, s'il s'y essaie, il ne sortira jamais du domaine des vraisemblances et des probabilités. En tout cas, l'introduction de la vérité absolue, ou point de vue de Dieu, dans un roman est une double erreur technique: tout d'abord elle suppose un récitant soustrait à l'action et purement contemplatif, ce qui ne saurait convenir avec cette loi esthétique formulée par Valéry, selon laquelle un élément quelconque d'une œuvre d'art doit toujours entretenir une pluralité de rapports avec les autres éléments. En second lieu, l'absolu est intemporel. Si vous portez le récit à l'absolu, le ruban de la durée se casse net; le roman s'évanouit sous vos yeux: il ne demeure qu'une languissante vérité *sub specie aeternitatis*.

Mais il y a plus grave: les appréciations définitives que M. Mauriac est toujours prêt à glisser dans le récit prouvent qu'il ne conçoit pas ses personnages comme il le doit. Avant d'écrire il forge leur essence, il décrète qu'ils *seront* ceci ou cela. L'essence de Thérèse, bête puante, désespérée prudente, etc., est complexe, je le veux bien, et ne saurait s'exprimer d'une seule phrase. Mais qu'est-ce au juste? Le plus profond d'elle-même? Regardons-y de près: "romanesque," Conrad avait bien vu que ce mot prenait son sens s'il traduisait un aspect du personnage *pour autrui*; ne voit-on pas que "désespérée prudent" et "bête puante" et "naufragée" et toutes ces formules bien frappées sont du même genre que ce petit mot placé par Conrad dans la bouche d'un marchand des Iles: raccourcis de moraliste et d'historien. Et lorsque Thérèse résume son histoire ("s'arracher à un bas-fond et y reglisser et se reprendre indéfiniment; pendant des années, elle n'avait pas eu conscience que c'était le rythme de son destin. Mais maintenant voici qu'elle est sortie de la nuit, elle voit clair ... "), elle n'a tant d'aisance à juger son passé que faute d'y pouvoir rentrer. Ainsi, M. Mauriac, lorsqu'il croit sonder les reins de ses personnages, reste dehors, à la porte. Il n'y aurait aucun mal s'il s'en rendait compte et il nous donnerait alors des romans comme ceux de Hemingway, où nous ne connaissons guère les héros que par leurs gestes et leurs paroles et les vagues jugements qu'ils portent les uns sur les autres. Mais quand M. Mauriac, usant de toute son autorité de créateur, nous fait prendre ces vues extérieures pour la substance intime de ses créatures, il transforme celles-ci en *choses*. Seules les choses *sont:* elles n'ont que des dehors. Les consciences ne sont pas: elles se font. Ainsi M. Mauriac, en ciselant sa Thérèse *sub specie aeternitatis,* en fait d'abord une chose. Après quoi il rajoute, par en-dessous, toute une épaisseur de conscience, mais en vain: les êtres romanesques ont leurs lois, dont voici la plus rigoureuse: le romancier peut être leur témoin ou leur complice, mais jamais les deux à la fois. Dehors ou dedans. Faute d'avoir pris garde à ces lois, M. Mauriac assassine la conscience des personnages.[1]

—"M. François Mauriac et la liberté," *Situations,* I, pp. 45–48.

The following is the opening paragraph of the "existential psychoanalysis" of Jean Genet. Already Sartre speaks of the fatal instant in Genet's life which turned him into a rascal. In the 570 pages that follow, Sartre interprets all Genet's life and writing as a consequence of this moment of decision and choice:

Genet s'apparente à cette famille d'esprits qu'on nomme au-jourd'hui du nom barbare de "passéistes." Un accident l'a buté sur un souvenir d'enfance et ce souvenir est devenu sacré; dans ses premières années, un drame liturgique s'est joué, dont il a été l'officiant: il a connu le paradis et l'a perdu, il était enfant et on l'a chassé de son enfance. Sans doute cette "coupure" n'est pas très aisément localisable: elle se promène au gré de ses humeurs et de ses mythes entre sa dixième et sa quinzième année. Peu importe: elle existe, il y croit; sa vie se divise en deux parties hétérogènes: avant et après le drame sacré. Il n'est pas rare, en effet, qu'une mémoire condense en un seul moment mythique les contingences et les perpétuels recommencements d'une histoire individuelle. Ce qui compte, c'est que Genet a vécu et ne cesse de revivre cette période de sa vie comme si elle n'avait duré qu'un instant. Or qui dit "instant" dit *instant fatal:* l'instant c'est l'enveloppement réciproque et contradictoire de l'avant par l'après; on est encore ce qu'on va cesser d'être et déjà ce qu'on va devenir; on vit sa mort, on meurt sa vie; on se sent soi-même et un autre, l'éternel est présent dans un atome

[1] For translation, see Appendix 16.

de durée; au sein de la vie la plus pleine on pressent qu'on ne fera plus que survivre, on a peur de l'avenir. C'est le temps de l'angoisse et de l'héroïsme, du plaisir et de la destruction: il suffit d'un instant pour détruire, pour jouir, pour tuer, pour se faire tuer, pour faire sa fortune sur un coup de dés. Genet porte en son cœur un vieil instant qui n'a rien perdu de sa virulence, vide infinitésimal et sacré qui termine une mort et commence une horrible métamorphose. Voici l'argument de ce drame liturgique: un enfant meurt de honte, surgit à sa place un voyou; le voyou sera hanté par l'enfant. Il faudrait parler de résurrection, évoquer les vieux rites initiatiques du chamanisme et des sociétés secrètes si Genet ne refusait catégoriquement d'être un ressuscité. Il y a eu mort, c'est tout. Et Genet n'est rien d'autre qu'un mort; s'il paraît vivre encore, c'est de cette existence larvaire que certains peuples prêtent à leurs défunts dans les tombeaux. Tous ses héros sont morts au moins une fois dans leur vie.

—*Saint Genet, comédien et martyr*, p. 9.

SELECTED WORKS

Baudelaire (Gallimard, 1947). Translated by Martin Turnell (New Directions, 1950).

Situations (Gallimard, 1947–1965), 7 vols. Essays from Vols. 1 and 3 translated by Annette Michelson as *Literary and Philosophical Essays* (Criterion, 1955); Vol. 4 translated by Benita Eisler (Braziller, 1965).

Saint Genet, comédien et martyr (Gallimard, 1952). Translated as *Saint Genet, Actor and Martyr* by Bernard Frechtman (Braziller, 1963).

REFERENCES

Diéguez, Manuel de. *L'Ecrivain et son langage* (Gallimard, 1962), "Sartre," pp. 234–293.

Girard, René. "Existentialism and Criticism," *Yale French Studies*, 16 (1955–1956), 45–52.

Hahn, Otto. "L'Œuvre critique de Sartre," *MLN*, May, 1965, pp. 347–363.

Hardré, Jacques. "Jean-Paul Sartre: Literary Critic," *Studies in Philology*, January, 1958, pp. 98–106.

Laufer, Roger. "Sartre as a Literary Critic," *Meanjin (Australia)*, Winter, 1959, pp. 427–434.

Thody, Philip. "J.-P. Sartre as a Literary Critic," *The London Magazine*, November, 1960, pp. 61–64.

JEAN STAROBINSKI

Born in Geneva in 1920, Jean Starobinski was trained both in letters and in medicine. He has made his career in the former. After teaching French in the United States for several years, he returned to Switzerland, where he teaches the history of ideas in the university of his native city. He is the author of several essays on literary subjects.

In reply to a survey of opinion on criticism conducted by *Les Lettres Nouvelles* (June 24, 1959), Starobinski gives a broad and tolerant definition of the critic. He sees merit in all approaches as long as they do not become exclusive. His own approach, according to what he states in prefacing his study of Jean-Jacques Rousseau, avoids imposing preestablished values or classifications. He tries simply to recognize, by careful reading, the symbols and ideas around which the thought of an author organizes itself. Does this mean that Starobinski attempts to establish the thematic substructure of an artist's work? In the case of Rousseau, does he present as basic structural elements the symbols of transparency and obstacle? The answer is yes, but with qualifications, because Starobinski's emphasis is on the author's personal obsessions rather than on their literary manifestations, and the symbols that translate them are as much Starobinski's as Rousseau's.

Starobinski's study of Rousseau is an analysis of the writer's personality—his conflicts, preoccupations, and their origins. It is indeed a study of the man behind the work, the latter being reduced to a source for clues and proof. Rousseau's life-long worry over false appearances, the difficulties of communication, his longing for innocence and Edenic bliss seem to be the chief problems in his psychology. They can be symbolized as transparency versus opaqueness, figures of speech which Rousseau himself uses from time to time in his writings. The word "obstacle," likewise, translates a feature of his thinking and appears in his writings. It is equated with whatever prevents transparency. However, Starobinski is not really studying—as do Mauron and Weber—the transformation of a psychological experience into a literary motif. He is not analyzing here an artistic phenomenon but the author himself.

č

The interest in Starobinski's thesis lies in his reduction of Rousseau's thought to a basic obsessional pattern. Whether Rousseau is railing against the theater or confessing his trivial sins, working out a new system for musical notation or advocating a return to nature, he would seem to envisage his problem in terms that can be symbolized by the antitheses of transparency and opaqueness (obstacle). The darkness of theaters offends him, and plays seem arch examples of deception and false appearances. He explains the purpose of his *Confessions:* "rendre mon âme transparente aux yeux du lecteur." If he is dissatisfied with the conventional system of musical notation, it is because it represents a complicated opaqueness. A return to nature means a return to innocence—limpidness, transparency. Through ten very substantial chapters Starobinski demonstrates this characteristic pattern rooted, he believes, in a childhood trauma (émotion première) and not without relation to the libido:

Aux yeux d'une critique soucieuse d'atteindre sinon à la totalité d'une œuvre et d'un écrivain, du moins aux principes qui rendent l'ensemble intelligible, les anomalies sexuelles de Rousseau, consignées dans l'œuvre elle-même, contribuent au *sens* de la totalité, au même titre que les échafaudages de pensée théorique. Pas plus qu'il n'est question de réduire l'idéologie de Rousseau à ses bases sentimentales, il n'est possible de limiter la vie "intime" à la pure anecdote: le vécu, explicitement repris dans l'œuvre, ne peut rester pour nous une donnée marginale. L'exhibitionnisme a été une phase aberrante du comportement sexuel de Jean-Jacques; mais, sous une forme transposée, il est au principe même d'une œuvre comme les *Confessions*. Rien n'autorise, certes, une interprétation régressive (dont la psychanalyse courante est coutumière) qui ramènerait les *Confessions* à n'être qu'une variante plus ou moins sublimée de l'exhibitionnisme juvénile de Jean-Jacques. A cette méthode régressive, nous préférons une interprétation "prospective," qui cherche à déceler, dans l'événement ou l'attitude chronologiquement antérieurs, des intentions, des choix, des désirs dont le sens dépasse la circonstance qui les a rendus manifestes pour la première fois. Même sans savoir d'avance que l'exhibitionnisme de Jean-Jacques dans les "allées sombres" et les "réduits cachés" de Turin préfigure déjà la lecture publique des *Confessions*, une analyse de son comportement sexuel resterait incomplète si elle n'aboutissait pas à la mise en évidence d'un certain type de "relation au monde." Le comportement érotique n'est pas une donnée fragmentaire; il est une manifestation de l'individu total, et c'est comme tel qu'il doit être analysé. Que ce soit pour le négliger ou pour en faire un sujet d'étude privilégié, on ne peut limiter l'exhibitionnisme à la "sphère" sexuelle: la personnalité entière s'y révèle, avec quelques-uns de ses "choix existentiels" fondamentaux. Au lieu donc de réduire l'œuvre littéraire à *n'être que* le déguisement d'une tendance juvénile ou infantile, l'analyse visera à découvrir, dans les faits premiers de la vie affective, ce qui les oblige à aller *jusqu'à* la forme littéraire, jusqu'à la pensée et à l'art.

Oui, tout semble vraiment commencer par la privation de l'amour maternel. "Je coûtai la vie à ma mère, et ma naissance fut le premier de mes malheurs." On a tout dit, ou presque, sur cette naissance qui a peut-être donné à Jean-Jacques le sentiment du péché d'exister. A partir de là, on peut construire une série d'explications qui s'agencent bien (et même trop bien). Le masochisme? Un besoin de payer pour la faute d'être né. Mme de Warens? L'évident désir du sein maternel. Les ménages à trois? La recherche symbolique du pardon et de la protection paternels. La passivité, le narcissisme? Conséquences d'une culpabilité, qui empêche Jean-Jacques de chercher des satisfactions "normales," c'est-à-dire de se poser en rival du Père auprès des femmes. Le sentiment de l'existence, les extases, l'appétit de l'immédiat? Un retour au ventre originel, dans une Nature apaisante. Et cette gourmandise pour les laitages? Le sens en est décidément beaucoup trop clair ...

Mais expliquer une conduite par ses fins secrètes ou par ses premiers prétextes, ce n'est pas encore comprendre toute cette conduite. El il ne suffit pas, non plus, de montrer que la conscience s'oriente vers des fins symboliques, qu'elle substitue à l'objet premier de son désir. Il faut chercher l'essentiel là où l'intérieur rejoint l'extérieur: dans la manière dont une conscience se rapporte à ses fins, dans la structure propre de ce rapport. Alors seulement l'on s'approche de la réalité d'une pensée et d'une expérience vécue. C'est accepter une conception assez pauvre de la causalité psychologique, que d'admettre la toute-puissance d'un complexe (en l'occurrence, le complexe d'Œdipe) qui orienterait tous les aspects de la personnalité. Le complexe est souvent allégué comme s'il était doué d'une énergie autonome et distincte, alors que la vie psychique réelle est, dès l'origine, une activité de la personne au contact du "milieu" environnant. Le moment capital d'un comportement n'est ni dans ses mobiles inconscients, ni dans ses motifs conscients, mais au point où une *action* s'articule sur les mobiles et les motifs, en d'autres termes, au point où l'homme s'engage dans une aventure où il devra créer les conditions de sa satisfaction. Une telle perspective, dans le cas de Rousseau, nous oblige à tenir compte non seulement de ce qu'il désire (consciemment ou symboliquement) mais surtout de la façon dont il se dirige vers la satisfaction désirée, de son "style d'approche" ...[1]

—*Jean-Jacques Rousseau, la transparence et l'obstacle,*
pp. 210–212.

In *L'Œil vivant,* a book made up of studies on several French authors, Starobinski pursues further his search for basic obsessional patterns. Those that he discusses here are tied up with various kinds of visual imagery or symbolism. But he is not describing an author's visual universe so much as his *libido sentiendi* in its relation to the world and to other

[1] For translation, see Appendix 17.

consciousnesses. He first takes up Rousseau again, whose feeling of always being watched, spied upon by a stern or malevolent eye, leads Starobinski to his guilt complexes. Turning next to Corneille, Starobinski analyzes "la gloire," the hero's drive to dazzle, the importance of presence, of spectacle. With Racine, he demonstrates that being seen is something to fear, to be equated with being found out. With Stendhal, he concentrates on the writer's play-acting, his resorting to masks as a means of eluding the ever-present eye. Again, in these essays, the man is more important than the work, the *thématique* being a manifestation of a basic psychological disposition. It is often Starobinski, not the author in question, who translates this disposition into visual terms. No one would question the contribution such studies make towards a deeper appreciation of the work itself and of how it came into being. On the other hand, the use of the word "looking" as with "obstacle" or "transparency" may be misleading. One expects a "mythology" that is the author's alone and a study of artistic transformation or sublimation through creative work; yet such a study is not pursued and the "mythology" is as much the critic's as the author's. However, if "theme" seems often only a thematic device for the critic, it is a very useful one, and it effectively ties together a series of brilliant essays on masters of French literature.

At the end of the prefatory chapter, "Le voile de Popée," Starobinski carries his theme of "looking" into a discussion of the critical function. In figurative language he restates what he said in his previous volume. Realizing the limitations both of external criticism and criticism by empathy, he would prefer simply to wait passively for the work itself to operate. Instead of looking at the work, let it look at you. Through that look which fixes itself upon us from the pages of a book, we can glimpse the personality behind literary creation:

Le critique est celui qui, tout en consentant à la fascination que le texte lui impose, entend pourtant conserver *droit de regard.* Il désire pénétrer plus loin encore: par-delà le sens manifest qui se découvre à lui, il pressent une signification latente. Une vigilance supplémentaire lui devient nécessaire, à partir de la première "lecture à vue," pour s'avancer à la rencontre d'un *sens second.* Qu'on ne se méprenne pourtant pas sur ce terme: il ne s'agit pas, comme pour l'exégèse médiévale, du déchiffrage de quelque équivalent allégorique ou symbolique, mais de la vie plus vaste ou de la mort transfigurée dont le texte est l'annonciateur. Souvent, il arrivera que cette recherche du plus lointain ramène au plus proche: aux évidences du premier regard, aux formes et aux rythmes qui, de prime abord, semblaient n'être que la promesse d'un message secret. Un long détour nous renvoie aux mots eux-mêmes, où le sens élit sa demeure, et où brille le trésor mystérieux que l'on croyait devoir chercher dans la "dimension profonde."

A la vérité, l'exigence du regard critique tend vers deux possibilités opposées, dont aucune n'est pleinement réalisable. La première l'invite à se perdre dans l'intimité de cette conscience fabuleuse que l'œuvre lui fait entrevoir: la compréhension serait alors la poursuite progressive d'une complicité totale avec la subjectivité créatrice, la participation passionnée à l'expérience sensible et intellectuelle qui se déploie à travers l'œuvre. Mais si loin qu'il aille dans cette direction, le critique ne parviendra pas à étouffer en lui-même la conviction de son identité séparée, la certitude tenace et banale de n'être pas la conscience avec laquelle il souhaite se confondre. A supposer toutefois qu'il réussisse véritablement à s'y absorber, alors, paradoxalement, sa propre parole lui serait dérobée: il ne pourrait que se taire, et le parfait discours critique, à force de sympathie et de mimétisme, donnerait l'impression du plus complet silence. A moins de rompre en quelque façon le pacte de solidarité qui le lie à l'œuvre, le critique n'est capable que de paraphrase ou de pastiche: on doit *trahir* l'idéal d'identification pour acquérir le pouvoir de parler de cette expérience et de décrire, dans un langage qui n'est pas celui de l'œuvre, la vie commune qu'on a connue avec elle, en elle. Ainsi, malgré notre désir de nous abîmer dans la profondeur vivante de l'œuvre, nous sommes contraints de nous distancer d'elle pour pouvoir en parler. Pourquoi alors ne pas établir délibérément une perspective panoramique, les *alentours* avec lesquels l'œuvre est organique-

ment liée? Nous chercherions à percevoir certaines correspondances significatives qui n'ont pas été aperçues par l'écrivain; à
interpréter ses mobiles inconscients; à lire les relations complexes
qui unissent une destinée et une œuvre à leur milieu historique
et social. Cette seconde possibilité de la lecture critique peut
être définie comme celle du *regard surplombant*: l'œil ne veut
rien laisser échapper de toutes les configurations que la mise à
distance permet d'apercevoir. Dans l'espace élargi que le regard
parcourt, l'œuvre est certes un objet privilégié, mais elle n'est
pas le seul objet qui s'impose à la vue. Elle se définit par ce
qui l'avoisine, elle n'a de sens que par rapport à l'ensemble de
son contexte. Or voici l'écueil: le contexte est si vaste, les relations si nombreuses, que le regard se sent saisi d'un secret
désespoir; jamais il ne rassemblera tous les éléments de cette
totalité qui s'annonce à lui. Au surplus, dès l'instant où l'on
s'oblige à situer une œuvre dans ses coordonnées historiques,
seule une décision arbitraire nous autorise à limiter l'enquête.
Celle-ci, par principe, pourrait aller jusqu'au point où l'œuvre
littéraire, cessant d'être l'objet privilégié qu'elle était d'abord,
n'est plus que l'une des innombrables manifestations d'une
époque, d'une culture, d'une "vision du monde." L'œuvre
s'évanouit à mesure que le regard prétend embrasser, dans le
monde social ou dans la vie de l'auteur, davantage de faits
corrélatifs. Le triomphe du regard surplombant n'est, lui aussi,
qu'une forme de l'échec: il nous fait perdre l'œuvre et ses
significations, en prétendant nous donner le monde dans lequel
baigne l'œuvre.

La critique complète n'est peut-être ni celle qui vise à la
totalité (comme fait le regard surplombant), ni celle qui vise
à l'intimité (comme fait l'intuition identifiante); c'est un regard qui sait exiger tour à tour le surplomb et l'intimité, sachant
par avance que la vérité n'est ni dans l'une ni dans l'autre tenta-
tive, mais dans le mouvement qui va inlassablement de l'une à
l'autre. Il ne faut refuser ni le vertige de la distance, ni celui de
la proximité: il faut désirer ce double excès où le regard est
chaque fois près de perdre tout pouvoir.

Mais peut-être aussi la critique a-t-elle tort de vouloir à ce
point régler l'exercice de son propre regard. Mieux vaut, en
mainte circonstance, s'oublier soi-même et se laisser surprendre.
En récompense, je sentirai, dans l'œuvre, naître un regard qui se
dirige vers moi: ce regard n'est pas un reflet de mon interrogation. C'est une conscience étrangère, radicalement autre, qui

me cherche, qui me fixe, et qui me demande de répondre. Je me sens *exposé* à cette question qui vient ainsi à ma rencontre. L'œuvre m'interroge. Avant de parler pour mon compte, je dois prêter ma propre voix à cette étrange puissance qui m'interpelle; or, si docile que je sois, je risque toujours de lui préférer les musiques rassurantes que j'invente. Il n'est pas facile de garder les yeux ouverts pour accueillir le regard qui nous cherche. Sans doute n'est-ce pas seulement pour la critique, mais pour toute entreprise de connaissance qu'il faut affirmer: "Regarde, afin que tu sois regardé."

—*L'Œil vivant*, pp. 25–28.

SELECTED WORKS

Montesquieu par lui-même (Seuil, 1953).

Jean-Jacques Rousseau, la transparence et l'obstacle (Plon, 1957).

"Psychanalyse et critique littéraire," *Arguments*, Jan.–March, 1959, pp. 37–41.

L'Œil vivant (Gallimard, 1961).

Preface to Jacques Ehrmann, *L'Amour et l'Illusion dans l'Astrée* (P.U.F., 1965).

"Les Directions nouvelles de la recherche critique," *Preuves*, June, 1965, pp. 23–32.

"Psychanalyse et critique littéraire," *Preuves*, March, 1966, pp. 21–32.

REFERENCES

Jones, P. Mansell. "*L'Œil vivant*," *French Studies*, July, 1962, p. 292.

Niklaus, Robert. "*L'Œil vivant*," *Modern Language Review*, July, 1962, pp. 450–451.

Poulet, Georges. "La pensée critique de Jean Starobinski," *Critique*, May, 1963, pp. 387–410.

JEAN-PAUL WEBER

In 1958 Jean-Paul Weber launched a double career in letters as a novelist with *Voyage au Zeud* and as an essayist with *La Psychologie de l'Art*. He has since become identified with the avant-garde in both genres, *Meurtre à l'Observatoire* bringing him into the group of New Novelists and *Genèse de l'Œuvre poétique* establishing him as a major figure among the New Critics. A continuation of the latter work appeared in 1963 under the title of *Domaines thématiques*. In addition to his literary career, Jean-Paul Weber, who is an agrégé de philosophie and a docteur ès lettres, pursues a career in teaching. In recent years he has been at Bryn Mawr (1961–1962) and then at the City College of New York.

In *Genèse de l'Œuvre poétique*, which is a thesis dedicated to his professors of literature and esthetics at the Sorbonne, Weber sets forth the principles of his own brand of thematic criticism. Art, he asserts, is a bit of childhood glimpsed through the gray haze of adulthood. What he means is that at the bottom of all esthetic creation there is some childhood experience. It may manifest itself forthrightly or symbolically, may be recognized consciously by the artist or not; but one may trace, through the infinite number of variations in a given artist's work, the inspiration of an event or a situation from his childhood.

Weber's method of investigation usually begins with a hypothesis (the conjecture of an obsession), proceeds with a search for manifestations (*analoga* or symbolizations), and concludes with evidence from biography. This type of work, which he calls "thematic analysis," does not presume to invalidate conventional criticism, source studies, or studies devoted to texts and variants. On the contrary, Weber believes that such investigations perform essential services. The thematic analysis does not invalidate psychoanalytical criticism either, indeed Weber has seemed inclined to view it as a corollary of psychoanalysis. However, vexed by the attacks upon his own work, he has recently been less indulgent, and between thematic analysis and psychoanalysis there are fundamental differences in concept of theme and in emphasis. In classic psychoanalysis, theme is multiple rather than single, common and general (Oedipus crisis, castration complex, etc.) rather than individual, and is, moreover, preponderantly sexual. Psychoanalytical criticism tends to subordinate the work of art to the man, whereas thematic analysis (Weber refers to himself as an esthetician) maintains the emphasis on the work of art.

❦

The authors chosen for analysis in *Genèse de l'Œuvre poétique* are eight major French writers from the nineteenth and twentieth centuries. Each reveals in his work a personal mythology rooted in something from childhood. This may be an object (the clock, with Vigny), a story (the legend of the Tower of the rats, Hugo), an event, a certain atmosphere, a taste—whatever it is, it has determined the basic configuration of the poet's work. A perusal of one of Weber's analyses will demonstrate how he tests his hypothesis to decide whether the theme that he suspects is really the key to the author's creative fantasies. He begins with Vigny and the clock. The frequency of clock motifs both in his prose and poetry suggests an obsession. The texts are examined scrupulously for references to clocks and their component parts, to time, to the hour of the day, to circularity and rotation, to movements to and fro. Then Weber turns to biography. In *Le Journal d'un poète*, he finds an episode involving a clock dating from the years when Vigny was seven or eight years old, the very age at which the poet himself situates the birth of his interest in verse. This discovery confirms the hypothesis. The task remaining is to go through the work again to trace the variation and modulation of the obsession, to show how the clock figures as an organic part of Vigny's creative art. Thus *Chatterton* is revealed as a drama of time and moment, *Moïse* as a poem structured on the topography of the clock (the ascension of Moses comparable to the minute hand, and so on). From the conclusion to the chapter, we take the following:

En supprimant l'Horloge, consciemment ou inconsciemment appréhendée, on supprimerait par là même les trois quarts de l'œuvre du poète. Au reste, nous avons réussi, croyons-nous, à discerner le *souvenir thématique*, qui est celui d'une "pendule noire" que le poète vit arriver dans sa nouvelle demeure lorsqu'il avait sept ou huit ans.

Il est aisé de comprendre le privilège thématique de cette pendule. Nous verrons que c'est aux environs de sept ans que la mémoire des poètes se révèle le plus apte à subir l'empreinte où se couleront, par la suite, les symboles de leur œuvre. D'autre part, la pendule noire n'est pas seulement pour Vigny, à cet âge, un objet nouveau, insolite, bizarrement animé; elle n'est pas seulement admirée, aimée par ses parents ("mon père l'aimait beaucoup"). Les noms poétiques, "les beaux noms" du calendrier révolutionnaire ("J'aimais les beaux noms de fructidor, thermidor et messidor") se gravent dans l'esprit de l'enfant à l'ombre de cette horloge, et aident sa vocation poétique à éclore. Les beaux récits, les récits passionnants de son père ("C'était pour moi une si grande fête de l'entendre ... ") déroulent leurs tragédies et leurs fastes devant la pendule noire toute empanachée de noms mélodieux, toute vibrante de rythme, toute jaillissante de carillons. L'Horloge, par son lexique, par son balancement régulier, par la musique des heures, par le discours captivant du père, par la tendresse des leçons maternelles qui s'y cristallisent, par l'affection paternelle qu'elle fait ressortir, l'Horloge, pour Vigny, est la Poésie même, éclat de mots sonores, nombre, mesure, musique, intrigue, sentiment—et aussi la nostalgie du Souvenir.

Mais l'Horloge et l'Heure, ainsi modulées, ne manifestent encore qu'un versant de la thématique du poète, son versant de clarté. Très rapidement, en effet,* l'univers horloger de Vigny s'enrichit de composantes sombres: lorsque l'Enfant écoute l'heure, non plus pour y projeter des mots mystérieux ou des récits pleins de tendresse et de feu, mais pour mettre un carcan de fer sur sa sensibilité, sur ses élans poétiques,† l'Horloge ne lui apparaît plus comme une région de féeries captivantes, mais comme la patrie même du Devoir tyrannique non moins que bienfaisant, et qui tient l'Enfant captif dans ses serres. Le rythme de l'Horloge n'est plus alors le pas souple de la poésie, mais roulement de tambour, ordre invincible, pas martelé des armées. De là, d'abord, l'ambivalence de la thématique affective: l'Heure-Poésie et l'Heure-Devoir engendrent, dans l'âme du poète, à côté d'un penchant insurmontable pour la parole et le vers, qui imprimera en filigrane l'image de la Pendule à la plupart de ses poèmes, une aversion secrète pour l'Ordre prestigieux que désormais l'Horloge personnifie et symbolise, et dont on trouvera maints échos dans *Servitude et Grandeur militaires*. De là, ensuite, l'ambivalence de l'idéologie du poète: nous ne doutons pas un instant que l'*Honneur* ne signifie, chez Vigny, thématiquement, l'*Heure*; la grandeur et l'absurdité de

*C'est en effet en 1807 que l'enfant Vigny entre comme demi-pensionnaire à l'institution Hix: il a alors dix ans. Cf. Lauvrière, *op. cit.*, p. 13.

† Cf. ces indications autobiographiques: "J'ai reçu une éducation très forte. L'habitude de l'application et d'un travail perpétuel . . ." (*Journal*, 1838, II, p. 1100.)—"Le temps le plus malheureux de ma vie fut celui du collège" (*ib.*, 1847, p. 1260). "Je me sentais d'une race maudite et cela me rendait sombre et pensif" (*ibid.*).—"Je ne vous ai parlé de ces détails, qui sont d'une petitesse à faire pitié, que pour vous donner un exemple de plus de *ces chagrins d'enfance qui laissent dans l'homme une teinte de sauvagerie difficile à effacer durant le reste de sa vie*. Ces peines . . . jettent une couleur sombre sur tout l'avenir" (*ibid.*, p. 1261).

Ajoutons à cela une *hantise du temps perdu*, qui tourmenta Vigny dès ses jeunes années: "Le temps me paraissant perdu s'il n'amenait une idée neuve et féconde" (*ibid.*, 1262), et probablement sa vie durant: "*Lorsqu'on fait des vers en regardant une pendule*, on a honte du *temps que l'on perd* à chercher une rime qui ait la bonté de ne pas trop nuire à l'idée" (1832; *ib.*, p. 941).

On le voit: le travail scolaire et la pensée créatrice ont très tôt défini un conflit et un remords (celui de *perdre son temps*), liés à l'horaire, au temps, à l'horloge, et qui n'ont cessé de bourreler l'inconscient et la conscience du poète.

l'honneur traduisent, sur le plan de l'idée, l'absurde majesté de l'Horloge; et en disant, par exemple: "l'honneur est la poésie du devoir", Vigny ne fait qu'accoler, en une formule unique, sonore, et un peu creuse, le double aspect de l'Horloge: *poésie et devoir.**

De là enfin, les destinées du poète. Amoureux de la pendule noire, il fit en son honneur des vers réguliers comme son rythme, traça des cercles mystérieux et mouvants, comme font sur le cadran les Aiguilles, dans ses poèmes, composa *Chatterton* comme un mécanisme horloger, poétisa jusqu'aux servitudes de l'obéissance passive et du pas cadencé. Mais aussi, esclave de l'Heure et de l'Horloge, il voulut d'abord les vaincre par l'esprit, apprenant les mathématiques sans doute pour apprendre à lire l'heure dans les astres, puis à comprendre le mécanisme savant qui va chercher ses ordres dans le ciel, pour nous les transmettre, parfait et vain Sous-officier, Adjudant stupide et terrible. C'est pour cela que Vigny aima les armes *savantes*, se prépara pour entrer à l'Ecole Polytechnique, mit des marins et des artilleurs dans ses récits. Il voulut aussi se confondre avec cette moitié sombre de son thème, comme il désira, se faisant poète, se fondre à la Poésie, à la Pendule noire de son enfance heureuse. Poète comme les mois révolutionnaires, il fut aussi soldat, officier, et toute sa vie il souhaita la guerre sans la trouver. C'est, en effet, être Pendule qu'être officier; Vigny nous l'expliqua abondamment, bien qu'à son insu; être officier, c'est scander le rythme de durées étrangères, c'est rythmer le pas d'une cohorte, c'est être inexorable comme le temps, obéi comme l'Horloge; c'est aussi recevoir les ordres d'en haut, comme le mouvement les reçoit des astres; c'est être une mécanique savante, meurtrière, mais à la merci d'un geste de gamin; c'est tuer à coup sûr, et être infiniment vulnérable; c'est être la terrible personnification et l'esclave de l'Honneur—comme l'Horloge est la personnification et l'esclave de l'Heure. Et peut-être la seule supériorité de Vigny, par rapport à l'Adjudant—que son inconscient voulut "ubuesque"—de *La veillée de Vincennes*, est d'être obscurément conscient de son statut d'Horloge, et de le crier, en prose comme en vers.

* Sur la philosophie du temps chez Vigny, qui refuse l'éternité au profit, à la fois, d'un étalement spatial du temps, faisant paraître simultanément ses trois "moments" ou *extases* (Heidegger), et d'une éthique de l'action dans la durée, cf. G. Poulet, *op. cit.*, pp. 263–290.

Thème unique, mais à deux têtes—*Janus bifrons*: et tout
Vigny en découle, poésie, symbolique consciente et inconsciente,
intrigues, idées, la religion de l'honneur et le stoïcisme, l'Ecole
Polytechnique, l'avancement à l'ancienneté, l'Académie, *Eloa*
et *Chatterton, Le Cachet rouge* et *le Docteur noir*.[1]
—*Genèse de l'Œuvre poétique*, pp. 87–90.

What may strike us as we study this passage typical of
Jean-Paul Weber is, besides the rich documentation, the
enthusiastic readiness to relate everything and anything in
Vigny to a clock fixation. Weber demonstrates eloquently
the tendency of the New Critics to obfuscate by emphatic
rhetoric the highly subjective character of their assertions.
Most people can remember having disliked school and lesson
practice, most people have felt guilty over time wasted; hap-
pily, few develop clock fixations. And many value honor
more than life, may even interest themselves in mathematics
or in a military career without subconsciously identifying
themselves with a clock. Here as elsewhere in the New
Criticism we might prefer a more sober exposition, less bold
affirmations, and stronger proof.

Weber's thesis has met with a variety of adverse criticism
from professors and journalists. Some find it too close to
psychoanalysis, others find it not close enough. (The psychoanalysts are apt to reproach thematic critics for not
"going all the way.") The suspicions have also been raised
that the themes Weber claims to find in his authors are
gratuitous and arbitrary, at least that their importance is
exaggerated. The reduction of all to one single theme seems
the most questionable aspect of his theory. In his introduction to *Domaines thématiques*, where he attempts to refute
his critics,[2] Weber concedes that a single theme may not

[1] For translation, see Appendix 18.
[2] He attempts to refute them again in *Néo-critique et Paléo-critique*,
published by Pauvert in the same series as Picard's incendiary pamphlet *Nouvelle Critique ou nouvelle imposture?*, to which it is a quite
unsatisfactory reply.

explain everything in an author. But he has not really retracted and, in this volume, he continues to analyze in the same fashion. Thus Poe's stories, he demonstrates, are structured on a clock fixation (why not his poems, too, if one single experience acts for all?), Lautréamont's works on a boyhood experience involving masturbation, Kafka's stories and poems on a childhood and school situation. Nerval, Weber allows, has two themes orienting his creative imagination: that of a portrait and a girl and that of lighting a fire. The first one, which juxtaposes a picture and a real person, is "modulated" by antithetical objects and situations. One remembers Richard's emphasis on the pairs of opposites in Nerval, which he saw, not as involving a specific trauma, but as a phenomenological attitude, that is, a fundamental aspect of the poet's reaction to the world.

Of course one interpretation does not necessarily invalidate the other. It should be remembered, in the defense of the thematic critics, that they do not claim to explain everything in the author they study. Weber's traumatic analysis does not deny the possibility of Richard's phenomenology: Nerval can have a portrait fixation and still have a special sensitivity to depth. The angle from which each critic approaches the subject is different; it is not necessarily contradictory.

SELECTED WORKS

La Psychologie de l'art (P.U.F., 1958).

Genèse de l'Œuvre poétique (Gallimard, 1960).

Domaines thématiques (Gallimard, 1963).

Néo-critique et paléo-critique ou contre Picard (Pauvert, 1966).

REFERENCES

Albérès, R.-M. "Pour les psychiatres," *Les Nouvelles Littéraires,* January 2, 1964, p. 5.

Attal, Jean-Pierre. "Deux détectives littéraires," *Critique,* April, 1961, pp. 319–329.

Greene, Tatiana. *"Genèse de l'Œuvre poétique," The Romanic Review,* April, 1964, pp. 156–158.

APPENDICES 1–18
Translation of Selected Passages

GASTON BACHELARD

A philosopher who has evolved his entire thinking from the fundamental themes of the philosophy of science, and followed the main line of the active, growing rationalism of contemporary science as closely as he could, must forget his learning and break with all his habits of philosophical research, if he wants to study the problems posed by the poetic imagination. For here the cultural past doesn't count. The long day-in, day-out effort of putting together and constructing his thoughts is ineffectual. One must be receptive, receptive to the image at the moment it appears: if there be a philosophy of poetry, it must appear and re-appear through a significant verse, in total adherence to an isolated image; to be exact, in the very ecstasy of the newness of the image. The poetic image is a sudden salience on the surface of the psyche, the lesser psychological causes of which have not been sufficiently investigated. Nor can anything general and co-ordinated serve as a basis for a philosophy of poetry. The idea of principle or "basis" in this case would be disastrous, for it would interfere with the essential psychic actuality, the essential novelty of the poem. And whereas philosophical reflection applied to scientific thinking elaborated over a long period of time requires any new idea to become integrated in a body of tested ideas, even though this body of ideas be subjected to profound change by the new idea (as is the case in all the revolutions of contemporary science), the philosophy of poetry must acknowledge that the poetic act has no past, at least no recent past, in which its preparation and appearance could be followed.

Later, when I shall have occasion to mention the relation of a new poetic image to an archetype lying dormant in the depths of the unconscious, I shall have to make it understood that this relation is not, properly speaking, a *causal* one. The poetic image is not subject to an inner thrust. It is not an echo of the past. On the contrary: through the brilliance of an image, the distant past resounds with echoes, and it is hard to know at what depth these echoes will reverberate and die away. Because of its novelty and its action, the poetic image has an entity and a dynamism of its own; it is referable to a direct *ontology*. This ontology is what I plan to study.

.　　.　　.　　.　　.　　.　　.　　.　　.　　.

To say that the poetic image is independent of causality is to make a rather serious statement. But the causes cited by psychologists and psychoanalysts can never really explain the wholly unexpected nature of the new image, any more than they can explain the attraction it holds for a mind that is foreign to the process of its creation. The poet does not confer the past of his image upon me, and yet his image immediately takes root in me. The communicability of an unusual image is a fact of great ontological significance. We shall return to this question of communion through brief, isolated, rapid actions. Images excite us—afterwards—but they are not the phenomena of an excitement. In all psychological research, we can, of course, bear in mind psychoanalytical methods for determining the personality of a poet, and thus find a measure of the pressures—but above all of the oppressions—that a poet has been subjected to in the course of his life. But the poetic act itself, the sudden image, the flare-up of being in the imagination, are inaccessible to such investigations. In order to clarify the problem of the poetic image philosophically, we shall have to have recourse to a phenomenology of the imagination. By this should be understood a study of the phenomenon of the poetic image when it emerges into the consciousness as a direct product of the heart, soul and being of man, apprehended in his actuality.

—*Poetics of Space*, Introduction, pp. xi–xiv.

The phenomenological situation with regard to psychoanalytical investigation will perhaps be more precisely stated if, in connection with poetic images, we are able to isolate a sphere of *pure sublimation;* of a sublimation which sublimates nothing, which is relieved of the burden of passion, and freed from the pressure of desire. By thus giving to the poetic image at its peak an absolute of sublimation, I place heavy stakes on a simple nuance. It seems to me, however, that poetry gives abundant proof of this absolute sublimation, as will be seen frequently in the course of this work. When psychologists and psychoanalysts are furnished this proof, they cease to see anything in the poetic image but a simple game, a short-lived, totally vain game. Images, in particular, have no significance for them—neither from the standpoint of the passions, nor from that of psychology or psychoanalysis. It does not occur to them that the significance of such images is precisely a poetic significance. But poetry is there with its countless surging images, images through which the creative imagination comes to live in its own domain.

For a phenomenologist, the attempt to attribute antecedents to an image, when we are in the very existence of the image, is a sign of inveterate psychologism. On the contrary, let us take the poetic image in its being. For the poetic consciousness is so wholly absorbed by the image that appears on the language, above customary language; the language it speaks with the poetic image is so new that correlations between past and present can no longer be usefully considered.

The examples I shall give of breaks in significance, sensation and sentiment will oblige the reader to grant me that the poetic image is under the sign of a new being.

This new being is happy man.

Happy in speech, therefore unhappy in reality, will be the psychoanalyst's immediate objection. Sublimation, for him, is nothing but a vertical compensation, a flight upwards, exactly in the same way that compensation is a lateral flight. And right away, the psychoanalyst will abandon ontological investigation of the image, to dig into the past of man. He sees and points out the poet's secret sufferings. He explains the flower by the fertilizer.

The phenomenologist does not go that far. For him, the image is there, the word speaks, the word of the poet speaks to him. There is no need to have lived through the poet's sufferings in order to seize the felicity of speech offered by the poet—a felicity that dominates tragedy itself. Sublimation in poetry towers above the psychology of the mundanely unhappy soul. For it is a fact that poetry possesses a felicity of its own, however great the tragedy it may be called upon to illustrate.

Pure sublimation, as I see it, poses a serious problem of method for, needless to say, the phenomenologist cannot disregard the deep psychological reality of the processes of sublimation that have been so lengthily examined by psychoanalysis. His task is that of proceeding phenomenologically to images which have not been experienced, and which life does not prepare, but which the poet creates; of living what has not been lived, and being receptive to an overture of language. There exist a few poems, such as certain poems by Pierre-Jean Jouve, in which experiences of this kind may be found. Indeed, I know of no oeuvre that has been nourished on psychoanalytical meditation more than Jouve's. However, here and there, his poetry passes through flames of such intensity that we no longer need live at its original source. He himself has said: "Poetry constantly surpasses its origins, and because it suffers more deeply in ecstasy or in sorrow, it retains greater freedom." Again, on page 112: "The further I advanced in time, the more the plunge was controlled, removed from the contributory cause, directed toward the pure form of language." I cannot say whether or not Pierre-Jean Jouve would agree to consider the causes divulged by psychoanalysis as "contributory." But in the region of "the pure form of language" the psychoanalyst's causes do not allow us to predict the poetic image in its newness. They are, at the very most, opportunities for liberation. And in the poetic age in which we live, it is in this that poetry is specifically "surprising." Its images are therefore unpredictable. Most literary critics are insufficiently aware of this unpredictability, which is precisely what upsets the plans of the usual psychological explanations.

—*Ibid.*, pp. xxv–xxvii.

We may then realize that an image is a plant that needs earth and sky, substance and form. Images that man finds evolve slowly, painfully; and we can understand Jacques Bousquet's profound remark: "An image costs humanity as much work as a new character costs a plant." Many images that are proposed cannot live because they are merely formal inventions, because they are not really adapted to the subject which they are supposed to adorn.

.   .   .   .

Strong in all these convictions, we could dispense with worn-out knowledge, with formal and allegorical mythologies that survive in a lifeless, strengthless way of teaching literature. We could also dispense with the innumerable poems of fakery, in which commonplace rhymesters struggle to create as many diverse and confused echoes as possible. If we have emphasized mythologies, it is because we have recognized in them a permanent effect, an unconscious effect on the souls of today. A mythology of water, as such, would be nothing but a story. We have tried to write a psychology, we have tried to tie together literary images and dreams.

—*L'Eau et les Rêves*, p. 4.

. . . if our research were to merit attention, it should afford some means, some new instruments, for literary criticism. That is the purpose of introducing the notion of cultural complex in literary psychology. We give this name to the *unconscious attitudes* that determine even the workings of consciousness. In the field of the imagination, they are the favorite images that are thought to be taken from the world about us yet are only *projections* of an obscure soul.

—*Ibid.*, p. 25.

In its excessive mythological overlay, the example of Pierre Louys' *swan* illustrates precisely what is meant by a *cultural complex*. Most often the cultural complex is a product of a school culture, that is, a traditional culture. . . . Pierre Louys had recourse to school culture in writing his story [*Leda*]. Only those with a *school* knowledge of myths can understand it. But if such readers are satisfied, their satisfaction remains impure. They do not know whether they enjoy the content or the form; they do not know whether they invoke images or passions. Often symbols are brought together without regard for their symbolic evolution. Whoever speaks of Leda must speak of the swan and the egg. The same work will connect the two stories without going into the mythic character of the egg. In Pierre Louys' work, Leda even has the idea that she could "cook the egg in hot ashes as she had seen satyrs do."

—*Ibid.*, pp. 57–58.

ROLAND BARTHES

The confidant. Between failure and bad faith, there is, however, one possible way out, that of dialectics. Tragedy does not ignore this possibility; but it has been able to admit it only by banalizing its functional figure: the confidant. In Racine's day, the role's popularity was waning, which perhaps increases its significance. The Racinian confidant (and this is in accord with his origin) is linked to the hero by a kind of feudal tie, a *devotion;* this liaison designates him as a true double, probably delegated to assume all the triviality of the conflict and of its solution, in short, to establish the nontragic part of the tragedy in a lateral zone where language is discredited, becomes *domestic.** As we know, the hero's dogmatism is continually countered by the confidant's empiricism. Here we must recall what has already been observed apropos of the tragic enclosure. For the confidant, the world exists; leaving the stage, he can enter reality and then return from it: his insignificance authorizes his ubiquity. The first result of this *droit de sortie* is that for him the universe ceases to be absolutely antinomic:† essentially constituted by an alternative construction of the world, alienation yields once the world becomes multiple. The hero lives in the universe of forms, alternations, signs; the confidant in the world of content, causality, accident. Doubtless he is the voice of reason (an utterly stupid reason, yet with something of Reason all the same) against the voice of "passion"; but this means, in particular, that he voices the possible against the impossible. Failure constitutes the hero, it is transcendent to him; in the confidant's eyes, failure *touches* the hero, it is contingent to him. Whence the dialectical nature of the solutions he (unsuccessfully) proposes, which always consist in mediatizing the alternative.

---

* Phaedra makes Oenone responsible for ridding her of the *business* of the act, so that she retains, nobly, and childishly, only the tragic result:
  To sway him, make use of every means. (*Phèd.* III, 1)
† "It is only in social existence that such antinomies as subjectivism/objectivism, spiritualism/materialism, activity/passivity lose their antinomic character . . ." Marx, *Economic and Philosophic Manuscripts of 1844.*

For the hero, then, the confidant's medicine is therefore aperitive, it consists first of all in opening up the secret, defining the exact status of the hero's dilemma; the confidant tries to produce an illumination. His technique seems crude, but it is a tested one: he must provoke the hero by naïvely representing to him a hypothesis contrary to his impulse, in a word, the confidant must "blunder"‡ (in general, the hero "reacts" to the strategy, but rapidly conceals it under a flood of justifying words). As for the behavior which the confidant recommends for dealing with the conflict, it is always dialectical, that is, subordinates the end to the means. Here are the most frequent examples of such behavior: to *escape* (which is the nontragic expression of tragic death); to *wait* (which, again, is to oppose time-as-repetition by reality's time-as-maturation);§ to *live* (*vivez!* this injunction, in the mouths of all confidants, stigmatizes the tragic dogmatism as a desire for failure and death: if only the hero would make life a value, he would be saved). In all three forms, the last one imperative, the viability recommended by the confidant is indeed the most antitragic value possible. The confidant's role is not only to represent it, but also to counter the alibis by which the hero masks his will to fail by a *ratio* external to the tragedy and in a sense explanatory of it. He *sympathizes* with the hero, in other words, attenuates his responsibility: he believes him free to escape but not to do wrong, forced into failure yet accessible to its outcome. This is quite the contrary of the tragic hero, who claims utter responsibility when it is a question of taking on himself an ancestral transgression he has not committed, but declares himself impotent when it is a question of transcending it; who seeks to be free, in a word, by being a slave, but not free by being free. Perhaps in the confidant, though he is clumsy and often utterly stupid, we already have a hint of that whole line of irreverent valets who will oppose the lord and master's psychological regression by a supple and happy mastery of reality.

—*On Racine*, pp. 53–55.

‡ Theramenes says to Hippolytus that it is precisely a matter of fulfilling the latter's love for Aricia:
Then do you yourself, my lord, turn against her? (*Phèd.* I, 1)
§ Yield, brother, to this seething frenzy: Alexander and time will make you the stronger. (*Alex.* III, 3)
Give this torrent a chance to subside. (*Bér.* III, 4)
But this success, Lady, is still uncertain. Be patient. (*Baj.* III, 3)

It seems that here we are approaching the heart of the matter. For if we turn now towards the reasons why university criticism is bound by principle not to admit the other criticism, we see immediately that this opposition is in no wise the banal fear of something new; university criticism is neither retrograde nor old-fashioned (a little slow, perhaps): it is perfectly capable of adapting. Thus, although for years it practiced a conformist psychology based on normalcy (inherited from Théodule Ribot, Lanson's contemporary), it has just "recognized" psychoanalysis and has approved (by a doctoral dissertation exceptionally well received) the strictly Freudian criticism of Ch. Mauron. But by this very approval, university criticism exposes its line of resistance: for psychoanalytical criticism is *still* a psychology, it postulates an *elsewhere* of the work (which is the writer's childhood), a secret of the author, material to decipher, which is still the human mind even though the vocabulary is new: a psychopathology of a writer is better than no psychology at all; in connecting the details of a work with the details of a life, psychoanalytical criticism continues to practice an esthetic of motivations founded entirely upon external connections: it is because Racine was himself an orphan that there are so many fathers in his plays: biographical transcendence is safe: there is, there will always be writers' lives to "delve into." In sum, what university criticism is disposed to admit (little by little and after resisting successively) is, paradoxically, the very principle of interpretative criticism or, if one prefers (although the word still frightens), of ideological criticism; but what it will not admit is that this interpretation and this ideology should decide to operate in a purely internal field of the work; in brief, what is objected to is immanent analysis: everything is acceptable provided the work can be connected to *something other* than itself, that is to say something other than literature: history (even though it becomes Marxist), psychology (even though it turns into psychoanalysis)—these *elsewheres* of the work will be gradually admitted; what will not be is a study that locates itself *within* the work and establishes its connection with the world only after having described it fully from the inside, in its functions or—as one says today—in its structure; what is rejected *en bloc* is phenomenological criticism (which *explicits* the work instead of explaining it), thematic criticism (which reconstitutes the inner metaphors of the work), and structural criticism (which considers the work to be a system of functions).

Why this refusal of immanence (the principle of which is moreover so often misunderstood)? For the moment one can give only contingent answers; perhaps it is out of obstinate submission to the ideology of determinism, which sees the work as the "product" of a "cause," and considers external causes to be more "causes" than the others; perhaps also because to move from a criticism of functions and meanings would imply a deep conversion of the norms of knowledge, hence of technique, hence even of the type of work the university does; one should not forget that since research is not yet separated from teaching, the university works but also it gives diplomas; it therefore needs an ideology articulated upon a technique sufficiently difficult to constitute an instrument of selection; positivism supplies it with the obligation of a vast, difficult, and patient learning; immanent criticism—or so it seems to it—asks before the work only a capacity of *astonishment*, difficult to measure: one can understand its reluctance to change its demands.

—*Modern Language Notes*, December, 1963, pp. 451–452.

It is precisely through the admission, on the part of criticism, that it is only a language (or, more accurately, a meta-language) that it can, paradoxically yet genuinely, be objective and subjective, historical and existential, totalitarian and liberal. The language that a critic chooses to speak is not a gift from heaven; it is one of the range of languages offered by his situation in time and, objectively, it is the latest stage of a certain historical development of knowledge, ideas and intellectual passions; it is a *necessity*. On the other hand, each critic chooses this necessary language, in accordance with a certain existential pattern, as the *means of exercising* an intellectual function which is his, and his alone, putting into the operation his "deepest self," that is, his preferences, pleasures, resistances and obsessions. In this way the critical work contains within itself a dialogue between two historical situations and two subjectivities, those of the author and those of the critic. But this dialogue shows a completely egotistical bias towards the present; criticism is neither a "tribute" to the truth of the past nor to the truth of "the other"; it is the ordering of that which is intelligible in our own time.

—*The Times Literary Supplement*, September 27, 1963, p. 740.
In French in *Essais Critiques*, p. 257.

ALBERT BÉGUIN

Although there was no event that one can date, Balzac experienced a true conversion. Conversion to life—if it is possible to think that a man who bore within him life itself had need to discover it. Considering only the short works of *The Human Comedy*, or the stories scattered in periodicals, one may already see that the Balzacian imagination possesses two registers very different but bound together by an almost perfect analogy. On the one hand, there are the contemplations, the autonomous visions, in which purity belongs to angels, evil to Satan and his fiends, with the events unfolding in a universe which only distantly resembles our temporal world. But on the other hand, stories more dramatic than fantastic put before our eyes simple human adventures, as in *The Red House*, for example, or in the terrible tale of *La Grande Bretèche*, which is a hallucinatory masterpiece. And yet these works, situated in a time which is absolutely "normal," far from the frontiers where the laws of the temporal ease their tyranny, are not exempt from mysterious presences, diabolic or divine. Supernatural influences, although without any of their legendary characteristics, are none the less perceptible. No Satan in person nor minor demons, but in the hearts of men insinuations of passion, lust for gold, power, criminal inclinations. No Seraphitus-Seraphita angel, but love and its luminous hopes, the mysteries of sympathetic understanding, the silent marriage of souls across distance. Above all, the terrestrial reign of suffering, failures, catastrophes. All that exists, makes sense, only in relation to a heaven and a hell, which are not specifically evoked, but which orient every destiny, torn between their contradictory appeals.

The world of Balzac's tales proposes to the reader's meditation, in dramas of prodigious intensity, a constant interrogation on the subject of human nature, or rather of the limits of the person. It is not irrelevant that everything in them is explained by magnetism, the contact of souls, the muted influence of images and colors. The big question of Balzac is always the same: where are our frontiers? What am I? To what am I exposed? On what communications with other people, on what exchanges with everything that surrounds me should I make my acts and my destiny depend? The fantastic story evokes the perceptible presences of Satan and of God, exercising their influences, intervening in our acts, guiding our destiny, and the person in it appears not as a closed being, one that could determine itself, but as one open to supernatural forces. The dramatic story, in its turn, discloses other exchanges, other intrusions: the maternal presentiment in *The Conscript* shows that a loved one leads his life outside of us and another one—or the same one—within us, so that a mother can read in her own heart what happens to her son. In *The Red House*, the criminal impulse of one of the two friends mysteriously incites the other's crime, and all the panic anxiety which reigns in this story comes from this frightening thought: we may be subject to a will that is not in ourselves but in another being.

Man then is situated at the intersection of diverse influences, and his true personality, at each instant, is constituted by the living mechanism of forces beyond his control. Balzac thus translates his own fear of being invaded, of giving way before the pressure of nature or of a world of aggressive spirits. What resistance can be made to this invasion, how can one escape the abyss of threatening madness? The stories of dreamers and seekers of the absolute give Balzac's answer to this question: man has, for his defense, the power of his intelligence, the gifts that enable him to understand and to command the friendly or enemy forces that surround him. By deciphering reality, reading its signs, one acquires the means of dominating it. To be sure Balthazar Claes and Frenhofer, by aiming their thought or their art at the discovery of a magic formula or a limitless power, condemn themselves to catastrophe. But, if the conclusion of *The Quest of the Absolute* or of *The Unknown Masterpiece* is tragic, if the painter who strives for divine perfection ends up with nothing, and if Claes cannot cry out Eureka before the hour of his death, they are none the less heroes, and their quest is a noble quest. Who is right, one may ask, Balthazar Claes, who sacrifices the happiness of his family to his philosophical strivings, or Marguerite, his wife, who defends her life inch by inch against this mad destruction? They are both right, for Balzac does not take sides; the tragic confrontation of husband and wife symbolizes a struggle which has never been resolved in Balzac's own mind, and which, in his eyes, goes on eternally in every human being. This struggle is the law of life, everyone divided between the desire for happiness and the ambition for knowledge or power, torn by contradictory wishes for temporal tranquillity and triumphs of the mind. Mind is deadly for all who follow its imperious demand, it wears life out, and turns its back on it and denies it; but one cannot, for all that, refuse the spiritual vocation for the sake of life. The paradox remains unsolvable, eternity cannot be possessed either by resignation to the modest happiness of mortals or by the heroic conquest of the intelligence. It lies on the other side of death.

Having reached this conclusion, Balzac is at the point of discovering the beauty of life, of understanding that it is a beauty of the imperfect and the unsatisfactory. From the plunge into mystery that he has taken in writing his tales, he brings back, moreover, the feeling that a person is open through and through and made up of far more things than we ordinarily know. But taught by the very experience of his fantastic vision, he will perceive that this openness and this complexity of beings—each destiny made up at the juncture of multiple influences—can be read and deciphered without explicit recourse to the supernatural. It is thus that he becomes definitively a novelist.

—*Balzac Visionnaire*, pp. 199–204.

It is then "our" experience—if it is true that the experience of poets that we adopt becomes absorbed into our personal essence . . . to help us face deep anguish—it is our experience that I hoped to find in the study that I undertook. And I have not given up either this hope or this direction to my investigation.

.   .   .   .

This book does not propose then to reduce to a clearly analyzable system the ambitions and the works of a "school" of poetry. Such a project seems to me meaningless. To devote one's effort to the definition of a historical reality, without any other goal, is a strange undertaking and perhaps a hopeless one. Although objectivity can, and doubtless must, be the law of the descriptive sciences, it cannot fruitfully be applied to the sciences of the mind. Any "disinterested" activity in that direction implies an unpardonable betrayal of oneself and of the "object" studied. A work of art and of mind *interests*, in effect, like memories and dreams, that most secret part of ourselves where, detached from our apparent individuality and turned towards our real personality, we have but one concern: making ourselves ready for warnings, for signs, and for experiencing the amazement we feel when we contemplate for an instant the human condition in all its strangeness, with its risks, all its anxiety, its beauty, and its disillusioning limitations.

.   .   .   .

To write history, the same search that the individual makes to find his own melody must be undertaken for humanity. That is why a historical work, and particularly an essay on spiritual history, forbids an author to abstract himself. Of course he is not at liberty to ignore the truth of facts or to manipulate them as he pleases. But honesty of documentation is an insufficient virtue, merely the preliminary condition for a study which one would like to sense is a personal and vital interrogation.

.   .   .   .

What was this German romanticism to which I was drawn by so many seductive appeals? If I wanted to grasp its spiritual meaning, pin down what it has to say to men of our times, I should have to turn from reading works to studying them, drawing lines of demarcation, hunting for features common to all romantic faces. For a long time I went from disappointment to disappointment. I had begun with the innumerable works in which German criticism has, for some years, been desperately trying to arrive at a formula for romanticism. There are many profound, vital, perspicacious views and analyses in these books. But the over-all synthesis that would absolutely define the romantic spirit seems to elude all the attempts.

.   .   .   .

The impossibility of classifying decided me: I would choose instinctively *my* romantics.

.   .   .   .

It is by these romantic principles that I have attempted to guide my research, convinced as I am, with my poets and philosophers, that one knows only what one carries within one, and that one can speak of romanticism only romantically. The failure of too many critics eager to judge the contemporaries of Goethe from a Goethean point of view, should have sufficed, moreover, to put me on guard against any method other than that of kindred feeling.

—*L'Ame romantique et le Rêve*, Introduction, pp. xvi–xxii.

MAURICE BLANCHOT

That we should think of Joubert as a writer near to us, nearer than the great literary names whose contemporary he was, is not due only to the obscurity (an obscurity that was, moreover, distinguished) in which he lived, died, then survived. Being in one's lifetime a name without brilliance does not, as Stendhal hoped, suffice to shine brightly one or two centuries later. It is not even sufficient for a great work to be great and to develop in a dark corner for posterity, one day in grateful recognition, to set it in full daylight. It may be that humanity one day will know everything—beings, truths, and worlds—but there will always be some work of art (perhaps even all art) to fall outside this universal knowledge. That is the privilege of artistic activity: what it produces, even a god often is unaware of.

It is true, notwithstanding, that many works are prematurely exhausted from being too much admired. The great blaze of glory that writers and artists in their old age enjoy, burns up within them a substance in which their work will henceforth be lacking. Young Valéry used to seek in every illustrious book the error that caused it to be known: an aristocratic judgment. But one often feels that death will finally bring silence and calm to the work left to itself. During his lifetime, even the most detached and negligent of writers fights for his books. He is alive, that suffices; he stands behind them with the life he has left and of which he makes them a present. But his death, even if it passes unnoticed, shuts the door and locks up the meaning. How can it, being all alone, expand or contract, disintegrate or develop, realize itself or fail? Yet will it ever be alone? Even those who seem to have deserved it by the gift of great discretion which they possess, are not always rewarded by being forgotten.

Joubert possessed this gift. He never wrote a book. He only got ready to write one, resolutely seeking the right conditions for writing one. Then he forgot even his intention. More exactly, what he was looking for, the source of writing, the space to write it, the light to encircle in space, demanded of him, brought out in him, dispositions which made him unfit for an ordinary literary work or caused him to turn away from it. All this made of him one of the first really modern writers, preferring the center to the sphere, sacrificing the results to the discovery of what might bring them about, and not writing to add one book to another but to capture the site whence all books seemed to originate and which, once found, would make it unnecessary for him to write any.

—Le Livre à venir, pp. 63–64.

Let us admit that literature begins just when literature becomes a question. . . . The question that it asks does not concern, properly speaking, its value or its right. If it is difficult to discover the meaning of this question, it is because the question tends to put art itself on trial, its powers and its objectives. That literature rises out of its own ruins is a commonplace paradox for us. But we must still find out whether this doubt about art itself—which has constituted the most illustrious aspect of art for the last thirty years—does not imply a shifting, a relocation, of a force at work deep within artistic creations and loath to come out in the open, a work originally quite distinct from any depreciation of literary activity or of the literary Thing.

Let us note that literature, as self-negation, has never meant the mere denunciation of art or of the artist as a mystification or fraud. To be sure literature may not be legitimate, may be something of an imposture. But some have discovered more: literature is not only illegitimate but nonexistent, and this nonexistence perhaps constitutes an enormous, marvelous strength on condition that it be isolated, reduced to a pure state. One of the tasks that surrealism pursued was to turn literature into the exposure of its empty inside, to open it up completely to the part of it that is nothing, to make it realize its own unrealness; so that, although it is exact to recognize that surrealism was a powerful negative movement, it is no less true to see in it a great creative ambition, for when literature coincides for a moment with nothing and immediately it is all, then the all begins to exist: how wonderful!

We are not trying to mistreat literature; we are trying to understand it and see why it can be understood only by depreciating it. It has been noted with surprise that the question: "What is literature?" has never received other than trivial replies. But here is something even stranger: in the form of such a

question something appears that takes away from it all seriousness. It is possible to ask: what is poetry? what is art? or even:
what is a novel? and it has been done. But literature, which is
poem and novel, seems to be the element of emptiness—present
in all that is grave yet upon which reflection, with its own
gravity, cannot operate without losing its seriousness. If imposing
reflection approaches literature, literature becomes a caustic
force, capable of destroying in itself and in reflection whatever
might be imposing. If reflection moves away, then literature
becomes, in effect, something important, essential—more important than philosophy, religion, and the life of the world that
it embraces. But if reflection, astonished by this dominion,
considers this power and asks it what it is, it is penetrated immediately by a corrosive and volatile element and can only
scorn a thing so vain, so vague, and so impure, and in this scorn
and this vanity be consumed in its turn, as was so well shown
in the story of Monsieur Teste.

One would be wrong in making the powerful contemporary
negative movements responsible for this volatile and volatizing
force which literature seems to have become. About 150 years
ago a man who held art in as high esteem as one can imagine—
since he saw how art can become religion and religion art—this
man (called Hegel) described all the ways by which one who
chooses to be a man of letters condemns himself to belong to the
"animal kingdom of the mind." From the first step he takes,
Hegel says, a person who wishes to write is stopped by a contradiction: to write one must have the gift of writing. But, in itself,
the gift is nothing. So long as he has not sat down and written a
work, a writer is not a writer, and he has no idea whether he has
the capacity of becoming one. One has talent only after having
written, but it is necessary to have it in order to write.

—*La Part du Feu*, pp. 305–307.

Thus we arrive at the idea that criticism is in itself almost
without reality. . . . One must hasten to add that such a depre-
ciatory view does not shock criticism but rather is welcomed,
received with a curious humility, as if this manner of being
nothing was its most profound truth. When Heidegger makes his
comments on Hölderlin's poems, he says (I am quoting approxi-
mately): whatever the commentary can do in regard to the

poem, it must always consider itself superfluous; and the last step of the interpretation, the most difficult, is the one that causes it to vanish before the pure affirmation of the poem. Heidegger uses this figure: in the noisy tumult of nonpoetic language, poems are like a bell suspended in free air, which vibrates if the lightest snow falls upon it—so light as not even to be felt, yet capable of setting it in harmonious motion. Perhaps a commentary is only a little snow causing the bell to vibrate.

. . . .

Why, between the reader and the work, between the story and the work, should come this ugly hybrid of reading and writing, this man who, although a specialist of reading, can read only while writing, writes only about what he reads, and must at the same time, while reading and writing, give the impression that he is doing nothing, nothing but letting the depth of the work speak . . . ?

. . . .

Let us accept for a moment Heidegger's delicate image: this snow which causes the bell to vibrate, this white motion, impalpable and rather cold, which disappears in the warm movement that it sets going. Here critical discourse, lacking duration and reality, desires to vanish before creative affirmation: it never does the speaking when it speaks; it is nothing; remarkable modesty; but perhaps not so modest. It is nothing, but this nothing is precisely what permits the silent, the invisible work be what it is: word and light, affirmation and presence, speaking as if by itself, without alteration, in this first quality emptiness which critical intervention has the mission to produce. Critical discourse is that sound chamber in which, for a moment, is transformed and encircled into speech, the dumb, indefinite reality of the work. And so, by modestly and obstinately claiming to be nothing, it makes itself out to be—not distinguishing itself from the other—creative speech, of which it is like the necessary realization or, metaphorically speaking, the epiphany.

—*Arguments*, Jan.–March, 1959, pp. 34–36.

ROBERT CHAMPIGNY

However, from the beginning, Meursault may seem a stranger to one person: the reader of the book. The study that I have undertaken concerns Meursault and treats the book entitled *The Stranger* only as a document, the only document that I possess on Meursault. In other words, instead of considering Meursault as a character in a novel, I place myself within the fiction according to which the story was written by Meursault. What does Meursault tell about himself that may make him appear as a stranger?

What I have said so far is founded on a reading of the book. Now, it has seemed to me that, in the first part, Meursault does not feel himself in any way a stranger and the other characters do not consider him a stranger. Under these conditions, how could he appear a stranger to the reader? I do not of course mean to say that Meursault will necessarily appear to the reader a stranger: various readers will react variously, the same reader may vary his reaction. But I can at least say that Meursault *may*, from the beginning, appear a stranger to the reader, although he does not seem a stranger either to himself or to the others.

—*Sur un héros païen*, pp. 24–25.

Throughout his story, Meursault will thus appear careful not to say what he does not know—even concerning details that may seem to us negligible. For it is not negligible for him to mark the limits of what he knows. As for stating facts themselves, he tries to be as complete as possible. But when he does not remember, he says so—he does not invent. Likewise he says so, when he does not understand. . . .

There is an expression that turns up frequently in Meursault's story that demonstrates how extremely careful he is to be precise. It is the expression "in a sense," a common enough expression but one which Meursault takes out of the ordinary by using it at rather unexpected moments. Here are some examples: "He noticed that time passed quickly and, in a sense, this was true. . . . In a sense, that upset me. But, in another, it killed time . . . In a sense, it was an advantage . . . In a sense, it interested me to see a trial. . . . Consequently, what was vexing was that the condemned man should have to hope that the apparatus was in good working order. This, I thought, was a flaw in the system. In a sense, this is true. But in another sense, I had to admit that it proved the efficiency of the system. In sum: the condemned man was obliged to collaborate morally . . ."

—*Ibid.*, pp. 81–82.

When it is a question of treating subjects such as the one here, one may do three things: rationalize one's taste, rationalize other people's taste, or just rationalize. My taste, rather than other people's, may furnish a base for the essay I am writing: for I know other people's only very partially and doubtfully—by hearsay. That does not mean that all my tastes, whatever they may be, are to be justified at any cost: rationality excludes rationalistic excessiveness. All I should like to do is pin down the coherence I feel among certain of my tastes. The correct explanation of this coherence is what guides and may justify this essay. Therefore, just as it opposes the excesses of rationalism, my method opposes, not impressions but impressionism, whether it presents itself as "subjective" (personal) or "objective" (collective).

In literary criticism, to presume to be "objective," apparently one must abstain from judging (from criticizing), or pretend to abstain, or else make the judgment so vague as to echo the average of all previously formulated judgments. Now, if the language of an essay on poetry is somehow to resemble that of a scientific treatise, it will not be by its "objectivity," by its search for universality, but by its coherence. Search for universality, in an essay like this one, would not make its language scientific prose but political oratory; it would be running with the hare and hunting with the hounds. In science, universality and coherence go together; in a critical essay such as this, they are incompatible.

—*Le Genre poétique*, pp. 26–27.

MANUEL DE DIÉGUEZ

But the work of Rabelais, like any great work, is a town constructed by one man alone, a town that is worn down day by day by the step of this man, who could not otherwise find *guide de Dieu et compaignie*. If we ask whence come these stones or how to pry some loose to construct or reconstruct our own cities, we are simply barbarians. In order to understand with whom and about what this man is speaking through the stones, we must not read the inscriptions on the façades, we must scrutinize the extraordinary action itself of one who retires into the desert to tear his town out of silence. Present-day Rabelais criticism would interrogate the spiritual mystery that is called art and which lends voices to an immense night. In such a way the most inner Rabelais may appear, the Rabelais who questions, and whose work opens out upon a solitude, the Rabelais who fights step by step to anchor his order (the true one, the imaginary) in the chaos of the other city; the Rabelais who, carried away by his myth, clings to it, wears himself out on it, destroys himself by it.
—*Rabelais par lui-même*, pp. 130–131.

But in the *Prologue* [to the *Tiers Livre*] we clearly see that Rabelais has given away his secret as a writer, the form of his defiance to the world through style: a sort of marvelous rivalry of words with the entire universe. One feels that Rabelais makes his reply to silence, outside of any philosophical system, as a great writer, that is, by a certain writing modeled upon his deepest behavior, which is to take up the challenge of matter, to oppose it with an equal mass, to substitute the verb for all flesh. This *Prologue* has a thickness and a time quality that are gripping— the real has been drowned in a verbal torrent. But, as with Balzac, flesh is made verb through a spiritual insurrection: the words do not rival the lethargy of the world and its grayness, as with Flaubert, but rather represent a victory over the lethargy of matter. There is a Rabelaisian breath, without which the mass of words would not destroy anguish and would not equal creation.
—*Ibid.*, p. 85.

Chateaubriand and Bossuet betray the same obsession of the abyss, of immensity, of silence. But Pascal alone maintains pure vertigo. What would an existential psychoanalysis of Pascal's style yield? We can only sketch one here.

"I do not know who brought me into the world, or what the world is, or what I am. I am in terrible ignorance of all things: I do not know what my body is, my senses, my soul and that part of me that thinks what I say, that reflects upon everything and upon itself, and knows itself no better than the rest. I see the terrifying spaces of the universe that enclose me, and I find myself fixed in a spot of this vast expanse without knowing why I am placed here rather than elsewhere, or why this little time that is given me to live is assigned to me at this moment rather than at another of all the eternity that has preceded me and that will follow me. Everywhere I see only infinities, which enclose me like an atom and like a shadow that remains only an instant never to return. All I know is that soon I am to die; but what I know least about is this death that I cannot escape."

This panting fusion of logic with vertigo, this respiration of a mind as if exhausted yet capable always of holding out until the finish line, this style as if armed with a last breath and which murmurs, in haste, irrevocable statements—all this is not "pure melody." In connection with Sartre, we have seen that Pascal's primordial intuition of nothingness, his vision of man as a stranger in the world, his modern look at the vanity of scientific knowledge and at death, his liberty tied to anguish, make of him the most existentialist of great writers; yet it so happens that this existentialist completely escapes an existentialist psychoanalysis of style according to the method of Sartre. Why? Because for Sartre man is meaningful, whereas Pascal's approach aims at pulverizing human meanings, reducing them to a tragic absurdity by a simple look which organizes terror. And that is why Pascal cannot be grasped except by a psychoanalysis of the simple look—this look is the heart of things, blasting, destroying, terrorizing, by means of the most irrefutable logic. At times, glory inhabits this astonished brain; then pride overcomes the dismay at seeing itself thus, flung among things. But almost always this mind beyond the world comes looking for indications, traces, or vestiges of its inexplicable adventure, and some hope for a destiny that may escape the absurd. No one ever stopped like that on the path to the abyss, with this distracted and all-powerful look, nourished by a vertigo straight from the physical world, with this murmur so terribly firm, and in this dying rhythm that destroys the flesh through reason alone: so that the verb is born miraculously from the flesh that it effaces immediately.

Now such an enterprise of language will not tolerate organizing the world by means of the word—filling the emptiness into which we are cast by the splendors and the finery of Chateaubriand—or even filling it with the vaulted phrase of great cosmic oratory, Bossuet's. Hence this constantly broken rhythm, this breath on the point of going out yet prolonged beyond breath. The pure emptiness must be maintained—and the anguish of this emptiness—by a sentence which cannot be enclosed in any structure and which remains forever pure suspense. "True eloquence cares little . . ." For all eloquence, by the very fact that it proposes an architecture of the sentence, escapes nothingness and models the universe on a form that stands for some answer. Any order fills up the emptiness. But a style of pure terror and pure statement refuses all modes of organization of the verb—therefore of being—which would throw over the emptiness some veil or some armor, some panoply, some disdainful laconism, some minute network of equivalences.

Pascal feels for all *procedures* a horror that goes beyond scorn of rhetoric: he is well aware that a *procedure* is an ontological alibi, and that a tissue of *procedures* suffices to blind man by filling up the abysses.

—*L'Ecrivain et son langage*, pp. 304–307.

MICHEL FOUCAULT

Reduced to this self-destruction, which is as well the chance of its birth, the problematic and necessary language of Roussel cuts a strange figure: like all literary language, it is a violent destruction of everyday clichés, but it holds the emblematic pose of this murder indefinitely; like everyday language, it keeps on repeating but not for the purpose of collecting and continuing; it keeps what it repeats in the abolition of a silence that projects a necessarily inaudible echo. Roussel's language, right off, opens up to triteness, which it welcomes in the most disorganized form of chance: not in order to say better what has been already said but to subject the form to a second explosive destruction and, from these inert and shapeless scattered pieces, create, by leaving them in place, the most extraordinary meanings. Far from being a language seeking to begin, it is the second shape of words already spoken: it is the language of always, eroded by destruction and death. That is why its refusal to be original is essential. It does not seek to discover, but, beyond death, rediscover the very language it has just massacred, rediscover it identical and entire. It is repetitious by nature. Speaking, for the first time, of objects never seen, of machines never conceived, of monstrous plants, cripples that Goya would never have dreamed of, of crucified medusas, of glaucous-blooded adolescents, this language carefully hides the fact that it says only what has been said. Or rather, it has revealed it at the last moment in the posthumous declaration, thus opening up, by a voluntary death, an inner dimension to language which is that of the suicide of language and of its resurrection from the pulverized splendors of its corpse. It is this sudden emptiness of death in the language of always, and immediately the birth of stars, which define the distance of poetry.

—*Raymond Roussel,* pp. 61–62.

If language were as rich as real being, it would be the useless and mute copy of things; it would not exist. And yet without a name to name them, things would remain in the night. Roussel felt this illuminating lacuna of language to the point of anguish, of obsession, if you wish . . .

—*Ibid.*, p. 208.

FRANÇOIS GERMAIN

Logically connected by a dialectic of compensation, Paradise and Hell, in the domain of images, constitute an organic whole, which is, strictly speaking, the universe of Vigny. We arrive thus at a global structure, very simple, that of the circle and sometimes that of the sphere. At the end of the eighteenth century, the word circle was a favorite of fashion. It designated not only a social gathering, but a domain, an environment, a field of activity—and in a sense that can be very abstract. This extension of meaning, at a time when literature was fond of describing, naturally favored the appearance of circular pictures. "In the east, spring flowers; in the south, autumn fruits; in the north, the ice of winter" (Rousseau, *N.H.*, t.I, p. 52). "An immense horizon spread around us in a circle," writes Chateaubriand. "One could see, to the East, the summits of Horeb and Sinai, the desert of Sur and the Dead Sea; to the South the mountain chains of Thebaid; to the North the sterile plains where Pharaoh pursued the Hebrews; and to the West, beyond the sands where I had lost my way, the fruitful valley of Egypt" (*Martyrs*, t.II, p. 19). To be sure Mme de Staël does not describe many landscapes, but in the society pictures that she creates, the main character—Delphine in her drawing room, Corinne on the Capitoline Hill or on Cape Misena—is always in the center of a circle of admirers (*Delphine*, t.I, p. 195; *Corinne*, t.I, p. 93; t.II, p. 137, 164, 228), and this arrangement is not only picturesque: "I felt myself outside life's order: on the edge of the circle of existence; but, having returned to morality, I am in the center of life; and, far from being agitated by universal movement, I see it turn about me" (*Delphine*, t.III, p. 122). Vigny was greatly inspired by these models, but he goes farther than they. In their geometrical nudity, the circle and the sphere ultimately stand for the work of art and the genius that creates it.

—*L'Imagination d'Alfred de Vigny*, pp. 226–227.

RENÉ GIRARD

The masochist is at once more lucid and more blind than other victims of metaphysical desire. He is more lucid in that he possesses that lucidity, increasingly prevalent in our time, which permits him alone among all desiring subjects to perceive the connection between internal mediation and the obstacle; he is more blind because, instead of following out the implications of this awareness to their necessary conclusion, instead of giving up misdirected transcendency, he tries paradoxically to satisfy his desire by rushing toward the obstacle, thus making his destiny one of misery and failure.

The source of this ill-starred lucidity which characterizes the last stages of ontological sickness is not difficult to discover. It is the increased proximity of the mediator. Enslavement is always the final result of desire, but at first it is very distant and the desiring subject cannot perceive it. The eventual result becomes increasingly clear as the distance between mediator and subject decreases and the phases of the metaphysical process are accelerated. Every metaphysical desire thus tends toward masochism, because the mediator is always growing nearer and the enlightenment which he brings with him is incapable, by itself, of curing ontological sickness; this insight only provides the victim with the means of hastening the fatal evolution. Every metaphysical desire proceeds toward its own truth and toward the desiring subject's awareness of this truth; masochism occurs when the subject himself enters into the light of this truth and eagerly collaborates in its advent.

.   .   .   .

Masochism clearly reveals the contradiction which forms the basis of metaphysical desire. The impassioned person is seeking the divine through this insuperable obstacle, through that which, by definition, cannot be crossed. It is this metaphysical meaning which has escaped most psychologists and psychiatrists. Often the subject is said simply to desire shame, humiliation, and suffering. No one has ever desired any such thing. Every victim of metaphysical desire, including the masochist, covets his mediator's divinity, and for this divinity he will accept if necessary—and it is always necessary—or even seek out, shame, humiliation, and suffering. The masochist cannot be understood unless we recognize the triangular nature of his desire. The conception has always been of a linear desire and, starting from the subject, the sempiternal straight line is traced; and this line always runs into the familiar disappointments. These in turn are thought to be the *object* of his desire; it is asserted in short that the masochist desires what *we* would never desire.

—*Deceit, Desire, and the Novel*, pp. 179–182.

LUCIEN GOLDMANN

The solitude of the tragic hero, the abyss that separates him both from the world and from God, has posed for Racinian tragedy another problem of composition, that of the *chorus*. Racine, like all modern tragic writers probably, has continually been preoccupied by it. He has always sought for a way of introducing, in the manner of the tragic authors of antiquity, a chorus in the plays that he wrote. But the problem was and remains unsolvable. The chorus has a precise significance. It is *the voice of the human community* and, for that very reason, the voice of the gods. Greek tragedy told the destiny of a hero who, in a homogeneous universe regulated by the agreement of the community and the divinity, having violated the traditional order of things by his "hubris" and having separated himself from the one and irritated the other, had brought down upon his head the anger and the vengeance of the gods.

On the contrary, in Racinian tragedy—and in all great modern tragedy—the authentic community of men disappeared so long ago that no memory of it remains. The world, which is no longer bound to the hero, is a jungle of rapacious egoisms and unconscious victims—it is the world of which Pascal said that it crushed man, but a man greater than it because man knows that he is being crushed whereas the world does not. That is why he could never again be the terrified or even impassive witness of events.

—*Jean Racine, dramaturge*, pp. 27–28.

Rationalism continued to grow and develop in this way in France until the twentieth century, but in the seventeenth it stood at a turning-point. It had then, thanks to the work of Descartes and Galileo, found a philosophical system and a system of mathematical physics which were unmistakably superior to the old Aristotelian framework. It was against this background that, in connection with other factors, the Jansenist attitude which found its most coherent expression in the great tragic works of Pascal and Racine was developed.

The nature of the tragic mind in seventeenth-century France can be characterized by two factors: the complete and exact understanding of the new world created by rationalistic individualism, together with all the invaluable and scientifically valid acquisitions which this offered to the human intellect; and, at the same time, the complete refusal to accept this world as the only one in which man could live, move and have his being.

Reason is an important factor in human life, one of which man is justly proud and which he will never be able to give up; however, it by no means constitutes the whole man, and it should not and cannot be taken as a sufficient guide to human life. This is true on every plane, even on that of scientific research, where reason seems so pre-eminently at home. This is why, after the amoral and a-religious period of rationalism and empiricism, the tragic vision represents a return to morality and religion, of religion in the wider meaning of faith in a set of values which transcend the individual. However, the tragic vision never actually reaches the stage of offering either a set of ideas or an art which are capable, by offering a new community and a new universe, of taking the place of the atomistic and mechanistic universe set up by individual reason and, from this point of view, it must be considered as essentially a transitional phase. It accepts that the world of rationalist and empirical thought is definite and unchangeable—although it perceives the ambiguity and confusion which lie behind its apparent clarity—and can offer as a challenge to it only a new set of demands and a new scale of values.

—*The Hidden God*, pp. 33–34.

In studying the works of Malraux, one is struck by the fact that between his first writings: *Fantastic Kingdoms, Paper Moons, The Temptation of the West*, which announce the death of the Gods and the universal decomposition of values, and the following writings: *The Conquerors, The Royal Way, Man's Fate*, there is not only a difference in content but a difference in form. Although in both cases the works are fiction, only the second ones create a realistic universe in which the characters—in spite of being imaginary—are individual and living, and for that reason possess a novel-like quality, whereas the first ones are either . . . essays . . . or fantastic and allegorical stories.

If we assert, moreover, that all the subsequent novels of Malraux will create universes governed by positive and universal values and that the first work indicating a new crisis, *The Duel with the Angel,* will be at once the last and the least novel-like, the most intellectual of Malraux's works of fiction, we may be able to formulate a first hypothesis: *In these works dominated by the crisis of values which characterized western Europe at the time they were being written, the really novel-like part corresponds to the period when the writer believed himself capable, towards and against everything, of protecting certain authentic universal values.*

—*Pour une sociologie du roman,* pp. 41–42.

Now the problem of a sociology of the novel has always preoccupied the sociologists of literature without, up to now, inspiring them to take a decisive step in the path of its elucidation. Since the novel was at bottom a biography and social chronicle during all the first part of its history, it has always been possible to show how a social chronicle reflected more or less the society of the period—an assertion that one truly need not be a sociologist to make.

Then again, the transformation of the novel since Kafka has been related to the Marxist analyses of reification. Here too one must say that serious sociologists ought to have seen a problem rather than an explanation. If it is evident that the absurd world of Kafka, of *The Stranger* by Camus, or the world of relatively autonomous objects of Robbe-Grillet correspond to the analysis of reification such as it has been developed by Marx and subsequent Marxists, the problem arises as to why, although this analysis was worked out in the second half of the nineteenth century and it concerned a phenomenon of an even earlier date, this same phenomenon does not appear in the novel until after World War I.

In brief, all these analyses had to do with the relationship of certain elements of the *content* of fiction with a social reality that they reflected almost without transposing or by means of a more or less transparent transposition.

Now the very first problem which a sociology of the novel should have attacked is that of the relationship between the *form of fiction* and the *structure* of a social milieu within which it has developed—that is to say, of the novel as a literary genre and of the modern individualistic society.

It seems to us today that by bringing together the analyses of Lukàcs and Girard—although neither is the result of specifically sociological preoccupations—we can accomplish, if not a complete elucidation of this problem, at least a decisive step towards its elucidation.

—*Ibid.*, pp. 22–23.

Unfortunately, as genetic structuralism, psychoanalysis—at least as Freud developed it—is not sufficiently consistent and is far too tainted by the scientism that dominated the university at the end of the nineteenth century and the beginning of the twentieth. This is brought out on two important points.

In the first place, the future dimension is completely lacking in Freudian explanations. Influenced by the determinism of his time, Freud entirely neglects the positive forces of counterbalance that operate in all human structure whether individual or collective; he seeks all his answers in the experiences of childhood, in the forces instinctively repressed or suppressed, while entirely neglecting the positive function that consciousness and the relation to reality could have.

In the second place, for Freud a person is an absolute subject, for whom others can be only *objects* of satisfaction or frustration; this fact explains perhaps the absence of future that we have spoken of.

Doubtless it would be false to reduce the Freudian libido to the sexual domain; it is nevertheless true that it is always *individual* and that, in the Freudian vision of humanity, there is no place for the collective subject and the satisfaction that a collective action can bring to the individual.

. . . .

The integration of works into the individual biography can, in effect, only reveal their individual meaning and their relation to the biographical and psychological problems of the author. This means that research of this type, however valid and scientifically exact, places the work outside its cultural and esthetic context, on the same level as all the individual symptoms of such and such a patient cared for by the psychoanalyst.

—*Ibid.*, pp. 225–227.

CHARLES MAURON

Will the experiment we have made with texts of Mallarmé give comparable results if we superimpose texts of a different poet? For example, Baudelaire. I will begin with some prose poems.

The first is *A Hemisphere in Tresses*.[1] It swarms with Baudelairian themes: invitations to voyages, fine ship, idleness and perfume of warm countries, etc. Neither its external sources nor its meaning permit the slightest doubt. Let us begin from the last sentence of this text:

"Let me bite slowly thy heavy black tresses. When I nibble at thine elastic and rebellious tresses, it seems to me that I eat memories."

Our analyses of Baudelaire and Mallarmé thus have comparable points of departure. But they will immediately separate. In the text of the prose poem, the adjective "heavy" applied to a woman's hair most certainly constitutes a Baudelairian leitmotif: "Slowly and forever! My hand in thine heavy mane . . ."* (*The Tresses*) ". . . her tresses which hung down her back, heavy as horsehair . . ." (*The Vocations*) We shall not be astonished to find in another prose poem, *The Fair Dorothy*, obviously linked in subject to the preceding, the following sentence: ". . . The weight of her enormous blue-black tresses draws backward her delicate head . . ."* The heaviness has become intensified: it pulls the head back. However, we are not justified in seeing here anything but a charming detail to indicate a girl's beauty. Still this text evokes another, not less familiar although quite different. I am thinking of the letter addressed by Baudelaire to Asselineau on March 13, 1856, in which the poet tells his friend one of his dreams. Here is the story: the poet sees a monster perched on a pedestal, apparently bored to death. The fantastic monster must, to a certain extent, represent the dreamer himself, since Baudelaire admits having awakened in the posture he attributed to the monster. Now the latter has, wound around his body, an appendage that begins at his head: ". . . something elastic, like rubber, and so long, so long that, if

[1] The quotations from Baudelaire are generally from the Arthur Symons translation (The Casanova Society, 1925). An asterisk indicates that the translation is my own.

he wound it on his head like a hairpiece, it would be much too heavy, and absolutely impossible to carry." Here we have both the too weighty chignon that pulls the head back (*The Fair Dorothy*) and the elastic heaviness of Jeanne Duval's tresses (*A Hemisphere in Tresses*).

Meanwhile the dream explains further what troubles the monster has with his tail: ". . . If he let it drag on the ground, it would pull his head over backwards" . . . in the evening, ". . . he is obliged . . . to stagger, with his rubber appendage, as far as the supper room . . ." Does not this comic and pitiful gait, encumbered by something dragging on the ground, evoke in its turn a famous poem from *The Flowers of Evil: The Albatross?*

> They lay them on the deck; and instantly
> Cumbrous and shamed, the empyrean's kings
> Let trail along their sides distressfully,
> Like oars, their once magnificent white wings.[2]

Shall we hesitate before this comparison? By its very subject, *The Albatross* is linked to the themes of the ship, the voyage, therefore the hair. The albatross represents the poet:

> Prince of the clouds, the Poet is like you.

But we have seen that the monster, in a grotesque oneiric transformation, represented him also (terribly bored, immobilized on his pedestal, ridiculous when he walks while men circulate around him). Moreover, in *The Flowers of Evil*, we will slip without any trouble from the Albatross to the Swan, and from the Swan to the Girl from Malabar, which brings us immediately back to the fair Dorothy of the Prose Poems. By its total coherence, the network of associations thus sketched reinforces the probability of each connection. From the fair Dorothy, passing by the dream of the monster (and incidentally the Albatross), we are then led to another prose poem: *To Everyone his Chimera*, where we find the same step, made heavier and heavier.

> All of them carried on their backs an enormous Chimera, as heavy as a sack of corn or of coals, as heavy as the accoutrement of a Roman foot-soldier.

[2] Translation by Lord Derwent. *Flowers of Evil* (London: Fanfare Press, 1940).

But the monstrous Beast . . . enveloped and oppressed its men with its elastic and powerful muscles; it hooked itself with its two vast claws to the man's breast; its fabulous head surmounted the man's forehead, like one of those terrible helmets by which the ancient warriors terrified their enemies.

The helmet recalls the hair (Mallarmé, in one of our three poems, had picked up the metaphor, and Valéry will pick it up in his turn). But the Chimera, weighing down upon the nape and the back, girdling the torso, is compared also to a docker's load (sack of coals, soldier's knapsack). She is none the less the Chimera, the Dream, demand rather than invitation to voyage, towards death, across the boredom of a terrain that resembles a wasteland. From these sad wanderers harassed by their burden which looks like some fantastic headgear, we pass easily to the figure of *The Evil Glazier*. Bent under a load fastened like a soldier's knapsack and ordinarily rising above his head, he wanders through the poor districts, gets stuck in the stairs he is made to climb, and falls beneath his load of panes that should be magically colored to make life look rosy:

. . . "What! You have no coloured glasses? Red, blue magical glasses, glasses worthy of Paradise? Impudent that you are! How dare you wander about in poor quarters, how dare you think of not having glasses that make one's life worth living?" And I pushed him violently in the direction of the staircase, where he stumbled, grumbling.

I went over to the balcony and I took up a little flowerpot, and when I saw the man just outside the door that gave on the pavement, I let fall perpendicularly my war engine on the outer edge of his hooks, and the shock making him fall backward he somehow managed to break under the poor back what remained to him of his itinerant fortune, which was shattered into tiny bits as if it were by a flash of lightning.

Thus pulled backward, the bearer of false chimeras falls.

The impeded gait is succeeded by the fall. And if we would appreciate the cruel meaning of this catastrophe (which, we suspect, rather than to a glazier happens to the poet, for whom the glazier—like the albatross—is the image) we must slip from this prose poem to another: *A Heroic Death*.

The Evil Glazier and *A Heroic Death* can be superimposed
exactly. The two poems describe the growing tension, then the
abrupt discharge of a perverse aggressive impulse. With a hiss,
the Prince causes the actor to tumble, as the poet does to the
glazier. The two aggressive characters coincide. They are artists,
bored and perverse—one of the images Baudelaire had of himself
and towards which he affected the attitude of a doctor, a moralist, and a theologian. The two aggressions present the same
characteristics: cruelty, unexpected violence, calculated execu-
tion, well-aimed shot, laughter. The two victims are broken by
life, forced to dispense a chimerical beauty, and falling under the
burden—evidently another image that Baudelaire had of himself.
A preconscious thought links up this series of images: Fancioulle—the evil glazier—the monster of the dream—the albatross—the swan—Andromache—the girl from Malabar—the fair
Dorothy. Many other figures could be added to this list. But we
sense enough already that the network exists and that it deeply
concerns Baudelaire's personality. What was closest to his
heart—his fate as a poet—is involved. I shall cite just two more
poems.

In *The Madman and the Venus*, we find an infantile image of
the buffoon that stands somewhere between Fancioulle and the
monster of the dream:

> . . . At the feet of a colossal Venus, one of these absurd
> fools, one of these obstinate clowns, whose chief business
> is to make Kings laugh when Remorse and Ennui obsess
> them, made more hideous by a ridiculous and bizarre cos-
> tume, wearing a fool's cap and bells, huddled against the
> pedestal, lifts his weeping eyes towards the immortal God-
> dess.

This enormous, implacable Venus, with mind far away, beyond reach, recalls both *The Giantess* and *Beauty*:

> I had loved to live near a young Giantess of Necromancy,
> Like a voluptuous cat before the knees of a Queen . . .
> To wander over her huge forms—nature deforms us—
> And to crawl over the slopes of her knees enormous . . .

and:

> I am beautiful as a dream of stone, but not maternal;
>
> .   .   .   .

The poets, before the strange attitudes of my gloom,
That I assume in my moods of alienation,
In austere studies all their days and nights consume . . .

By analogy (as in a dream), adult humiliations and embarrass-
ments certainly call up again infantile situations. But especially,
the Chimera has become too weighty, cold, and petrified. The
poet feels the overwhelming scorn of his own esthetic conscience.
The Chimera has detached herself from him and has united
herself to the Prince to show him a coldness as cruel as the
atmosphere is ardent. "Everyone knows love, seems to say the
Fool, monster or poet, except me, no longer on my pedestal."

This despondency is different from falling, as boredom is
different from an acute attack of depression. But their consequence is a feeling of ill-luck:

To lift a load so heavy and crazy
One must have your courage, Sisyphus!
If the heart of Tantalus is lazy,
Art's long, Time's short, for Tantalus.

And we are now in the dark regions of Baudelairian spleen:

Far from graves where vermin are feeding
On bodies in miasmic marshes,
My heart, my passionate heart is bleeding,
The very sense within me parches.

Under the effect of depression, the weight of hair, then of the
Chimera, becomes that of destiny and, finally, of the tomb.
—*Des Métaphores obsédantes au Mythe personnel,* pp. 58–63.

GEORGES POULET

The silence was everywhere; a sweetness seemed to emanate from the trees; she felt her heart begin beating again, and the blood circulate in her body like a stream of milk. Then she heard afar off, beyond the woods, over the hills, a faint and prolonged cry, a protracted voice, and she listened silently to its mingling, like a strain of music, with the last vibrations of her stirred nerves.

It is as if time, like a passing breeze, could be felt in the renewed beatings of the heart, in the blood that flows like a stream of milk. It is no longer the bitter consciousness of an interval, there is no more interval; there is only a gliding motion which carries away simultaneously the things and the sentient mind with the sense of an absolute homogeneity between the different elements that compose the moment. The mind, the body, nature, and life, all participate in the same moment of the same becoming.

—*Studies in Human Time*, p. 251.

There are, for Flaubert, other grand days in the sun when the mind is not open to the present sun, but to the "golden haze" still emanating from suns which have set long ago. There is for him a present that is the terminal place of recollected images as well as a present that is the terminal place of sensorial images.

—*Ibid.*, p. 252.

All distance is now abolished, as in the rarest and most perfect sensuous union. The reviviscence is, like pantheistic ecstasy, a pure viviscence. It has the same intensity, the same richness, it ends in the same synthesis of the object and the self.

—*Ibid.*, p. 252.

So then the descending movement of Flaubert's thought takes on the aspect of a prospective representation of life which, through a series of states, is brought out of the past up to the present and ends there by giving it the significance of being an effect that is the consequence of all the vast perceptible genetic travail in space and duration—a perspective similar to that which one has when, on the shore, one lifts his eyes slowly to the open sea in order to follow from out there the course of a wave that draws nearer and nearer, and finally perishes at one's feet—an experience that one also has when in writing, say, a periodic sentence (the periodic sentence of Flaubert), one finds that from the protasis to the apodosis the different elements are composed in a rising and falling synthesis which, in coming to its completion, affords the discovery in the written sentence of an indissoluble unity in which everything becomes present. From that point on, the problem of time is simply a problem of style.

—*Ibid.*, p. 261.

My thought is a space in which my thoughts take place, in which they take their place. I watch them arrive, pass on, wander aside or sink out of sight, and I distinguish them at spatial and temporal distances which never cease to vary. My thought is not made up solely of my thoughts; it is made up also, even more perhaps, of all the *interior distance* which separates me from, or draws me closer to, that which I am able to think. For all that I think is in myself who think it. The distance is not merely an interval; it is an ambient milieu, a field of union.

—*The Interior Distance*, Introduction, p. vii.

Thus from the beginning Mallarmean thought finds itself stricken as it were with paralysis. It does not move. It neither takes flight spontaneously, like the poetry of Lamartine or Vigny, nor even artificially, like the poetry of Baudelaire. And if to dream is to imagine, it does not even dream. It situates at an infinite distance an ideal of which it is entirely ignorant, except that the ideal depends upon its dream and it cannot dream it. Then it waits to be able to dream. Instead of a starting point, for Mallarmé there is only immobility and waiting:

I sink in myself till my ennui mounts . . .

Thus there is no initial movement. There is nothing except a negative state which can be prolonged indefinitely, eternally, like an empty time.

But still, if there is no initial movement, there is this initial situation. In the absence of any movement and any positive duration, there is something that exists or that would exist if it could be dreamed. There is, if you will, not yet a poetry, but the kind of vacancy which is formed in the sky of thought by forgetfulness of the things of the world and by the simple waiting for what has not yet taken place. The poetry of Mallarmé has thus, in spite of everything, a kind of beginning. It is neither a point nor a movement, it is an initial space.

—*Ibid.*, p. 236.

It is an absolutely virginal space, comparable on the one hand to the whiteness of the sheet of paper on which one will write, and on the other hand comparable to the uniformity of the blue sky. Among the poems of Mallarmé's youth, there is perhaps not a single one which does not have the Azure for its theme. But there is also perhaps not one of them that aims at describing it directly or at seizing upon the positive significance of it. The Azure is the symbol or the presence of an indefinite reality which can only be expressed under the negative form of space or the sky. An ineffable, indescribable presence which seems to get reflected in thought as the sky is mirrored in the water:

> . . . a high gushing fountain sighs toward the Azure!
> —Toward the softened Azure of pale, pure October,
> Which mirrors in great basins its infinite languor . . .

Hardly a faint pretense of movement is made here. No doubt the fountain rises, but this movement of ascension is immediately exhausted, it has only the worth of a sigh, of a sigh *toward* the azure. Nothing exists except in the most purely static relationship of a space to a thought, and of a thought to this space. But from the very fact that it has this relationship, the initial indetermination takes on a new significance. This is no longer simply a space, it is the space *toward which* this sigh rises. It is a positive space, the space of a desire. Besides, between this desire and this place there is another space, a negative space, a void, a distance. The Azure is then that which presents itself beyond its absence, that which affirms itself beyond that which denies it, that which exists beyond that which does not exist. It is a presence, but at a distance. Like an object glimpsed through a window, like a reflection in a mirror. It is in its absence that its presence appears; it is in the void that its fullness is mirrored.

—*Ibid.*, p. 237.

MARCEL RAYMOND

In his introduction to the anthology of "whimsical" poems published in *Vers et Prose* in October 1913, Francis Carco, after making his bow to Paul Fort, defined his own position and that of his group, placing it to the right of André Salmon, Apollinaire, Max Jacob, Henri Hertz, somewhere near Toulet and Tristan Klingsor "who gave a less heterogeneous character to fantasy." Apollinaire's group must be considered separately—it was the avant-garde that led poetry toward a certain literary cubism, which in turn paved the way for the new art of the postwar years. Jean-Marc Bernard, who figures among the "whimsical" poets in *Vers et Prose*, might be regarded as a neo-classicist, while Vincent Muselli and Léon Vérane might well be called neo-Romanist poets. Thus the movement extends on a wide front; after the armistice of 1918, the poets of this group continued together for a few seasons, largely in honor of P. Toulet, whose memory they wished to preserve.

But whatever master they chose, and whatever the various sources of their poetry, the *fantaisistes*, or whimsical poets, are moderns in spirit. They bade farewell to legends; as for regrets, pleasures, griefs, how could they forget them? No sooner do their dreams try to soar than they are caught in the troubled atmosphere, in the strong and bitter odor that hangs heavy over the landscape of our time. One must accept this twentieth century existence as it is; can poetry sustain itself by anything other than true sensations and emotions? In this sense impressionists, these poets are related to Jammes, Verlaine, Laforgue, even Corbière, and to the Rimbaud of the earliest poems; in short, to the decadents rather than the symbolists.

They are the libertines of modern bohemia; bohemians of the provinces whose wretched festivities plunge these young men into boredom; civil servants or soldiers, who love nothing so much as poetry and nothing so little as their trade; bohemians of Paris, who first gravitated to the *Lapin agile*, in Montmartre, before settling (toward 1910) in Montparnasse. The strange goddess, Fancy, oscillating between realism and chimera, awakened in the course of a sleepless night or under the pink and gray light of one of those morning twilights immortalized by Baude-laire. Several features of this contemporary bohemia remind one of the bohemia of Baudelaire and Banville, or of the *Jeune-France* movement; but the *fantaisistes* of today, even though they may have preserved something of romantic sentimentalism, have resolved to be without illusions. They know that people are no good. They have no thought of upholding the rights of art, passion or justice for the benefit of mankind. They love without believing in love, without believing in happiness, and a sense of modesty, the memory of former tears, and a certain self-detachment prevent them from opening their hearts without irony.

This humor, less natural than deliberate, or natural only as a result of a deliberately adopted habit, a humor that for a moment enables the poet to escape from the burden of his life, to pierce its illusions, to judge it, and to rediscover a possibility of free play, of freedom on the margin of oppressive reality, consti-tutes perhaps the only common characteristic of these minds which in other respects are quite different from one another. It is doubtless Laforgue, more than any one else, who set them the example of this theatrical attitude.

—From Baudelaire to Surrealism, pp. 131–133.

Long before him, Saint Augustine had written *Confessions*. Like Saint Augustine, Jean-Jacques could have said: I loved to love (*amabam amare*). But from the pen of the Bishop of Hippo, these formulas apply only to his youth. For him, confessing is assuming one's place as a creature sinful but pardoned, com-pletely turned to God and no longer towards one's self, more eager to know God than one's self. Even with the Greeks, self-knowledge was not an end in itself. The goal is wisdom (phi-losophy), the goal is to become "the demiurge of one's self," knowing what one wishes to be.

Rousseau's immediate predecessor is Montaigne, "master of us all," as he will say. Like the ancients, Montaigne sought wisdom, but becoming gradually convinced that the only living wisdom is one adapted to each individual, he ended up by painting himself. From the very beginning, Rousseau decides to tell all in order to make his book something unique; if necessary, in the process, he will divulge some secrets of wisdom, or rather, of happiness. On the contrary, it is only after having written the *Essays* that Montaigne murmurs: "I have told all." No, Rousseau protests, Montaigne painted himself only in profile. But he will admit in the fourth *Revery* that he too, "without realizing it" (an essential difference), painted himself in profile. Furthermore, the man described in the Confessions is not without resemblance to the man of the *Essays:* changeable, always different from what he was a minute ago, always in contradiction with himself. Before Rousseau, nobody had found more pleasure in studying himself than Montaigne. Few had been more vulnerable: "Each is dealt a blow [by the imagination], but some are knocked down by it. I am run through." Moreover, Montaigne, like Rousseau, grants extraordinary privileges to the self-cognitive subject: "Only you know if you are tender or cruel." The subjective consciousness is alone in the axis of truth; it refuses to recognize any judgment that another person—whether his intention be good or bad—might pass on it. Consciousness of self is consciousness of one's interiority and, already, of one's isolation in the world.

But with Rousseau autobiography has such a different atmosphere, so much stormier! Self-preoccupation turns into a fascination. Self-love combined with consciousness becomes passion and suffering.

Tormented by love of self, tormented by vision of self,

such is man, according to the poet of *The Shepherd's House,* such is his punishment. And another poet shows us Psyche whirling about, after her own shadow. But consciousness finally wears one out. Is not this the destiny of modern man, a destiny which has been following its course since the *Confessions,* through romanticism and existentialism? Man in the baroque age dallied between being and appearing, putting on one the mask of the other. Rousseau, on the contrary, makes a point of appearing only what he is, bent on following a vocation of sincerity without alibi and keeping his heart in a state of absolute transparency. But this is the path of pride; good intentions are not rewarded: one risks losing one's way, being reduced to lie, to embrace the shadows. Hence the throbbing hunger for exoneration all the while he is protesting his innocence. For his protest is full of anguish, although it rests on the persuasion that the self, loving itself without sense of rivalry, shares the innocence of nature. The feeling of guilt, always denied but permeating everything, settles here or there depending on the circumstances; constantly routed out by consciousness but always reforming at the zenith like a black dot. Rousseau is like a Christian who would refuse grace (too humiliating), but who would ask that his fundamental non-culpability be proclaimed for all eternity. He gives notice of appeal before God Almighty, he consents to recognize his baseness and despicable behavior—but only so that others might groan and suffer for them in his place. Perhaps his guilt is precisely believing himself without guilt; perhaps his sin is judging himself incapable of a sin that could be spontaneous. Be that as it may, in the case of Rousseau, deliverance or reprieve is possible only through forgetfulness, or by a temporary blotting out of a *self* that can no longer feel itself exist except through its sensations.

—*Œuvres complètes de Jean-Jacques Rousseau*, I, xii–xiv.

"People worry about what I have wanted to *say*, but it is what I have wanted to *do* that matters." Yet almost everywhere saying and doing are inextricably tied together. It is therefore legitimate to indicate the place of a poem in the field of Valéry's thought and to elucidate its meaning.

It is not said often enough that *The Young Fate* is a drama. The metaphysical debate which is its subject is charged with a high human—even tragic—potential. Tragic means extreme, irreparable. The whole poem develops the consequences of an event of this nature, of a metaphysical catastrophe. The action is presented or suggested by an ardent pantomime in the form of an extraordinarily modulated *récitatif* punctuated by blanks, in which pathos prevails over ethos—the heroine suffers her destiny.

She is alone, in this poem of interior solitude and of the divided being; a monologue of the *self*, a dialogue between the *self* and itself. The thought of another person is only glimpsed in one or two passages, and by refraction. As for the spirit of the serpent, it has infected the self with itself like a venom: it has become its consciousness. Having bitten, having accomplished its crime, it disappears.

What crime by myself or upon myself consummated?

asks the Young Fate: the serpent is none other than she—through her, herself, evil has come into the world.

Albert Thibaudet said that *The Young Fate* was considered the most difficult poem in literature. A reputation wholly undeserved.

If it is "the story of a consciousness during the course of a night," as Valéry has declared, its obscurity is that of a night shot through with lightning flashes. If in some verses—perhaps a dozen—obscurity seems to pile up, it is through an excess of superimposed and crisscrossed illuminations. But the overall meaning comes out more clearly with each reading. Its sense is universal—and specifically Valérian: the Young Fate is assailed by a double temptation, that of the negating consciousness (implacable urge towards lucidity and purity, which isolates her completely) and the temptation of life or of the urge to live (which is opposed to consciousness, but which is that of the world, to which man is attached by everything which in him is not his *pure self*).

—*Paul Valéry et la tentation de l'esprit*, pp. 129–130.

JEAN-PIERRE RICHARD

This fire blazes too in our body: it is what materially permits human radiation and personal intercourse. This carnal sun is nothing other than the blood. The blood has heat, pliancy, plenitude, continuity; into the most remote parts of the being it causes the secret liquid of life to flow. It illuminates, it burns; the reddening flame of a hearth can "inundate with blood an amber-colored skin." And, inversely, any sun may resemble a bleeding wound. Rich blood especially, can satisfy thirst; it too is a "nourishing father"; the lost blood in *The Fountain of Blood* spills out "turning the cobblestones into little islands," "quenching each creature's thirst"; in a still more disturbing way, the sadistically decapitated corpse of A Martyr

> . . . spreads out like a river
> On the quenchéd pillow
> A red and living blood which the cloth drinks up
> With the avidity of a meadow . . .

To drink fresh hot blood is to drink at the spring of life. Blood is thus the very symbol of expansion and the living antithesis of all paralysis.

Nevertheless it is itself susceptible to paralysis: let it slow down or cool off and it becomes coagulated blood. Coagulation is sanguinary petrification: this is why the setting sun or the winter sun, the dying sun, so often appears to Baudelaire in the guise of a sort of congealed clot. But blood may also incur the curse of immobility by ways entirely different: that, for example, of an internal decay. In the scale of life and death, tainted blood is scarcely better than coagulated blood; both signify stagnation, impotence, and both, in effect, may be found in the sluggish blood of the splenetic man. For, if it is true, as Baudelaire writes in his study on Poe, "that our destiny circulates in our arteries with each corpuscle," it is fitting that the symbol of a destiny doomed from the start—doomed by original sin, doomed by the very movement of consciousness—that the symbol of a wounded soul should be a blood which is also divided, at war with itself, therefore spiritless and devoid of that expansive heat which

Baudelaire calls *curiosity*. Spleen is nothing but lack of curiosity: what runs in the veins of a splenetic man is in effect a liquid of death, "in place of blood, the green water of Lethe."

What joy, on the other hand, to watch fresh blood flow! "The supernatural voluptuousness that man may feel by seeing his blood flow" is explained by the delight of a life heretofore protected, mysterious, but suddenly made present, marvelously and dangerously tangible. Our most distant reality, not really our nature but what Baudelaire names supernature, is exposed with it in broad daylight. And what makes this revelation especially astonishing is that it represents at the same time a threat to this supernature; something sacred betrays itself in it and dies. The grandeur of hemorrhaging lies in the fact that it combines thus an evidence of life and a fatality of death: it shows man that he exists and is powerful only through a surge of weakness. The nightmare of the dried-up spring or of the extinguished sun will thus be found in the world of flowing blood: the dream of hemophilia, which *The Fountain of Blood* describes, admirably translates this obsession of a life bled white.

This bleeding does not necessarily postulate a wound: the sanguinary vaporization called hemorrhaging is aggravated by all the porousness of bodies; here flesh permits blood to run through it in all directions. To bleed, it does not even need to be cut into. Everything filters through the epidermis—it is as if skin did not exist:

> It seems to me at times that my blood gushes forth
> Like a fountain with rhythmic sobs.
> I hear it well, flowing with a drawn-out murmur,
> But I touch and prod myself without finding the wound . . .

This same epidermic permeability, so painful when Baudelaire feels it on his own body, becomes, instead, infinitely precious when he discovers it in others. It indicates for him a possible welcome, a possible opening. It is for him the carnal symbol of a spiritual transparency. Beneath this skin which is hardly a barrier, he can see the blood beating as one listens to a soul palpitating; he watches it form droplets on the skin; he can almost feel, from the outside, its agitated warmth; as in the flesh of Rubens

> . . . where life flows and churns
> Like air in the sky and the sea in the sea.

he can almost directly grasp the biographical beating of a foreign existence. Still better; suppressing the obstacle of the skin, he succeeds at times in receiving the immediate emanation of another's blood. In *The Balcony,* that remarkable symphony of flame and shadow, each detail of the setting echoes the splendor of a fire hidden in the shadows, the fecundating softness of a black sun: coal gleams red in the fireplace, the sun illuminates a twilight about to darken, two pupils shine in the half-light. Under the veil of a dark skin, the presence can be guessed of a blood strong and hot as a breath, of which the lover, as he bends over it, can seize the vapor, breathe the odor.

I fancied myself breathing the perfume of your blood . . .

But skin can also grow hard, turn into metal or stone; then the blood retreats, withdraws into the carnal depths. A cold woman, with eyes of steel and flesh of marble, seems to have neither life nor blood, and deep within her as on the surface the same sterile desert extends:

I join a heart of snow to the whiteness of swans . . .

The icy epidermis no longer hides any warm interior: it is the triumph of dandyism, the misfortune of communication broken off.

Double-sided misfortune: for Baudelaire loves this sterility that protects him from the other, which prevents any encroachment. But it protects also the other against her own threat; at every movement of her desire she opposes an indifference, an excuse.

All slips off, all blunts itself on the granite of her skin.

And Baudelaire, with mounting fury, feels the urge to break this granite and violate this passivity. He would like to make the snow of that heart melt, to reach—under the petrified surface of the other—the warmth of a blood, the sign of a life. He is ready, if need be, to cut and tear at the body that is refused him, to seek out the source of its blood. The dream of the inflicted wound thus translates the desire to force a rebellious intimacy; for a wound is a rape, a means of making another expose himself. Against the dandyism of the other, Baudelaire's best weapon is his sadism.

—*Poésie et Profondeur,* pp. 118–121.

JEAN ROUSSET

If the work of art is a principle of exploration and a medium of organization, it will be able to utilize and recompose any kind of element taken from reality or memory, but it will do so only to serve its own requirements and its own life; it is cause before being effect, product, or reflection—as Valéry was found of reminding us; so analysis will be concerned with the work alone, in its incomparable solitude, such as it has come forth from the "inner regions where the artist has withdrawn in order to create." (Proust) And if there is no work except in the symbiosis of a form and a dream, we will read them conjointly and grasp the dream through the form.

But how can form be grasped? How can it be recognized? We can be sure from the first that it is not always where one expects to find it, that (being a gushing forth from the depths and a manifest revelation of the work unto itself) it will be neither a surface nor a mold nor a receptacle, that it is no more the technique than the art of composing, and that it is not necessarily the same thing as the search for form or the deliberate balance of parts or the beauty of elements. The active and unpredictable principle of revelation and apparition, it overflows rules and artifices, and cannot be reduced to a plan or an outline, or a corpus of procedures or ways and means. Every work is a form in so far as it is a work. Form in this sense is everywhere, even in poets who deride form or aim at destroying it. Montaigne has form, Breton has form, the formless or the destructive urge has form, just as intimate revery or lyrical explosion has form. And the artist who claims to go beyond forms will do so by forms—if he is an artist. "To each work its form": Balzac's word here takes on its full meaning.

But there is comprehensible form only where there can be discerned an agreement or connection, a line of force, an obsessive figure, a network of presences or echoes, a web of convergences; I shall give the name of "structures" to these formal constants, these linkings that indicate a mental universe and that each artist invents anew according to his needs.

Convergences, linkings, groupings; yet we must beware of

relating everything to the virtues of proportion and harmony. It is an old habit, a "classic" habit, and one that survives in a Valéry, to define form as the relation of the parts to the whole. Doubtless this is often the case, and I shall have recourse to that principle in my analysis of Proust's novel—the author expressly invites me to do so. However it is only one criterion among others. Balzac is right: "To each work its form." Neither the author nor the critic knows in advance what he will find at the end of the operation. The critical instrument must not be fashioned in advance of the analysis. The reader will remain uncommitted—just attentive and watchful for the stylistic signal, the unforeseen and revealing structural characteristic. In the case of the works studied here, it will be a certain alternation characterizing the *Princess of Cleves*, or, in Marivaux, a peculiar distribution of active and passive functions, while the Flaubert of *Madame Bovary* calls for an analysis of the "post-of-observation." The approaches are as free and diverse as the inventiveness of the writer.

It is true nonetheless that, even if it manifests itself in many ways, a tendency towards unity (what Proust calls the "organized complexity") marks the majority of works; it will often happen that one of the characteristics of composition to be noted is a characteristic of inner relationship. A work is a whole, and it should always be viewed as such. Fruitful reading should be global reading, alert to identities and correspondences, similarities and oppositions, repeats and variations—like the knots and foci where texture concentrates or spreads out.

In any case, if reading, which develops in time, is to be global, it must make the work simultaneously present in all its parts. Delacroix points out that a picture, which can be seen all at once, is not like a book: a book, like a "picture in movement," is discovered only by successive fragments. The task of the discriminating reader consists in reversing this natural tendency of books so that they present themselves in their entirety to the mind's eye. There is no complete reading unless it transforms the book into a simultaneous network of reciprocal relationships; it is only then that the felicitous surprises take place and the work emerges before our eyes, because we are in a position to perform properly a sonata of words, figures, and thoughts.

—*Forme et Signification*, Introduction, pp. x–xiii.

JEAN-PAUL SARTRE

And now here is the real reason for his failure. He once wrote that the novelist is to his own creatures what God is to His. And that explains all the oddities of his technique. He takes God's standpoint on his characters. God sees the inside and outside, the depths of body and soul, the whole universe at once. In like manner, M. Mauriac is omniscient about everything relating to his little world. What he says about his characters is Gospel. He explains them, categorizes them and condemns them without appeal. If anyone were to ask him how he knows that Thérèse is a cautious and desperate woman, he would probably reply, with great surprise, "Didn't I create her?"

No, he didn't! The time has come to say that the novelist is not God. We would do well to recall the caution with which Conrad suggests to us that Lord Jim may be "romantic." He takes great care not to state this himself; he puts the word into the mouth of one of his characters, a fallible being, who utters it hesitantly. The word "romantic," clear as it is, thereby acquires depth and pathos and a certain indefinable mystery. Not so with M. Mauriac. "A cautious and desperate woman" is no hypothesis; it is an illumination which comes to us from above. The author, impatient to have us grasp the character of his heroine, suddenly gives us the key. But what I maintain is precisely the fact that he has no right to make these absolute judgments. A novel is an action related from various points of view. And M. Mauriac is well aware of this, having written, in *La Fin de la Nuit*, that ". . . the most conflicting judgments about a single person can be correct; it is a question of lighting, and no one light reveals more than another." But each of these interpretations must be in motion, drawn along, so to speak, by the very action it interprets.

It is, in short, the testimony of a participant and should reveal the man who testifies as well as the event to which he testifies. It should arouse our impatience (will it be confirmed or denied by events?), and thus give us a feeling of the dragging of time. Thus, each point of view is relative, and the best one will be that which makes the reader feel most acutely the dragging of time. The participants' interpretations and explanations will all be hypothetical. The reader may have an inkling, beyond these conjectures, of the event's absolute reality, but it is for him alone to re-establish it. Should he care to try this sort of exercise, he will never get beyond the realm of likelihood and probability.

In any case, the introduction of absolute truth or of God's standpoint constitutes a twofold error of technique. To begin with, it presupposes a purely contemplative narrator, withdrawn from the action. This inevitably conflicts with Valéry's law of aesthetics, according to which any given element of a work of art ought always to maintain a plurality of relationships with the other elements. And besides, the absolute is non-temporal. If you pitch the narrative in the absolute, the string of duration snaps, and the novel disappears before your eyes. All that remains is a dull truth, *sub specie aeternitatis.*

But there is something even more serious. The definitive judgments with which M. Mauriac is always ready to intersperse the narrative prove that he does not conceive his characters as he ought. He fabricates their natures before setting them down, he decrees that they *will be* this or that. The essence of Thérèse, the evil-smelling animal, the desperate and cautious woman, is, I admit, complex, and not to be expressed in a single sentence. But what exactly is this essence? Her inmost depths? Let us look at it more closely. Conrad saw clearly that the word "romantic" had meaning when it expressed an aspect of character *for other people.* Such words as "desperate and cautious" and "evil-smelling animal" and "castaway" and other such neat phrases are of the same sort as the word that Conrad puts into the mouth of the merchant of the islands. When Thérèse resumes her story,

> For years she had been unaware that the pattern of her
> destiny had been a series of attempts to get out of a
> rut, each ending in failure. But now that she had
> emerged from the darkness, she saw clearly . . .

she is able to judge her past so easily only because she cannot return to it. Thus, when he thinks he is probing the hearts of his characters, M. Mauriac remains outside, at the door.

This would be quite all right if M. Mauriac were aware of it and wrote novels like Hemingway's, in which we hardly know the heroes except through their gestures and words, and the vague judgments they pass on each other. But when M. Mauriac, making full use of his creative authority, forces us to accept these exterior views as the inner stuff of his creatures, he is transforming his characters into *things*. Only things can simply *be*; they have only exteriors. Minds cannot simply be; they become. Thus, in shaping his Thérèse *sub specie aeternitatis*, M. Mauriac first makes of her a thing, after which he adds, on the sly, a whole mental thickness. But in vain. Fictional beings have their laws, the most rigorous of which is the following: the novelist may be either their witness or their accomplice, but never both at the same time. The novelist must be either inside or out. Because M. Mauriac does not observe these laws, he does away with his characters' minds.

—*Literary and Philosophical Essays*, pp. 14–16.

Genet is related to that family of people who are nowadays referred to by the barbaric name of *passéistes*. An accident riveted him to a childhood memory, and this memory became sacred. In his early childhood, a liturgical drama was performed, a drama of which he was the officiant: he knew paradise and lost it, he was a child and was driven from his childhood. No doubt this "break" is not easy to localize. It shifts back and forth, at the dictate of his moods and myths, between the ages of ten and fifteen. But that is unimportant. What matters is that it exists and that he believes in it. His life is divided into two heterogeneous parts: before and after the sacred drama. Indeed, it is not unusual for the memory to condense into a single mythical moment the contingencies and perpetual rebeginnings of an individual history. What matters is that Genet lives and continues to relive this period of his life as if it had lasted only an instant.

To say "instant" is to say *fatal instant*. The instant is the reciprocal and contradictory envelopment of the before by the after. One is still what one is going to cease to be and already what one is going to become. One lives one's death, one dies one's life. One feels oneself to be one's own self and another; the eternal is present in an atom of duration. In the midst of the fullest life, one has a foreboding that one will merely survive, one is afraid of the future. It is the time of anguish and of heroism, of pleasure and of destruction. An instant is sufficient to destroy, to enjoy, to kill, to be killed, to make one's fortune at the turn of a card. Genet carries in his heart a bygone instant which has lost none of its virulence, an infinitesimal and sacred void which concludes a death and begins a horrible metamorphosis. The argument of this liturgical drama is as follows: a child dies of shame; a hoodlum rises up in his place; the hoodlum will be haunted by the child. One would have to speak of resurrection, to evoke the old initiatory rites of shamanism and secret societies, were it not that Genet refuses categorically to be a man who has been resuscitated. There was a death, that is all. And Genet is nothing other than a dead man. If he appears to be still alive, it is with the larval existence which certain peoples ascribe to their defunct in the grave. All his heroes have died at least once in their life.

—*Saint Genet, Actor and Martyr*, pp. 1–2.

JEAN STAROBINSKI

In the eyes of a critic anxious to grasp, if not the totality of a work or a writer, at least the principles which render the whole intelligible, Rousseau's sexual abnormalities, recorded in the work itself, contribute to the meaning of the totality by the same right as the constructions of his theoretical thought. Just as we cannot reduce Rousseau's ideology to sentiment, we cannot limit his "intimate" life to pure anecdote: his personal experiences, explicitly taken up in the work, cannot remain for us marginal data. Exhibitionism was an aberrant phase of Jean-Jacques' sexual behavior; but, in a transposed form, it is at the very heart of a work like the *Confessions*. We are not advocating a regressive interpretation (usual with present-day psychoanalysis), which would make of the *Confessions* only a more or less sublimated variant of Jean-Jacques' juvenile exhibitionism. Rather do we prefer a "prospective" interpretation, which would seek to discover in a previous act or attitude, certain intentions, choices, desires—the meaning of which goes beyond the circumstance that first made them manifest. Even without knowing in advance that the exhibitionism of Jean-Jacques in the "dark paths" and "hidden spots" of Turin already prefigures the public reading of the *Confessions*, an analysis of his sexual behavior would be incomplete if it did not expose a certain type of "contact with the world." Erotic behavior is not a fragmentary datum; it is a manifestation of the total person and should be analyzed as such. Whether for the purpose of neglecting it or of making it a subject for special study, one may not limit exhibitionism to the sexual "sphere": the whole personality is revealed in it, with some of its fundamental "existentialist choices." Instead then of reducing the literary work to *nothing more than* the disguises of a juvenile or infantile tendency, analysis will aim at discovering, in the elementary data of the affective life, what obliged them to go *as far as* literary form, as far as thought and art.

Yes, everything really seems to begin with the privation of maternal love. "I cost my mother her life, and my birth was the first of my misfortunes." Everything has been said—or almost—about this birth which may have given Jean-Jacques his sense of guilt for existing. Starting with this, one can construct a series of explanations that fit together well (and even too well). Masochism? A need to pay for the sin of having been born. Mme de Warrens? Obvious wish for the maternal breast. The threesomes? A symbolic search for paternal forgiveness and protection. Passivity, narcissism? The consequences of a guilt feeling that prevents Jean-Jacques from seeking "normal" satisfactions—that is to say, from setting himself up with women as a rival of the Father. The sentiment of existence, the ecstasies, the appetite for the immediate? A return to the womb, in soothing Nature. And that fondness for milk products? Its meaning is definitely much too clear . . .

But explaining behavior by its secret goals or basic motives is still not understanding it completely. Nor does it suffice to show that consciousness moves towards symbolic goals, which it substitutes for the original object of its desire. The essential must be sought there where the inner meets the outer: in the manner in which consciousness relates to its goals, in the very structure of this relationship. There only, one approaches the reality of a thought and an experience. It is to accept a rather poor concept of psychological causality, to admit that one complex alone (here, the Oedipus complex) can orient all the aspects of the personality. Complexes are often spoken of as if they were endowed with an autonomous and distinct energy, whereas the real psychic life is, from the beginning, an activity of the person in contact with his environment. The capital moment of behavior is neither in its unconscious causes nor in its conscious motives but at the point when the causes and the motives produce an *act*—in other terms, at the point when man commits himself to an adventure in which he will have to create the conditions of his satisfaction. Such a perspective, in the case of Rousseau, obliges us to take into consideration not only what he desires (consciously or symbolically) but especially the way in which he proceeds towards the satisfaction desired, his "style of approach."

—*Jean-Jacques Rousseau, la transparence et l'obstacle*, pp. 210–212.

The critic is one who, although giving in to the fascination of the text, intends to hold fast to his *right to look*. He desires to

penetrate still further: beyond the manifest meaning which reveals itself to him, he senses a latent significance. After the first
"sight reading," he needs an extra watchfulness to advance
towards a *second meaning*. But let no one misunderstand this
expression: it does not mean—as for medieval exegesis—the
deciphering of some allegorical or symbolic equivalent, but the
vaster life or transfigured death which the text announces. It will
often be that this search for the most distant brings one back to
the most at hand: to what one saw first, to the forms and
rhythms which, at first, seemed only the promise of a secret
message. A long detour sends us back to the words themselves,
where meaning chooses to dwell and where shines the mysterious
treasure that one expected to find in the "profound dimension."
   In truth, the demands of the critical look tend towards two
opposite possibilities, neither of which is fully realizable. The
first invites it to lose itself in the intimacy of that fabulous
consciousness which the work lets it perceive: comprehension
would be then the progressive pursuit of a total harmonizing
with the creative subjectivity, the fervent participation in the
sensible and intellectual experience that spreads throughout the
work. But however far he goes in this direction, the critic will not
succeed in stifling in himself the conviction of his separate
identity, the tenacious and banal certitude of not being the
consciousness with which he wishes to fuse. However, let us
suppose that he really succeeded in being thus absorbed: then,
paradoxically, he would lose his own voice, he could only keep
silent, and the perfect critical discourse, by dint of empathy and
mimesis, would give the impression of the most complete silence.
Without somehow breaking the pact of solidarity which links
him to the work, the critic is capable of nothing but paraphrase
and pastiche: one must *betray* the ideal of identification in order
to acquire the power of speaking of this experience and of
describing, in a language which is not that of the work, the life
in common that one has known with it, in it. Thus, in spite of
our desire to submerge ourselves in the living depths of the work,
we are obliged to remain on the outside in order to speak of it.
Why then not deliberately establish a panoramic perspective, the
surroundings with which the work is organically linked? We
would try to discern certain significant correspondences that have
not been perceived by the writer, interpret his unconscious motives, decipher the complex relationships that unite a destiny and

a work with their historical and social setting. This second possibility for critical reading can be defined as that of the *look from above*: the eye wishes to let nothing escape of all the configurations that separating itself from the work permits it to see. In the broadened area that the look encompasses, the work is of course a special object, but it is not the only object in view. It is defined by what surrounds it, it has meaning only in relation to the whole of its context. Now here is the difficulty: the context is so vast, the relationships so numerous, that the eye is seized by a secret despair: never will it be able to assemble all the elements of this totality before it. Furthermore, from the moment we are obliged to situate a work among its historical co-ordinates, we can limit the investigation only by an arbitrary decision. The investigation, in principle, could go on until the literary work is no longer the special object it was in the beginning but only one of the innumerable manifestations of a period, a culture, a "vision of the world." The more correlative facts of the social world or the life of the author that the eye tries to take in, the more the work diminishes in importance. The triumph of the look from above is, it too, only a form of failure: it causes us to lose the work and its meanings in giving us the world surrounding the work.

Complete criticism is perhaps neither the kind that aims at totality (like the look from above) nor the kind that aims at intimacy (like identifying intuition); it is a look that can be now from above, now from within—knowing in advance that the truth may not be found either in one or the other but in the movement that goes tirelessly from one to the other. Neither the rapture of distance nor that of proximity is to be refused: this double excessiveness must be desired in which the eye is each time close to losing all power.

But perhaps, too, criticism is wrong in wishing to regulate to this extent what its eye should see. Ofttimes it is better to forget oneself and let oneself be surprised. As a reward, I will feel the presence in the work of an eye that looks at me: its look is not a reflection of my query. It is a foreign consciousness—radically another's—looking for me, staring at me, and asking me to reply. I feel myself *exposed* to this question which comes thus to meet me. The work questions me. Before speaking on my own behalf, I must lend my own voice to this strange power which calls to me; now, however docile I may be, I always run the risk of preferring to it the reassuring melodies that I invent. It is not easy to keep our eyes open to receive the look that is seeking us. Doubtless not only for criticism but for all intellectual investigations, one must say: "Look, in order that you may be seen."

—*L'Œil vivant*, pp. 25–28.

JEAN-PAUL WEBER

If one were to take out the Clock, whether consciously or unconsciously apprehended, one would be removing three-fourths of the work of the poet. Moreover, we feel certain that we have discovered the thematic memory, which is that of a "black clock" that the poet saw come into his home when he was seven or eight years old.

It is easy to see why this clock should figure as a theme. The memory of poets is most apt to undergo around the age of seven an influence that will give rise to the symbols of their work. Moreover, for Vigny at this age, the black clock is not only an object that is new, extraordinary, strangely animated; it is not only admired and loved by his parents ("my father was very fond of it"). The poetic names, "the beautiful names" of the revolutionary calendar ("I loved those beautiful names of fructidor, thermidor and messidor") engrave themselves on the mind of the child in the shadow of this clock and help his poetic vocation to blossom. His father's beautiful stories, fervent stories ("It was such a great delight for me to hear him . . .") roll out their tragedies and their epics before the black clock all adorned with melodious names, all vibrating with rhythm, all bursting with chimes. The Clock, by its language, by its swaying in measure, by the music of the hours, by the fascinating discourse of father, by the tenderness of maternal lessons that crystallize around it, by the paternal affection that it brings out, the Clock, for Vigny, is Poetry itself, peal of sonorous words, number, measure, music, story, sentiment—and also the nostalgia of Memory.

But the Clock and the Hour, thus modulated, still manifest only one side of the poet's thematic system, its sunny side. Very rapidly, in fact,* the clock universe of Vigny acquires dark components: when the Child listens to the time, no longer to project into it mysterious words or stories full of affection and enthusiasm, but to put an iron collar on his sensitivity, on his poetic drive,† the Clock no longer appears to him as a captivat-

---

* It is in fact in 1807 that young Vigny enters the Hix school as a day pupil: he is ten years old. Cf. Lauvrière, *op. cit.*, p. 13.
† Cf. these autobiographical items: "I had a very strict education. The habit of application and perpetual work . . ." (*Diary*, 1838, II, p. 1100).—"The most unhappy time of my life was my student days"

ing fairyland, but as the land of Duty just as tyrannical as it is beneficent, and which holds the child captive in its grip. The rhythm of the Clock is then no longer the flexible step of poetry, but drum roll, invincible order, the hammered step of armies. Hence the ambivalence of the affective thematic structure: Hour-Poetry and Hour-Duty engender in the soul of the poet—beside an insurmountable inclination for words and verse, which will stamp the image of the Clock on the majority of his poems—a secret aversion for the fearful Order which henceforth the Clock personifies and symbolizes, and of which one will find many echoes in *The Military Condition*. Hence also the ambivalence of the poet's ideology: we do not doubt an instant that in Vigny *Honor* thematically signifies *Hour*; the grandeur and the absurdity of honor translate, on the level of ideas, the absurd majesty of the Clock; and in saying, for example: "honor is the poetry of duty," Vigny is only yoking, in a single formula which is sonorous and a little hollow, the double aspect of the Clock: *poetry and duty.*‡

Hence also the destiny of the poet. In love with the black clock, in its honor he made verses as regular as its rhythm, traced in his poems mysterious and moving circles as the Hands do on the face of a clock, composed *Chatterton* like a clock mechanism, poetized even the servitudes of passive obedience and marching in time. But also, a slave to the Hour and to the Clock,

(*ib.*, 1847, p. 1260). "I felt myself to be of a race accursed and that made me somber and pensive" (*ibid.*).—"I have spoken to you of these details, which are frightfully petty, only to give you another example of *those childhood sorrows that leave in the adult man a tinge of diffidence hard to erase during the rest of his life.* These troubles . . . lend a dark color to the whole future" (*ibid.*, p. 1261).

Add to that the complex of wasting time, which tormented Vigny from his youth on: "Time seemed to me wasted if it brought me no new and fruitful idea" (*ibid.*, 1262), and probably for the rest of his life: "*When one writes verse while looking at a clock*, one is ashamed at the time one loses looking for a rime courteous enough not to vitiate entirely the idea" (1832; *ib.*, p. 941).

It is clear: school work and creative thought very early brought out a conflict and remorse (wasting one's time), linked to schedule, time, the clock, and which never stopped racking the unconscious and the consciousness of the poet.

‡ On the philosophy of time in Vigny, who refused eternity in favor at once of spreading time out in space, making simultaneously appear its three "moments" or *extases* (Heidegger), and of an ethic of action in duration, cf. G. Poulet, *op. cit.*, pp. 263–290.

he wished at first to conquer them by the mind, learning mathematics doubtless to read the hour in the stars, then to understand the complex mechanism which seeks its orders in the sky, so that he could transmit them to us like a perfect and pointless Junior Officer, a stupid and terrible Sergeant major. That is why Vigny was fond of complex weapons, prepared for the Ecole Polytechnique, put sailors and gunners in his stories. He wished also to fuse with the dark half of his theme, as he desired when he became a poet to fuse with Poetry, with the black Clock of his happy childhood. A poet like the revolutionary months, he was also a soldier, an officer, and all his life he wished for war without finding it. To be an officer is actually to be a Clock; Vigny has explained it to us abundantly, although without knowing so; to be an officer is to scan the rhythm of someone else's time, to put the step of a cohort in rhythm, it is to be inexorable like time, obeyed like the Clock; it is also to receive orders from above, as movement receives them from the stars; it is to be a complex mechanism, deadly, but one that a child can set off; it is to kill on the spot, and be infinitely vulnerable; it is to be the terrible personification and the slave of Honor—as the Clock is the personification and the slave of the Hour. And perhaps the only superiority of Vigny, in relation to the Sergeant major— that his unconscious wanted "ubuesque"—of *An Evening at Vincennes*, is to be obscurely conscious of his status as a Clock, and to shout it in prose and in verse.

The theme is unique, but two-headed—*Janus bifrons*: and all Vigny stems from it—poetry, conscious and unconscious symbols, plots, ideas, the religion of honor and stoicism, the Ecole Polytechnique, advancement to seniority, the Academy, *Eloa, Chatterton, The Red Seal* and *The Black Doctor.*

—*Genèse de l'œuvre poétique*, pp. 87–90.